D1265864

ULTIMATE COMICS THE ULTIMATES

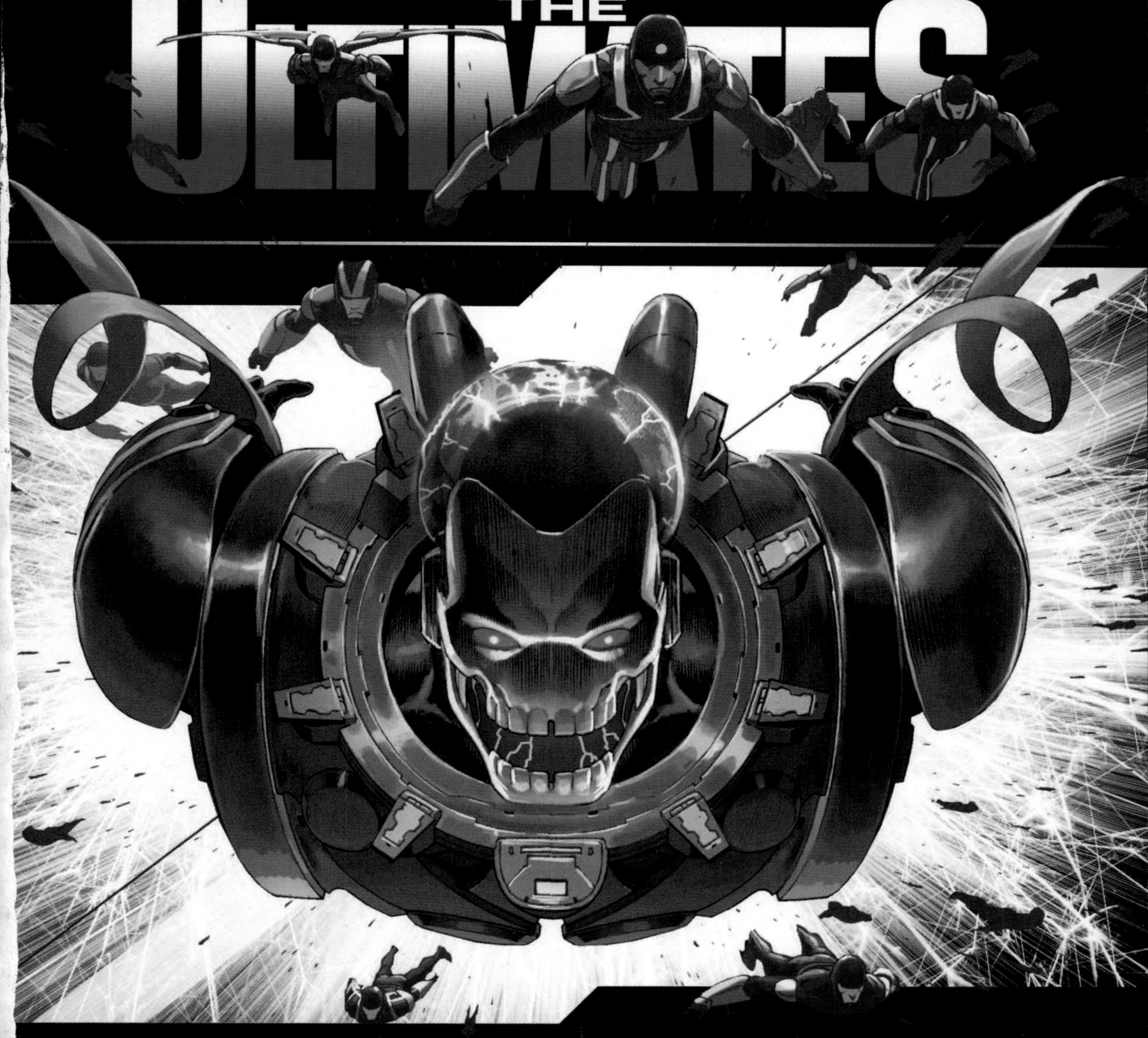

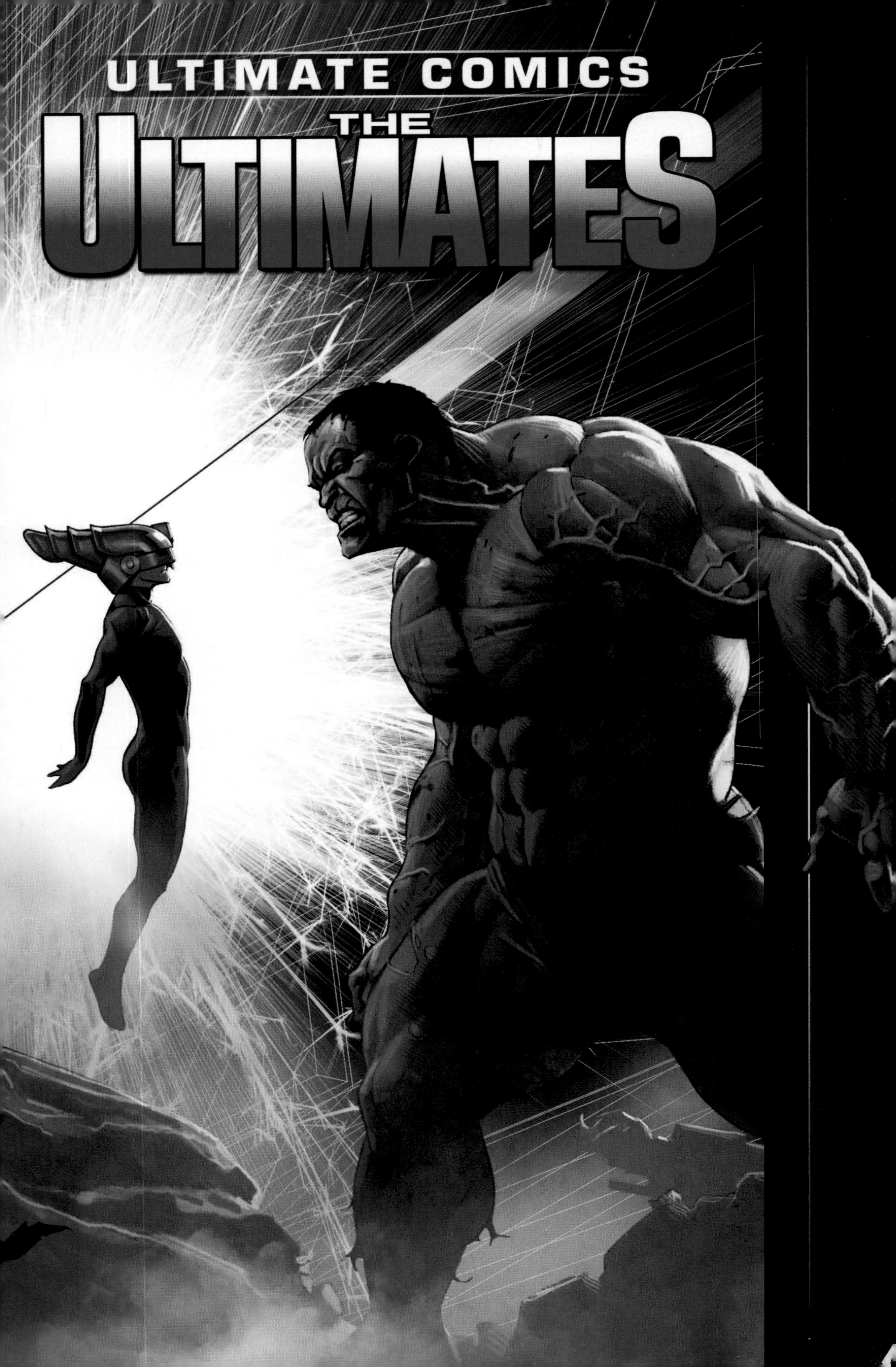
ULTIMATE COMICS
THE
ULTIMATES

WRITER: **JONATHAN HICKMAN** WITH **SAM HUMPHRIES** (#10-12)

#7-9 ARTIST: **ESAD RIBIC**   COLOR ARTIST: **DEAN WHITE**

#10 ARTIST: **LUKE ROSS** COLOR ARTIST: **MATTHEW WILSON**

#11 ARTISTS: **LUKE ROSS** (PP. 1-5 & 14-20), **BUTCH GUICE** (PP. 6-7),
LEONARD KIRK (PP. 8-9) & **PATRICK ZIRCHER** (PP. 12-13)
COLOR ARTISTS: **MATT MILLA** (PP. 1-5, 8-11 & 14-20)
& **JESUS ABURTOV** (PP. 6-7 & 12-13)

#12 ARTISTS: **LUKE ROSS** (PP. 1-13), **RON GARNEY** (PP. 14-18)
& **BUTCH GUICE** (PP. 19-20)   COLOR ARTIST: **MATT MILLA**

LETTERER: **VC'S CLAYTON COWLES**
COVER ART: **KAARE ANDREWS**
ASSISTANT EDITOR: **JON MOISAN** ASSOCIATE EDITOR: **SANA AMANAT**
SENIOR EDITOR: **MARK PANICCIA**

COLLECTION EDITOR: **JENNIFER GRÜNWALD**
ASSISTANT EDITORS: **ALEX STARBUCK** & **NELSON RIBEIRO**
EDITOR, SPECIAL PROJECTS: **MARK D. BEAZLEY**
SENIOR EDITOR, SPECIAL PROJECTS: **JEFF YOUNGQUIST**
SENIOR VICE PRESIDENT OF SALES: **DAVID GABRIEL**
SVP OF BRAND PLANNING & COMMUNICATIONS: **MICHAEL PASCIULLO**
BOOK DESIGNER: **RODOLFO MURAGUCHI**

EDITOR IN CHIEF: **AXEL ALONSO** CHIEF CREATIVE OFFICER: **JOE QUESADA**
PUBLISHER: **DAN BUCKLEY** EXECUTIVE PRODUCER: **ALAN FINE**

TWO CITIES. TWO WORLDS.

With the recent appearance of two new superhuman threats to the world—the People in Tian and Reed Richards' Children of Tomorrow in the City —S.H.I.E.L.D. and the Ultimates are doing everything they can to avert further disaster.

Sam Wilson (The Falcon) infiltrated the Children's City, but was soon discovered by Reed Richards, who offered to let him stay. Sam could have free rein of the City if he would explain humanity's coming extinction to the world.

The Ultimates needed help. After being turned down by Steve Rogers, Fury had no choice but to assemble the Ultimates and pay a visit to Tian…

ULTIMATE COMICS ULTIMATES BY JONATHAN HICKMAN VOL. 2. Contains material originally published in magazine form as ULTIMATE COMICS ULTIMATES #7-12. First printing 2012. Hardcover ISBN# 978-0-7851-5719-9. Softcover ISBN# 978-0-7851-5720-5. Published by MARVEL WORLDWIDE, INC., a subsidiary of MARVEL ENTERTAINMENT, LLC. OFFICE OF PUBLICATION: 135 West 50th Street, New York, NY 10020. Copyright © 2012 and 2013 Marvel Characters, Inc. All rights reserved. Hardcover: $24.99 per copy in the U.S. and $27.99 in Canada (GST #R127032852). Softcover: $19.99 per copy in the U.S. and $21.99 in Canada (GST #R127032852). Canadian Agreement #40668537. All characters featured in this issue and the distinctive names and likenesses thereof, and all related indicia are trademarks of Marvel Characters, Inc. No similarity between any of the names, characters, persons, and/or institutions in this magazine with those of any living or dead person or institution is intended, and any such similarity which may exist is purely coincidental. **Printed in the U.S.A.** ALAN FINE, EVP - Office of the President, Marvel Worldwide, Inc. and EVP & CMO Marvel Characters B.V.; DAN BUCKLEY, Publisher & President - Print, Animation & Digital Divisions; JOE QUESADA, Chief Creative Officer; TOM BREVOORT, SVP of Publishing; DAVID BOGART, SVP of Operations & Procurement, Publishing; RUWAN JAYATILLEKE, SVP & Associate Publisher, Publishing; C.B. CEBULSKI, SVP of Creator & Content Development; DAVID GABRIEL, SVP of Publishing Sales & Circulation; MICHAEL PASCIULLO, SVP of Brand Planning & Communications; JIM O'KEEFE, VP of Operations & Logistics; DAN CARR, Executive Director of Publishing Technology; SUSAN CRESPI, Editorial Operations Manager; ALEX MORALES, Publishing Operations Manager; STAN LEE, Chairman Emeritus. For information regarding advertising in Marvel Comics or on Marvel.com, please contact John Dokes, SVP Integrated Sales and Marketing, at jdokes@marvel.com. For Marvel subscription inquiries, please call 800-217-9158. **Manufactured between 5/21/2012 and 7/2/2012 (hardcover), and 5/21/2012 and 1/7/2013 (softcover), by R.R. DONNELLEY, INC., SALEM, VA, USA.**

10 9 8 7 6 5 4 3 2 1

7

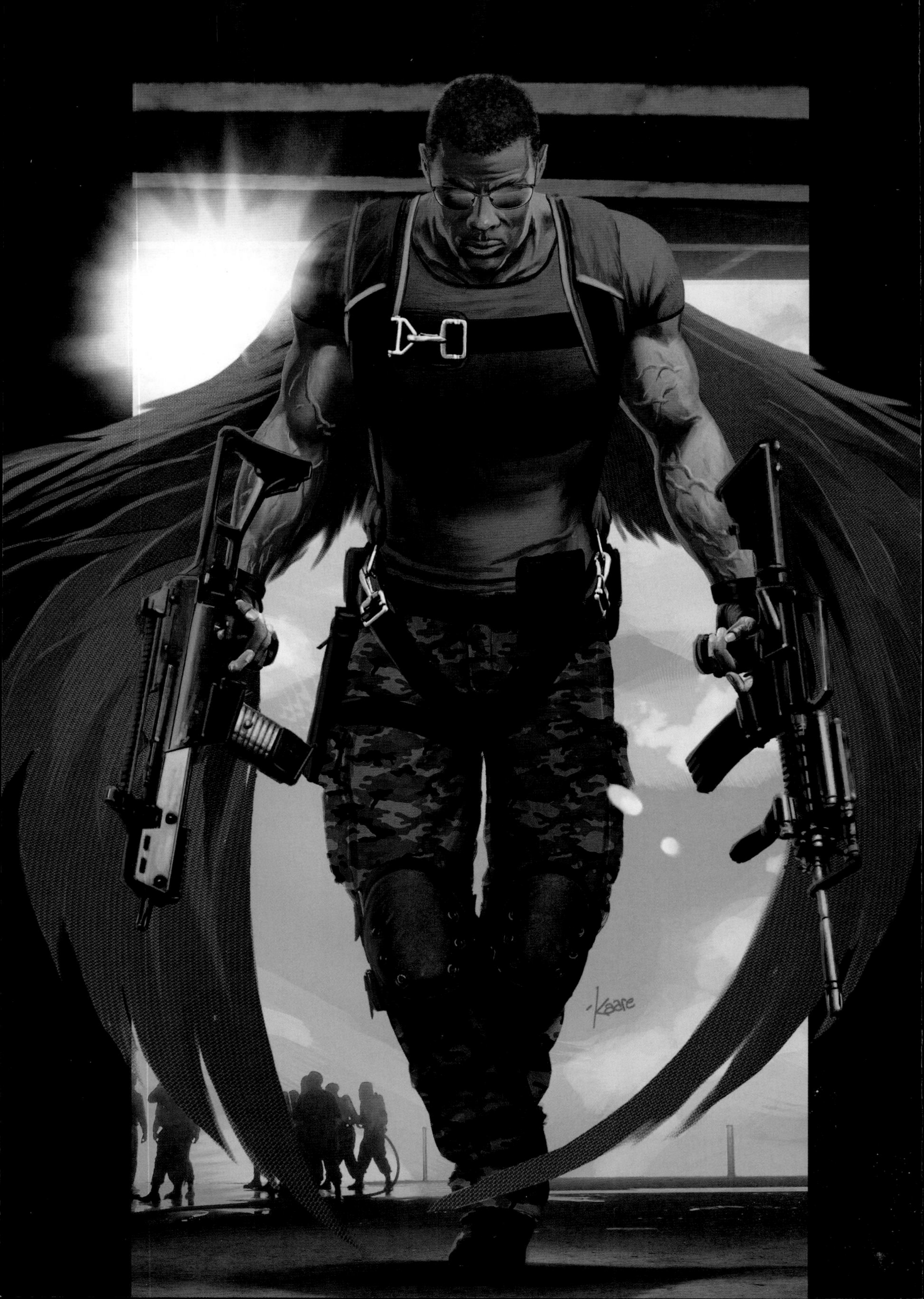

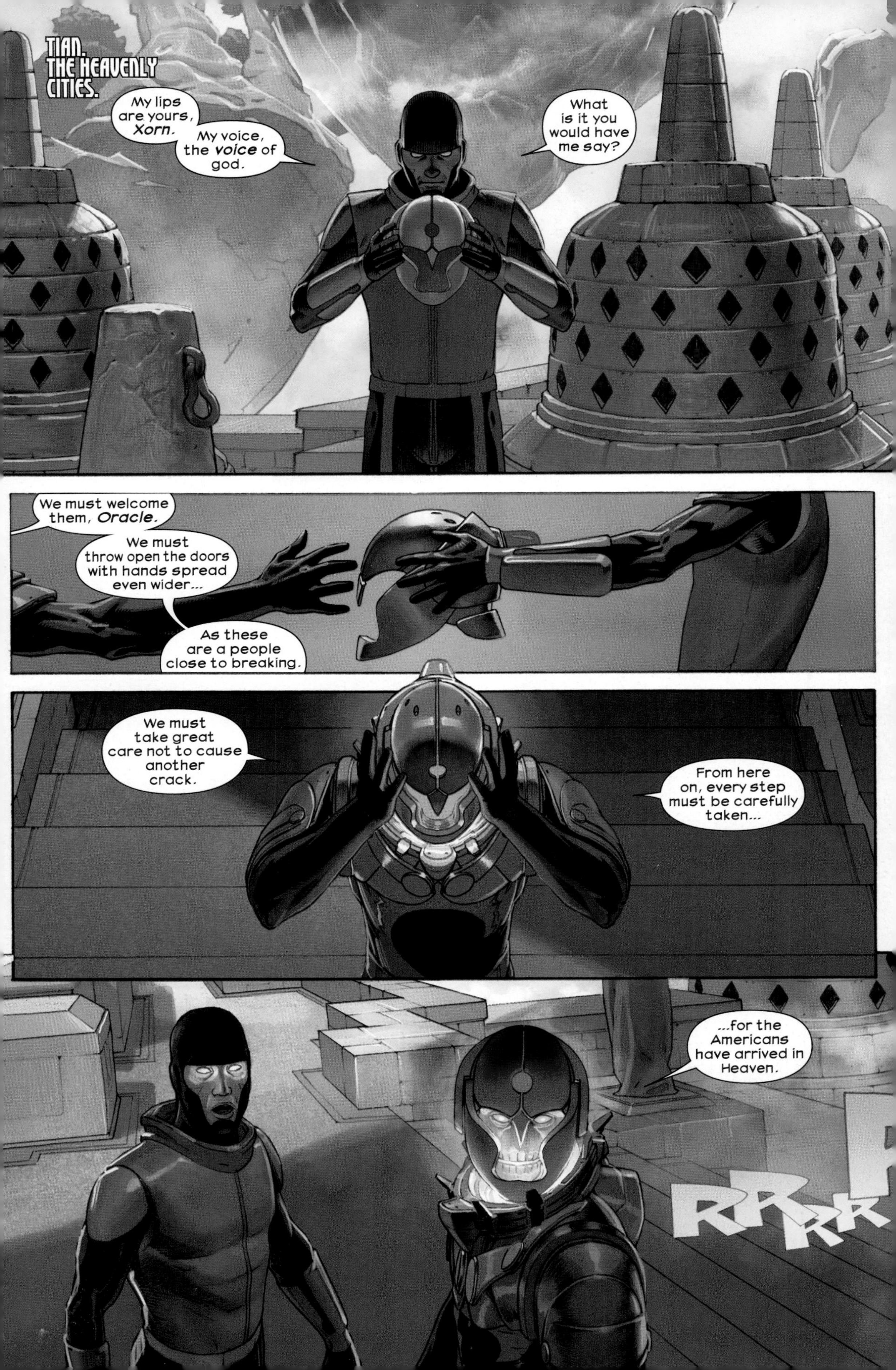
TIAN.
THE HEAVENLY CITIES.
My lips are yours, Xorn.
My voice, the voice of god.
What is it you would have me say?
We must welcome them, Oracle.
We must throw open the doors with hands spread even wider...
As these are a people close to breaking.
We must take great care not to cause another crack.
From here on, every step must be carefully taken...
...for the Americans have arrived in Heaven.
RRRRR

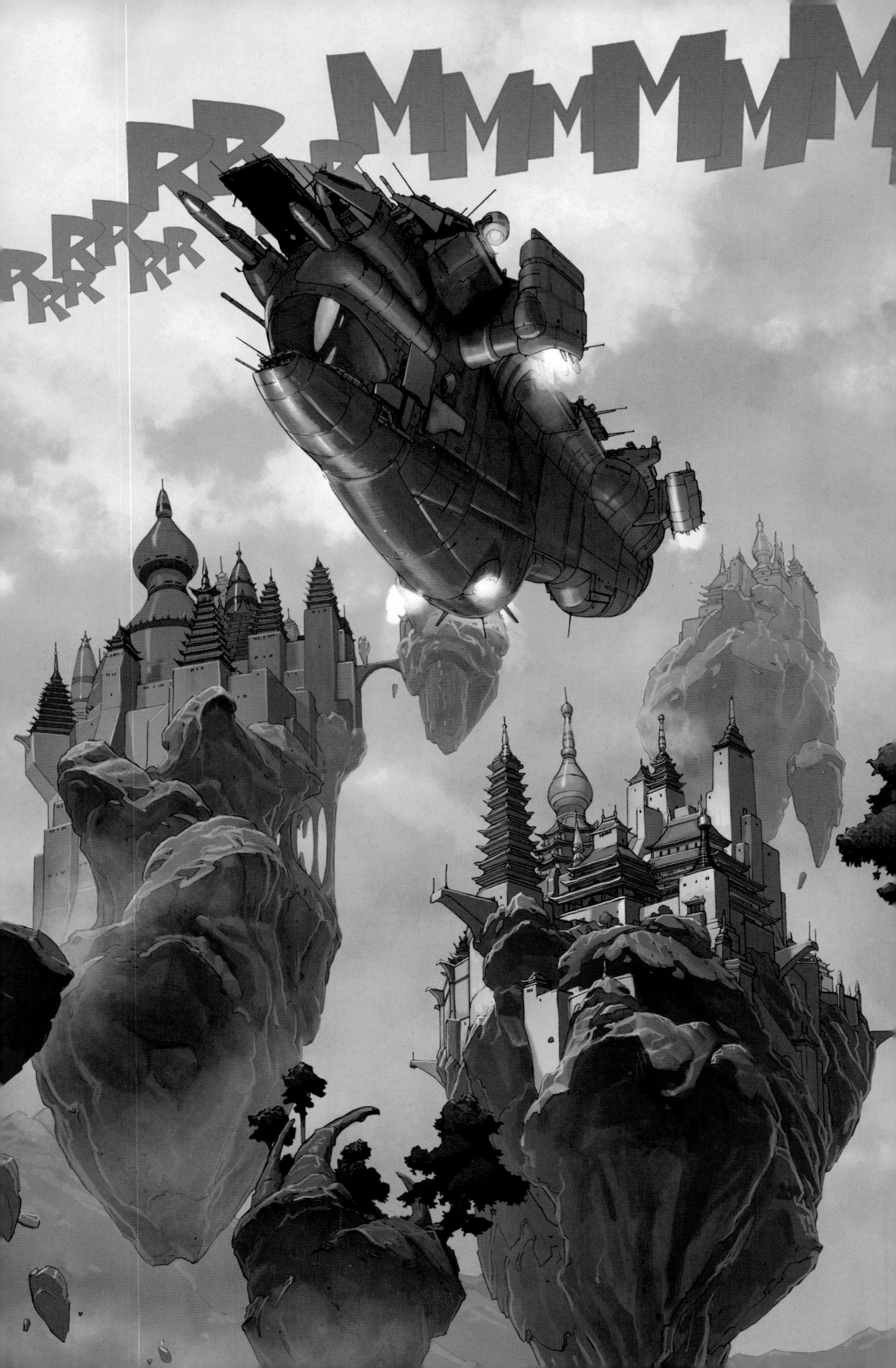
RRRRRRRRRRRMMMMMMMM

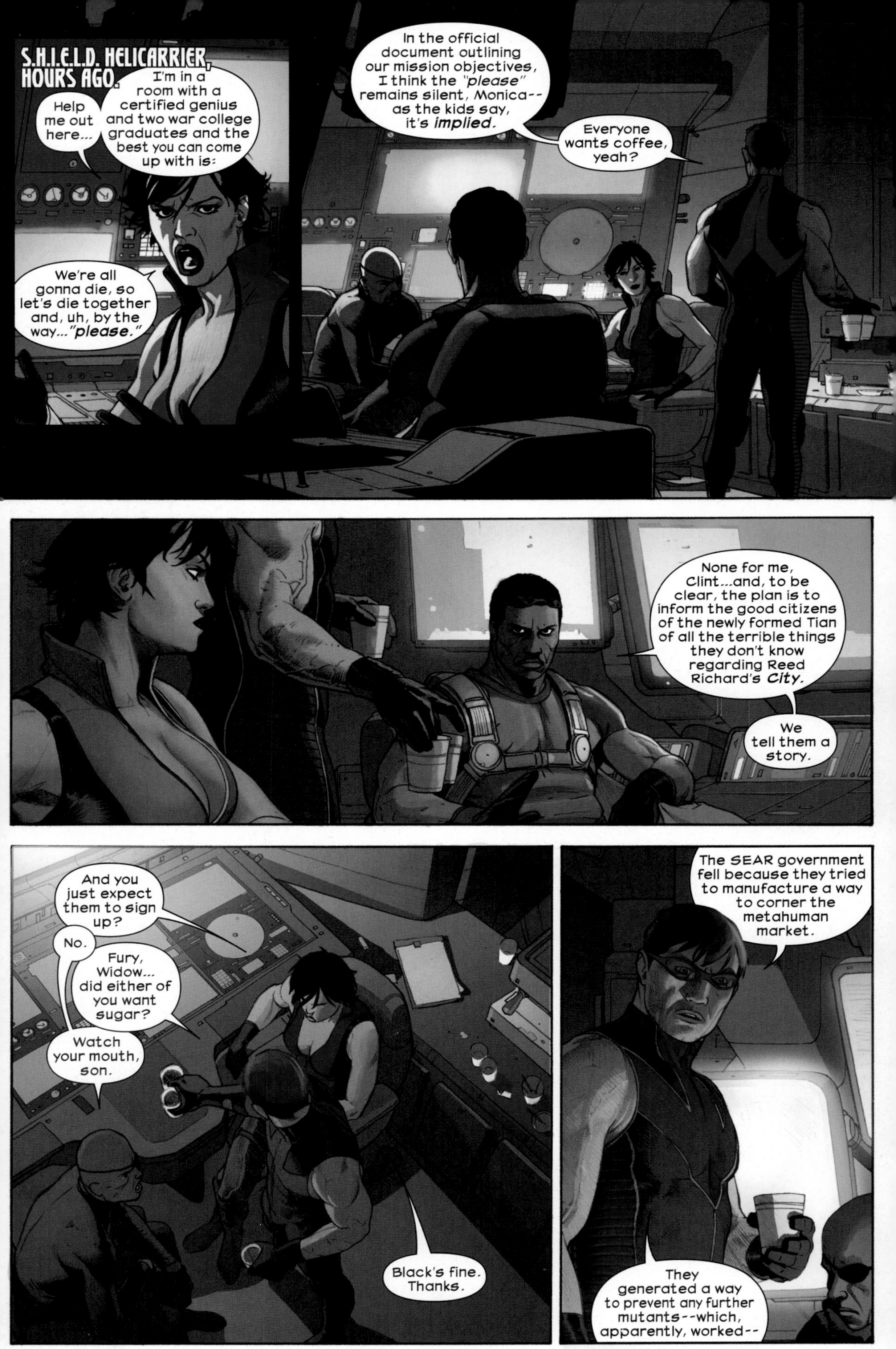

S.H.I.E.L.D. HELICARRIER, HOURS AGO.
Help me out here...
I'm in a room with a certified genius and two war college graduates and the best you can come up with is:
We're all gonna die, so let's die together and, uh, by the way..."please."
In the official document outlining our mission objectives, I think the "please" remains silent, Monica-- as the kids say, it's implied.
Everyone wants coffee, yeah?
None for me, Clint...and, to be clear, the plan is to inform the good citizens of the newly formed Tian of all the terrible things they don't know regarding Reed Richard's City.
We tell them a story.
And you just expect them to sign up?
No.
Fury, Widow... did either of you want sugar?
Watch your mouth, son.
Black's fine. Thanks.
The SEAR government fell because they tried to manufacture a way to corner the metahuman market.
They generated a way to prevent any further mutants--which, apparently, worked--

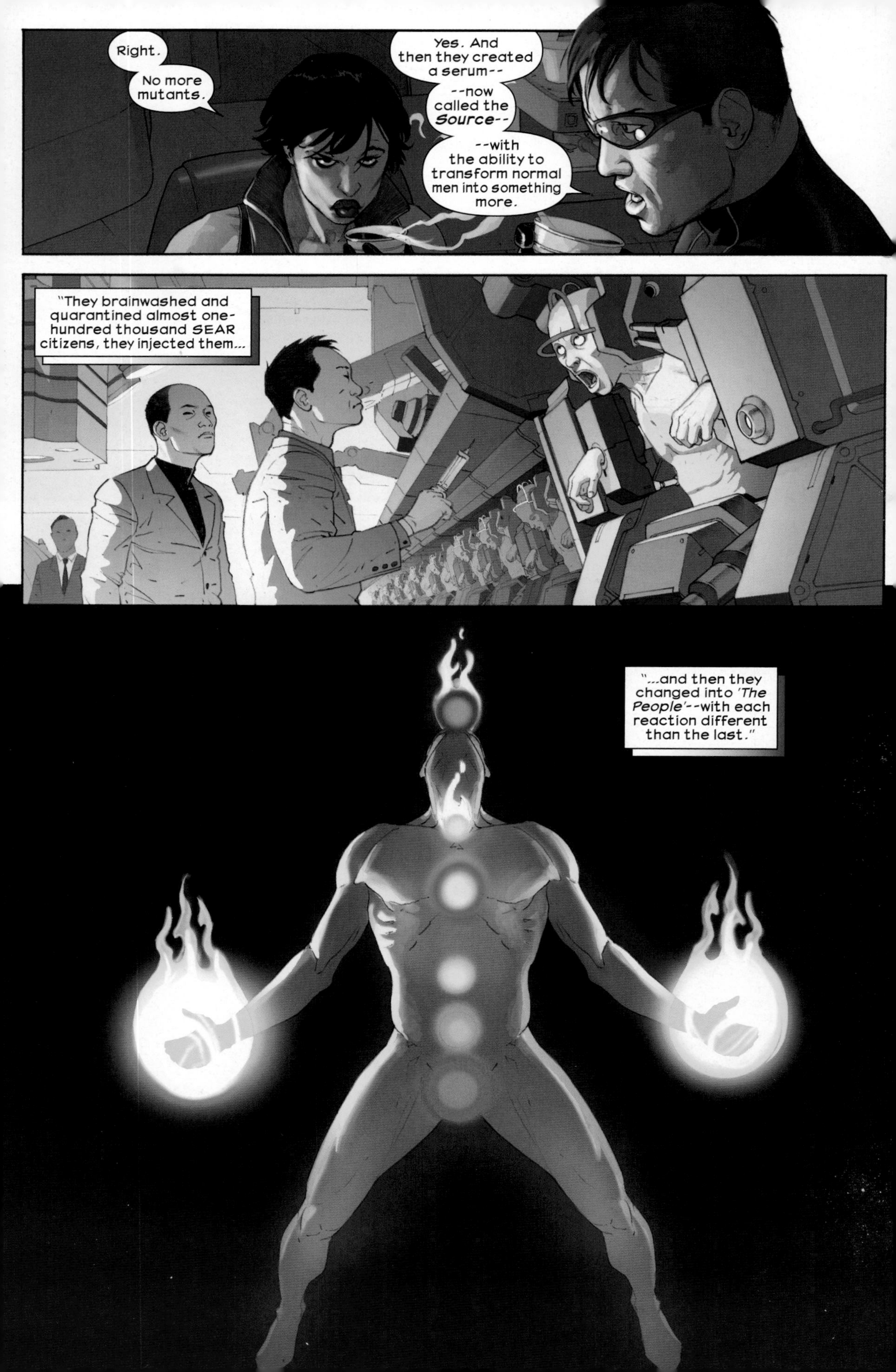

Right.
No more mutants.
Yes. And then they created a serum--
--now called the *Source*--
--with the ability to transform normal men into something more.
"They brainwashed and quarantined almost one-hundred thousand SEAR citizens, they injected them...
"...and then they changed into *'The People'*--with each reaction different than the last."

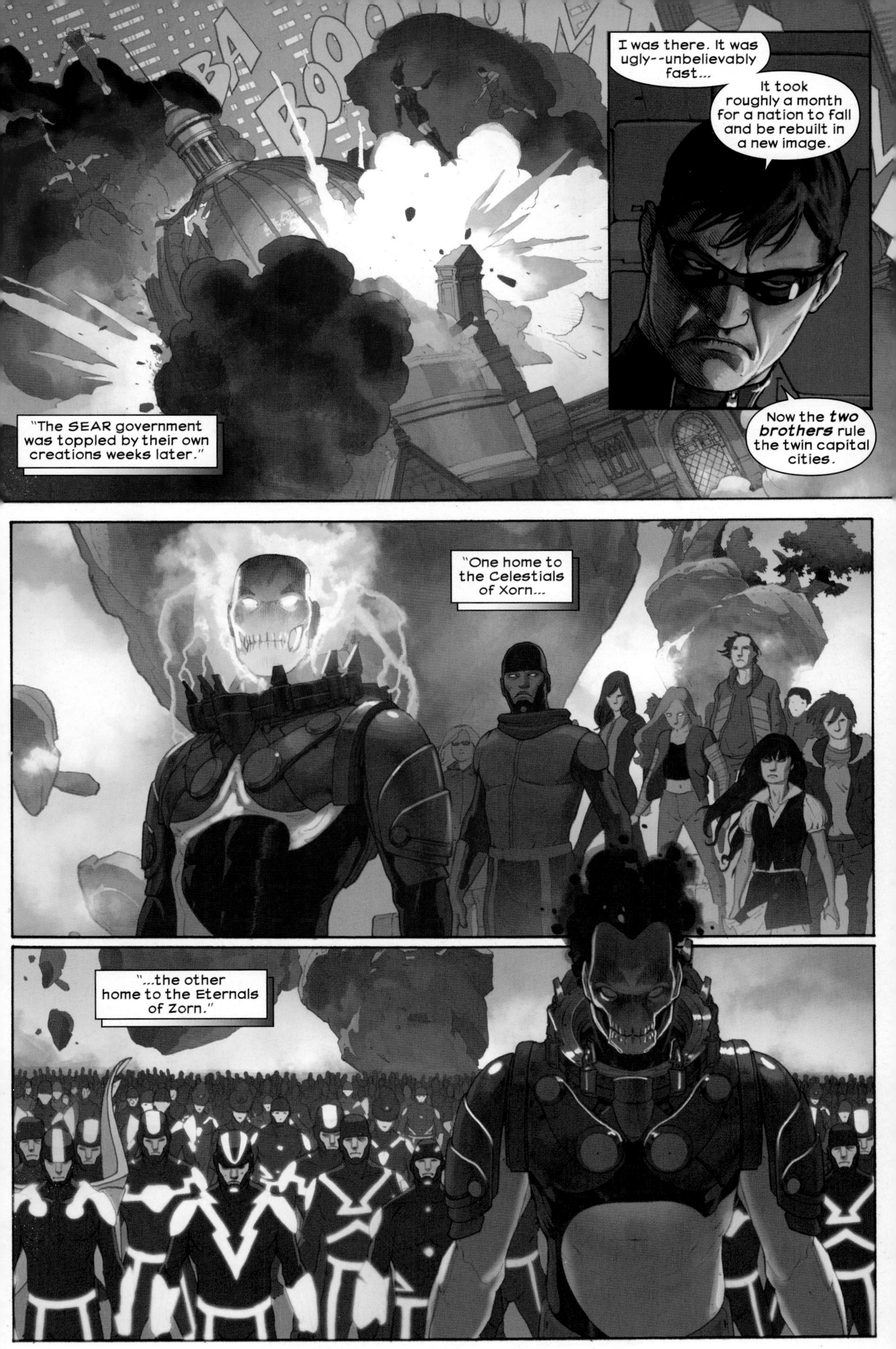

BA BOOM
I was there. It was ugly--unbelievably fast...
It took roughly a month for a nation to fall and be rebuilt in a new image.
"The SEAR government was toppled by their own creations weeks later."
Now the *two brothers* rule the twin capital cities.
"One home to the Celestials of Xorn...
"...the other home to the Eternals of Zorn."

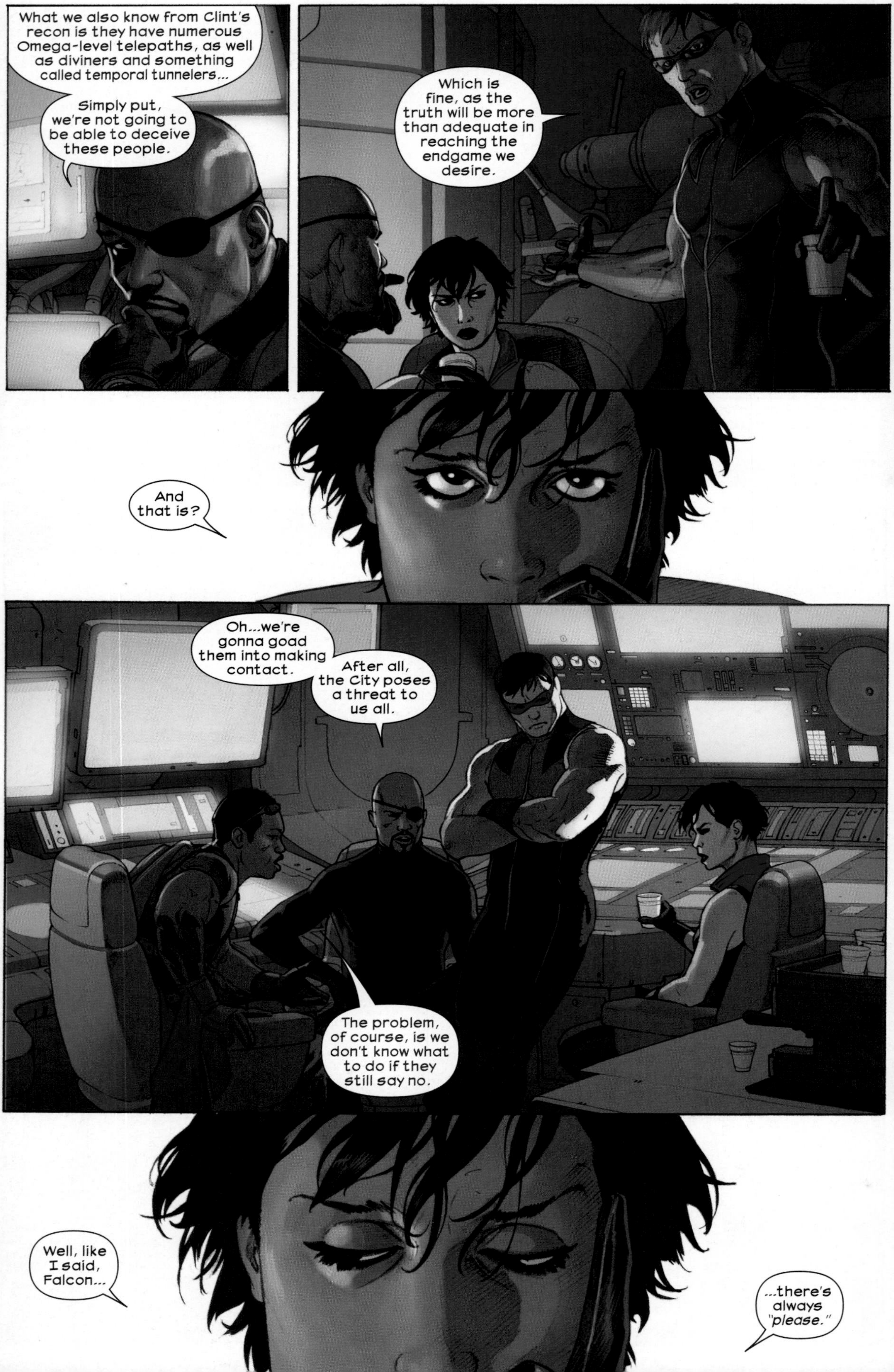
What we also know from Clint's recon is they have numerous Omega-level telepaths, as well as diviners and something called temporal tunnelers...
Simply put, we're not going to be able to deceive these people.
Which is fine, as the truth will be more than adequate in reaching the endgame we desire.
And that is?
Oh...we're gonna goad them into making contact.
After all, the City poses a threat to us all.
The problem, of course, is we don't know what to do if they still say no.
Well, like I said, Falcon...
...there's always *"please."*

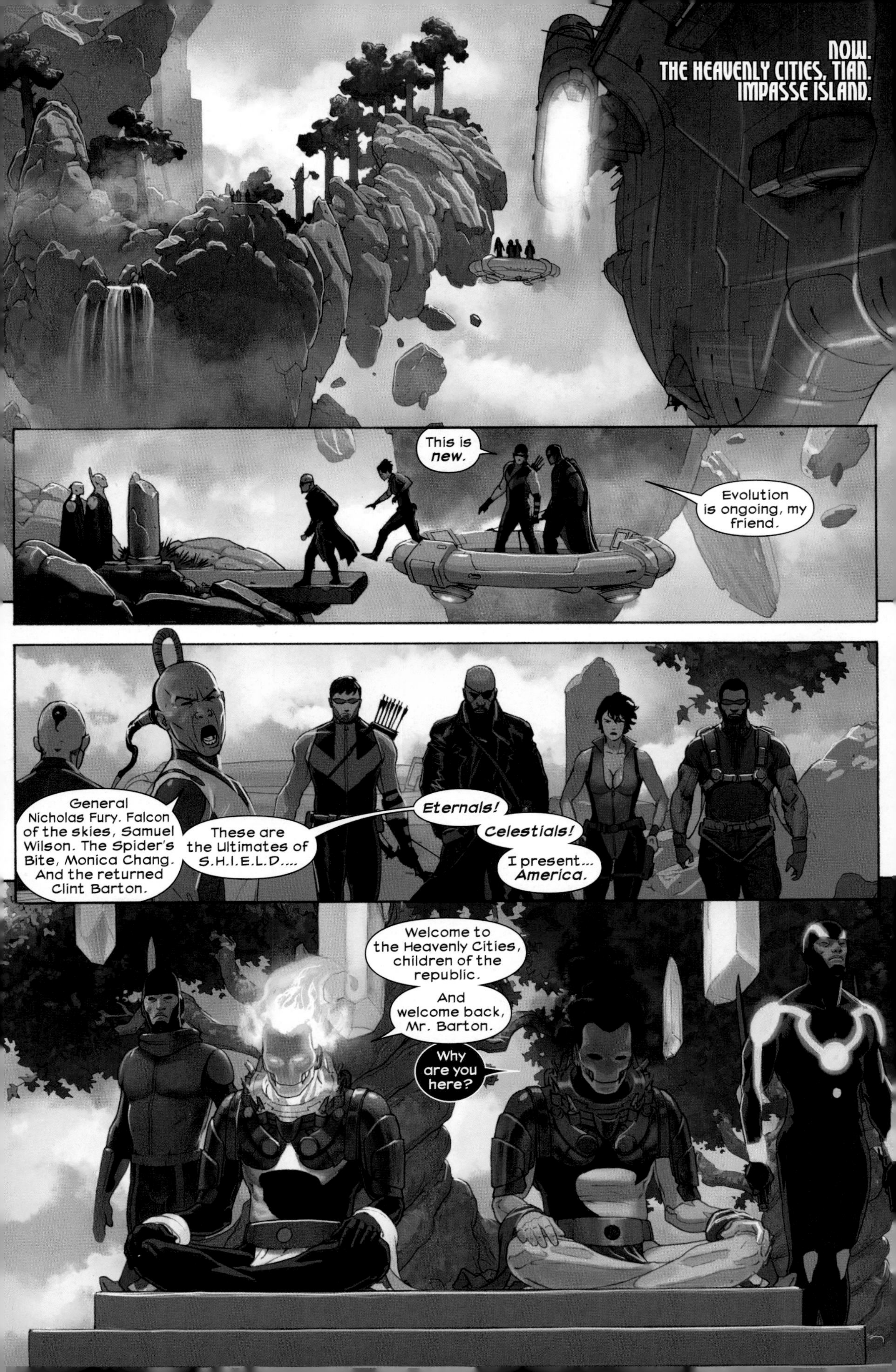
NOW.
THE HEAVENLY CITIES, TIAN.
IMPASSE ISLAND.
This is *new*.
Evolution is ongoing, my friend.
Eternals!
Celestials!
I present... *America*.
These are the Ultimates of S.H.I.E.L.D....
General Nicholas Fury. Falcon of the skies, Samuel Wilson. The Spider's Bite, Monica Chang. And the returned Clint Barton.
Welcome to the Heavenly Cities, children of the republic.
And welcome back, Mr. Barton.
Why are you here?

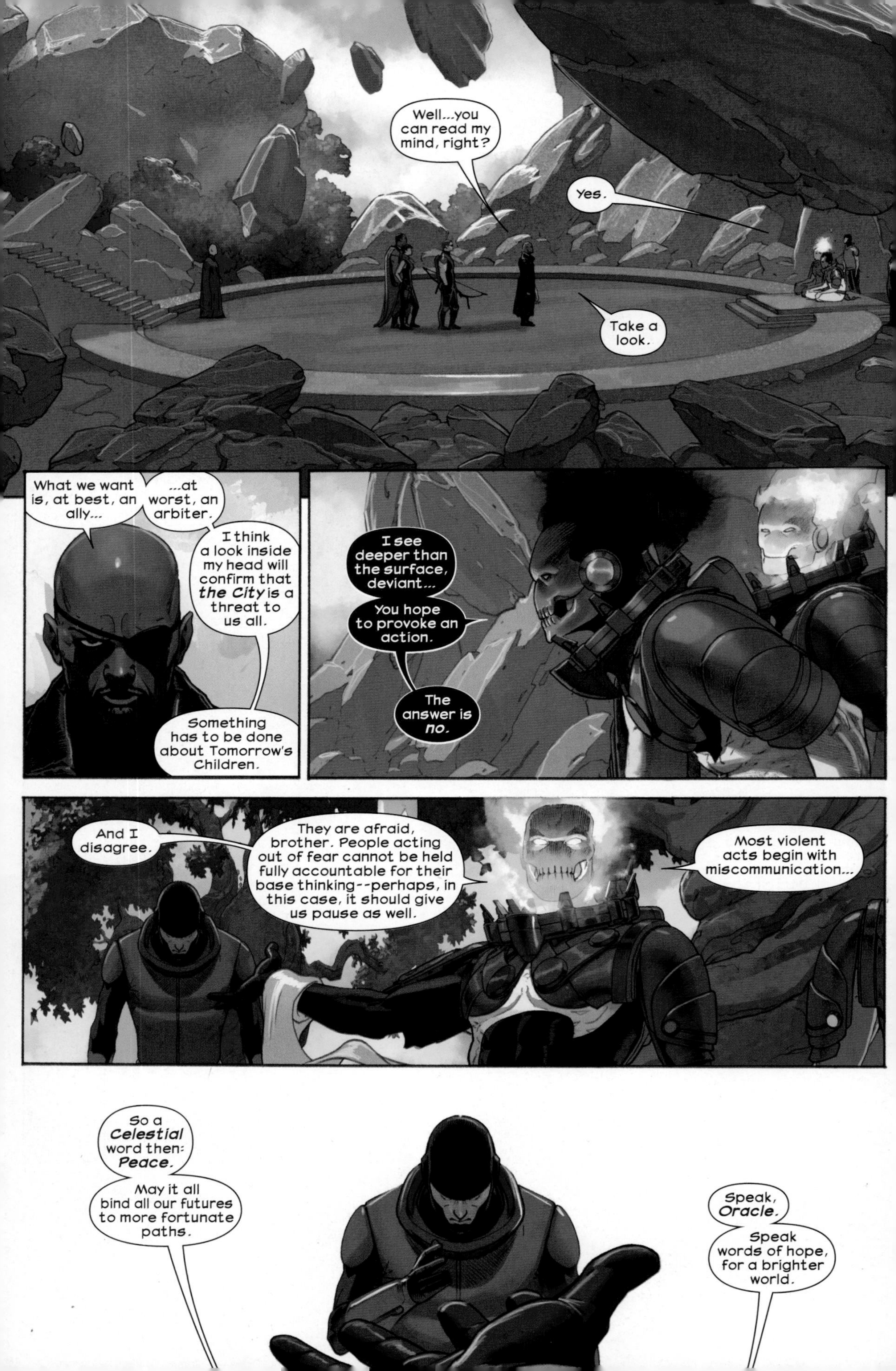
Well...you can read my mind, right?
Yes.
Take a look.
What we want is, at best, an ally...
...at worst, an arbiter.
I think a look inside my head will confirm that *the City* is a threat to us all.
Something has to be done about Tomorrow's Children.
I see deeper than the surface, deviant...
You hope to provoke an action.
The answer is *no.*
And I disagree.
They are afraid, brother. People acting out of fear cannot be held fully accountable for their base thinking--perhaps, in this case, it should give us pause as well.
Most violent acts begin with miscommunication...
So a *Celestial* word then: *Peace.*
May it all bind all our futures to more fortunate paths.
Speak, *Oracle.*
Speak words of hope, for a brighter world.

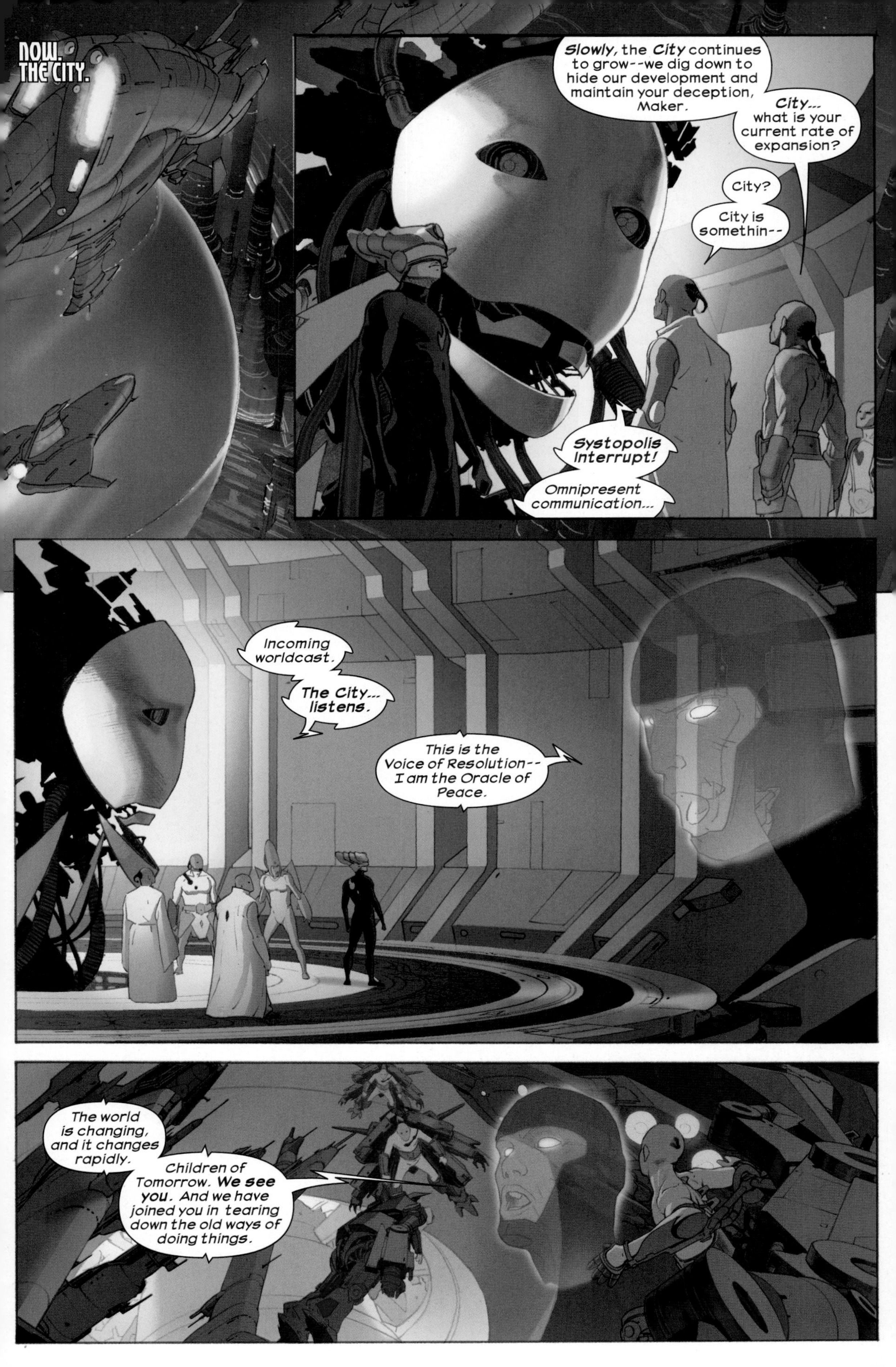
NOW. THE CITY.
Slowly, the City continues to grow--we dig down to hide our development and maintain your deception, Maker.
City... what is your current rate of expansion?
City?
City is somethin--
Systopolis Interrupt!
Omnipresent communication...
Incoming worldcast.
The City... listens.
This is the Voice of Resolution-- I am the Oracle of Peace.
The world is changing, and it changes rapidly.
Children of Tomorrow. We see you. And we have joined you in tearing down the old ways of doing things.

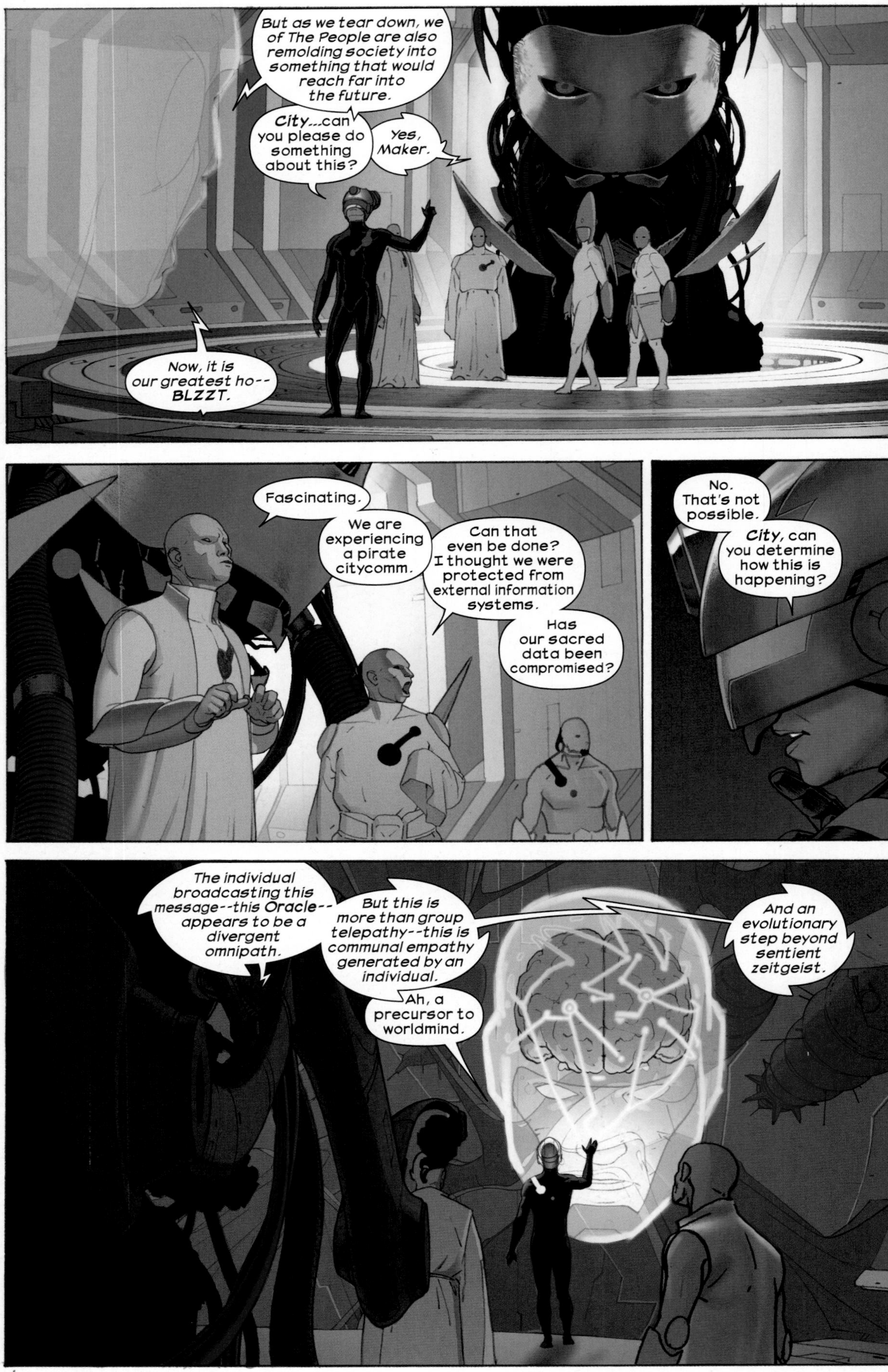
But as we tear down, we of The People are also remolding society into something that would reach far into the future.
City...can you please do something about this?
Yes, Maker.
Now, it is our greatest ho-- BLZZT.
Fascinating.
We are experiencing a pirate citycomm.
Can that even be done? I thought we were protected from external information systems.
Has our sacred data been compromised?
No. That's not possible.
City, can you determine how this is happening?
The individual broadcasting this message--this Oracle--appears to be a divergent omnipath.
But this is more than group telepathy--this is communal empathy generated by an individual.
And an evolutionary step beyond sentient zeitgeist.
Ah, a precursor to worldmind.

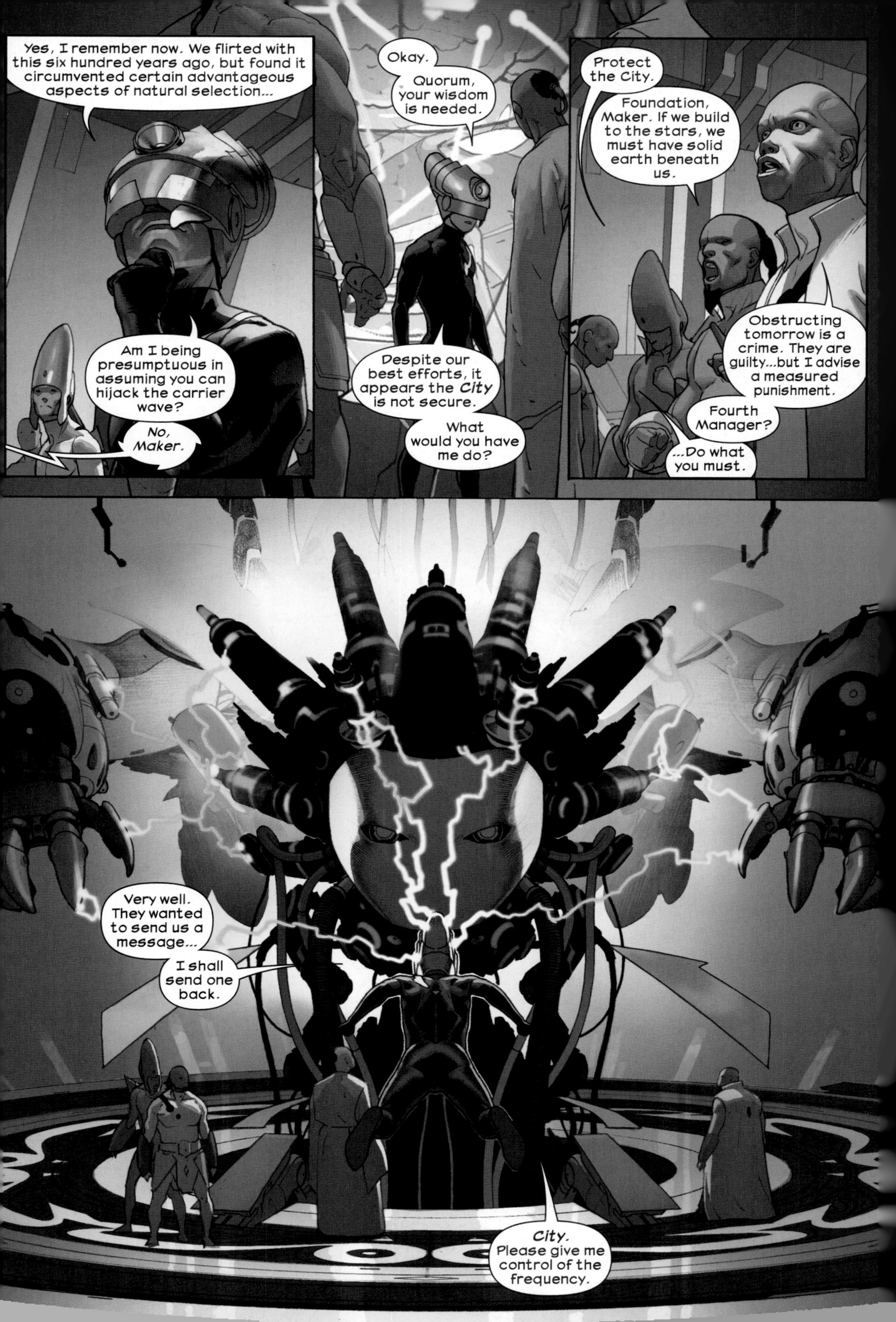
Yes, I remember now. We flirted with this six hundred years ago, but found it circumvented certain advantageous aspects of natural selection...
Am I being presumptuous in assuming you can hijack the carrier wave?
No, Maker.
Okay.
Quorum, your wisdom is needed.
Despite our best efforts, it appears the City is not secure.
What would you have me do?
Protect the City.
Foundation, Maker. If we build to the stars, we must have solid earth beneath us.
Obstructing tomorrow is a crime. They are guilty...but I advise a measured punishment.
Fourth Manager?
...Do what you must.
Very well. They wanted to send us a message...
I shall send one back.
City. Please give me control of the frequency.

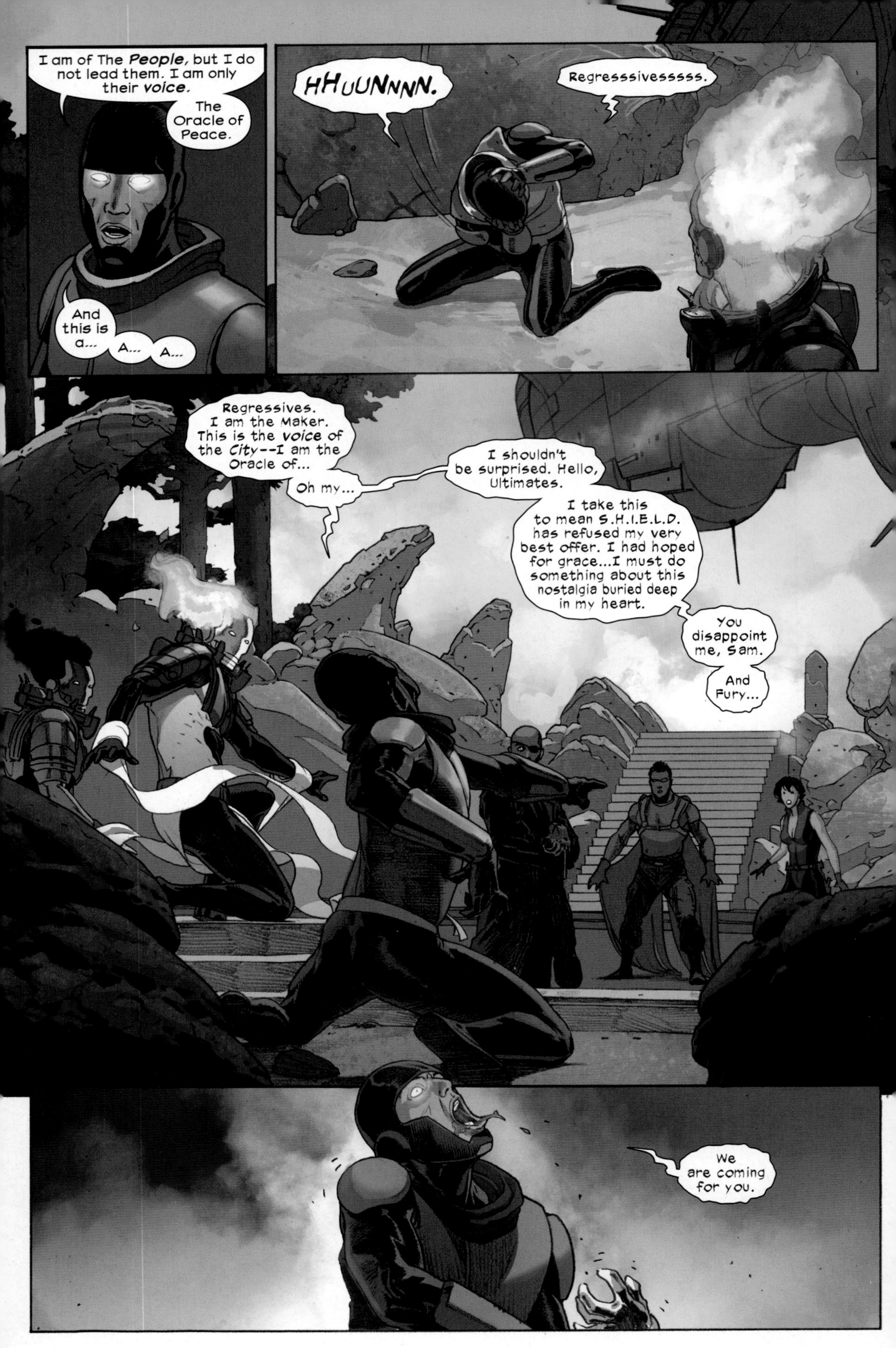
I am of The *People*, but I do not lead them. I am only their *voice.*
The Oracle of Peace.
And this is a...
A...
A...
HHUUNNNN.
Regresssivesssss.
Regressives. I am the Maker. This is the *voice* of the *City*--I am the Oracle of...
Oh my...
I shouldn't be surprised. Hello, Ultimates.
I take this to mean S.H.I.E.L.D. has refused my very best offer. I had hoped for grace...I must do something about this nostalgia buried deep in my heart.
You disappoint me, Sam.
And Fury...
We are coming for you.

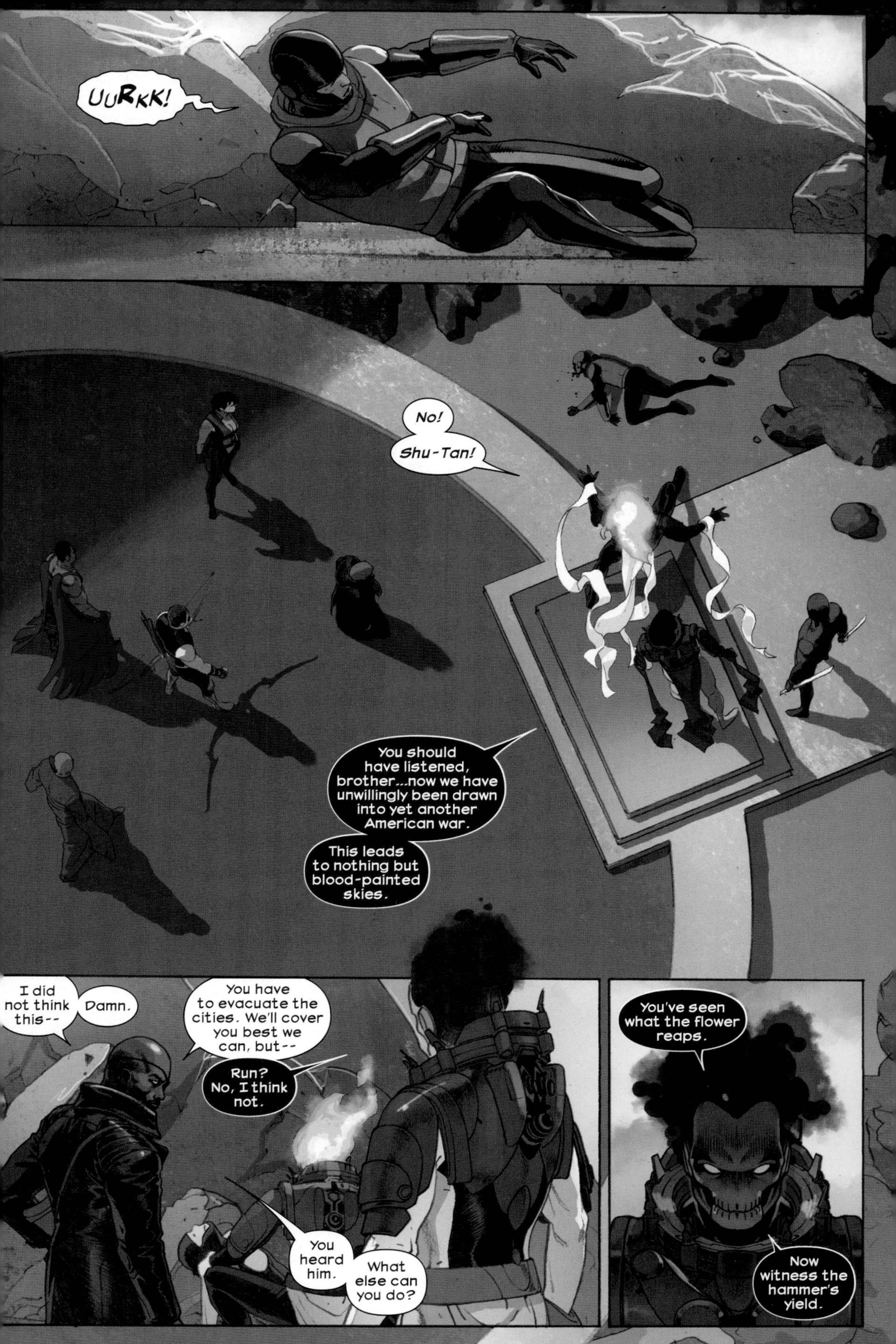
UURKK!
No!
Shu-Tan!
You should have listened, brother...now we have unwillingly been drawn into yet another American war.
This leads to nothing but blood-painted skies.
I did not think this--
Damn.
You have to evacuate the cities. We'll cover you best we can, but--
Run? No, I think not.
You heard him.
What else can you do?
You've seen what the flower reaps.
Now witness the hammer's yield.

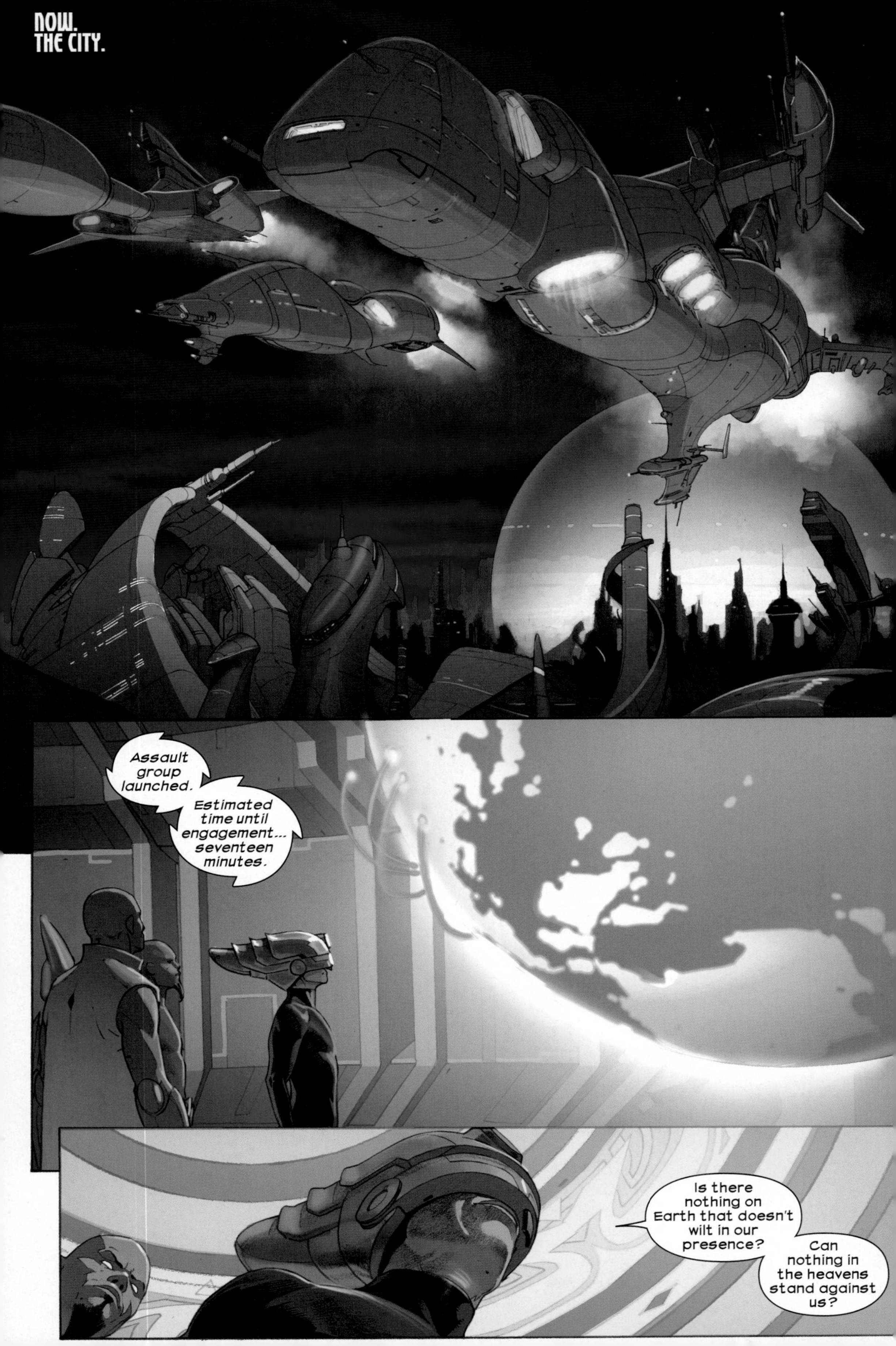
NOW.
THE CITY.
Assault group launched.
Estimated time until engagement... seventeen minutes.
Is there nothing on Earth that doesn't wilt in our presence?
Can nothing in the heavens stand against us?

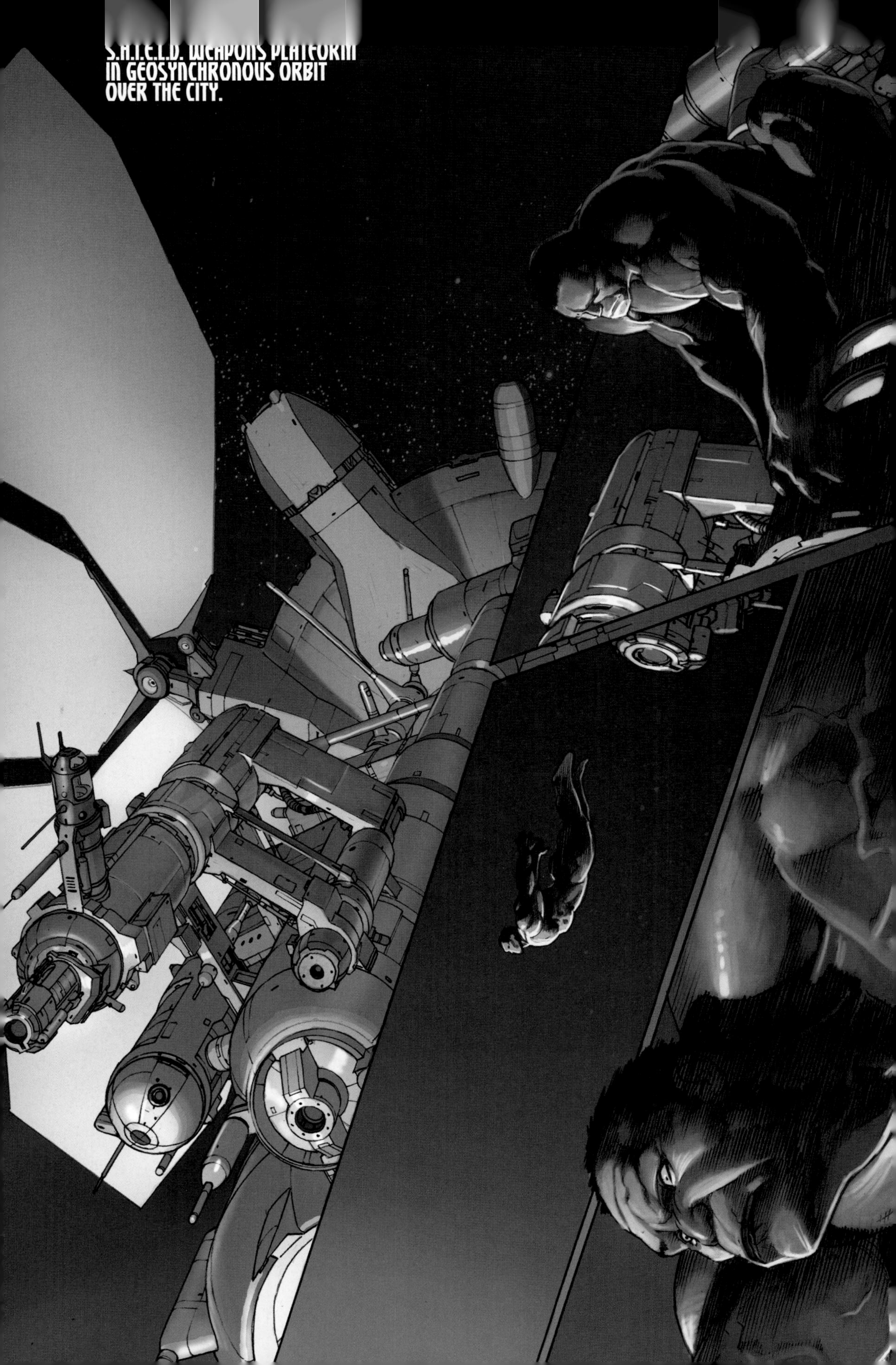
S.H.I.E.L.D. WEAPONS PLATFORM
IN GEOSYNCHRONOUS ORBIT
OVER THE CITY.

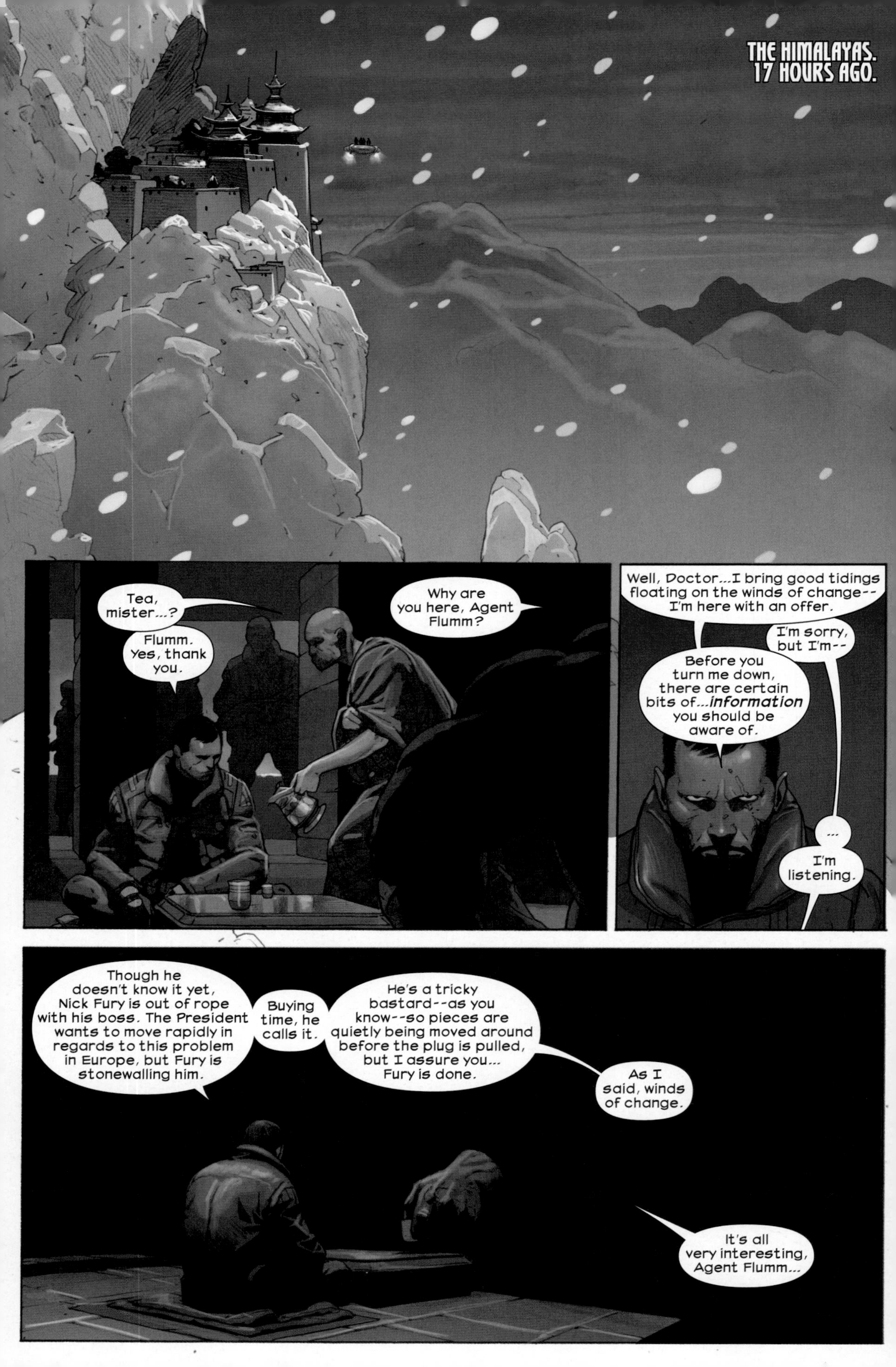
THE HIMALAYAS. 17 HOURS AGO.
Tea, mister...?
Flumm. Yes, thank you.
Why are you here, Agent Flumm?
Well, Doctor...I bring good tidings floating on the winds of change-- I'm here with an offer.
I'm sorry, but I'm--
Before you turn me down, there are certain bits of...*information* you should be aware of.
...
I'm listening.
Though he doesn't know it yet, Nick Fury is out of rope with his boss. The President wants to move rapidly in regards to this problem in Europe, but Fury is stonewalling him.
Buying time, he calls it.
He's a tricky bastard--as you know--so pieces are quietly being moved around before the plug is pulled, but I assure you... Fury is done.
As I said, winds of change.
It's all very interesting, Agent Flumm...

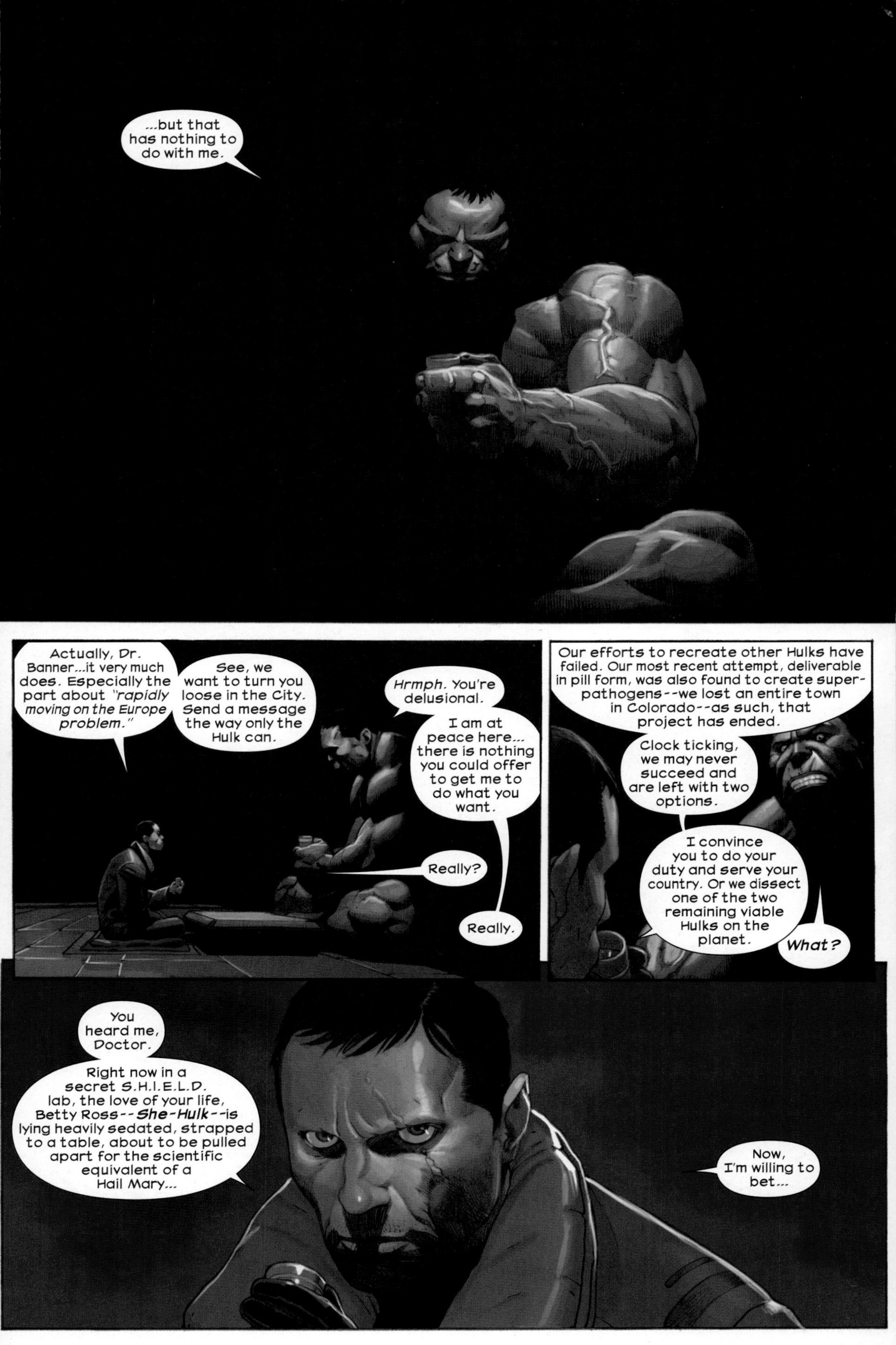

...but that has nothing to do with me.
Actually, Dr. Banner...it very much does. Especially the part about *"rapidly moving on the Europe problem."*
See, we want to turn you loose in the City. Send a message the way only the Hulk can.
Hrmph. You're delusional.
I am at peace here... there is nothing you could offer to get me to do what you want.
Really?
Really.
Our efforts to recreate other Hulks have failed. Our most recent attempt, deliverable in pill form, was also found to create super-pathogens--we lost an entire town in Colorado--as such, that project has ended.
Clock ticking, we may never succeed and are left with two options.
I convince you to do your duty and serve your country. Or we dissect one of the two remaining viable Hulks on the planet.
What?
You heard me, Doctor.
Right now in a secret S.H.I.E.L.D. lab, the love of your life, Betty Ross--*She-Hulk*--is lying heavily sedated, strapped to a table, about to be pulled apart for the scientific equivalent of a Hail Mary...
Now, I'm willing to bet...

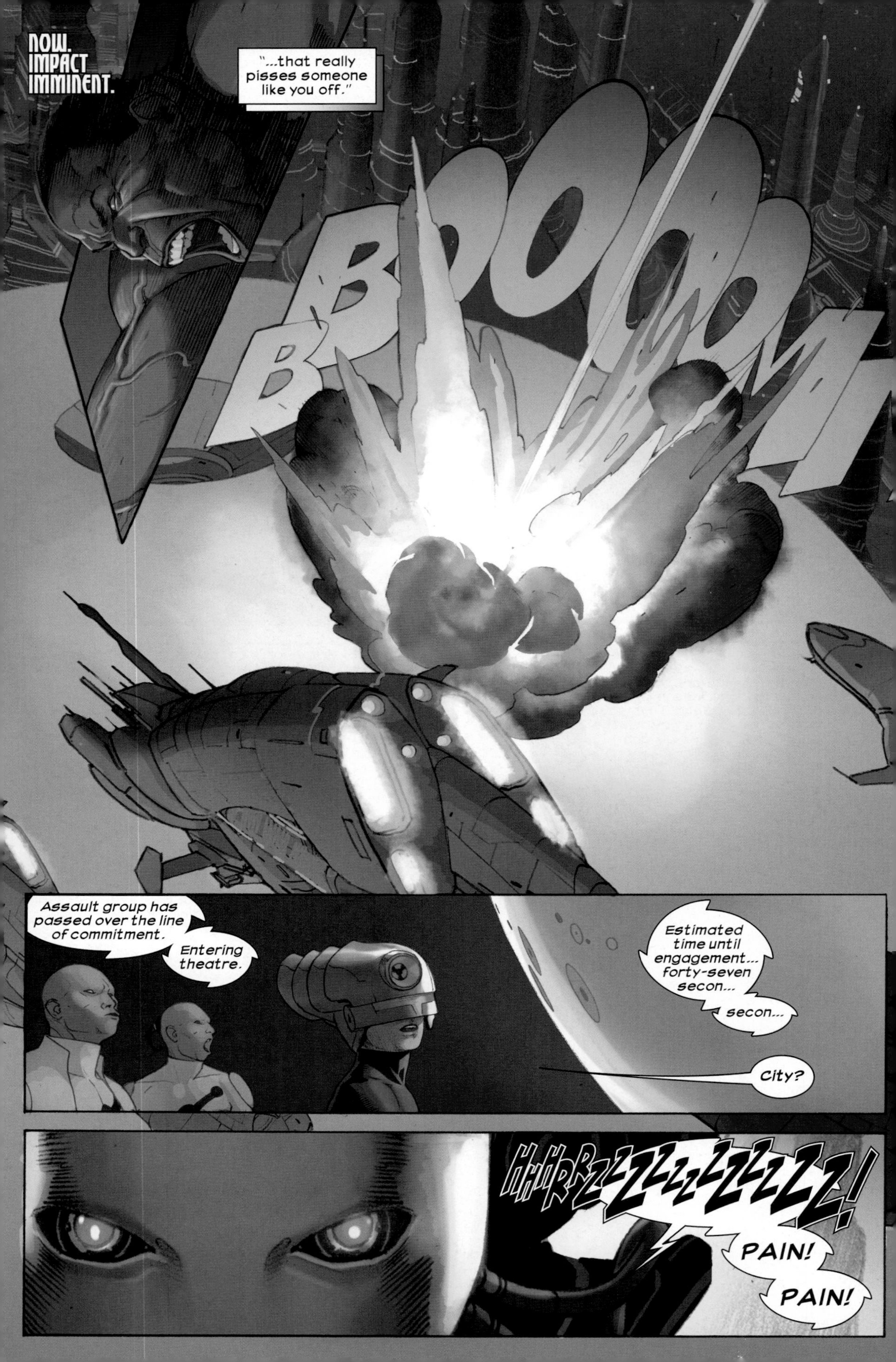
NOW. IMPACT IMMINENT.
"...that really pisses someone like you off."
BOOOOOM!
Assault group has passed over the line of commitment.
Entering theatre.
Estimated time until engagement... forty-seven secon...
secon...
City?
HHHRRZZZZZZZZZZ!
PAIN!
PAIN!

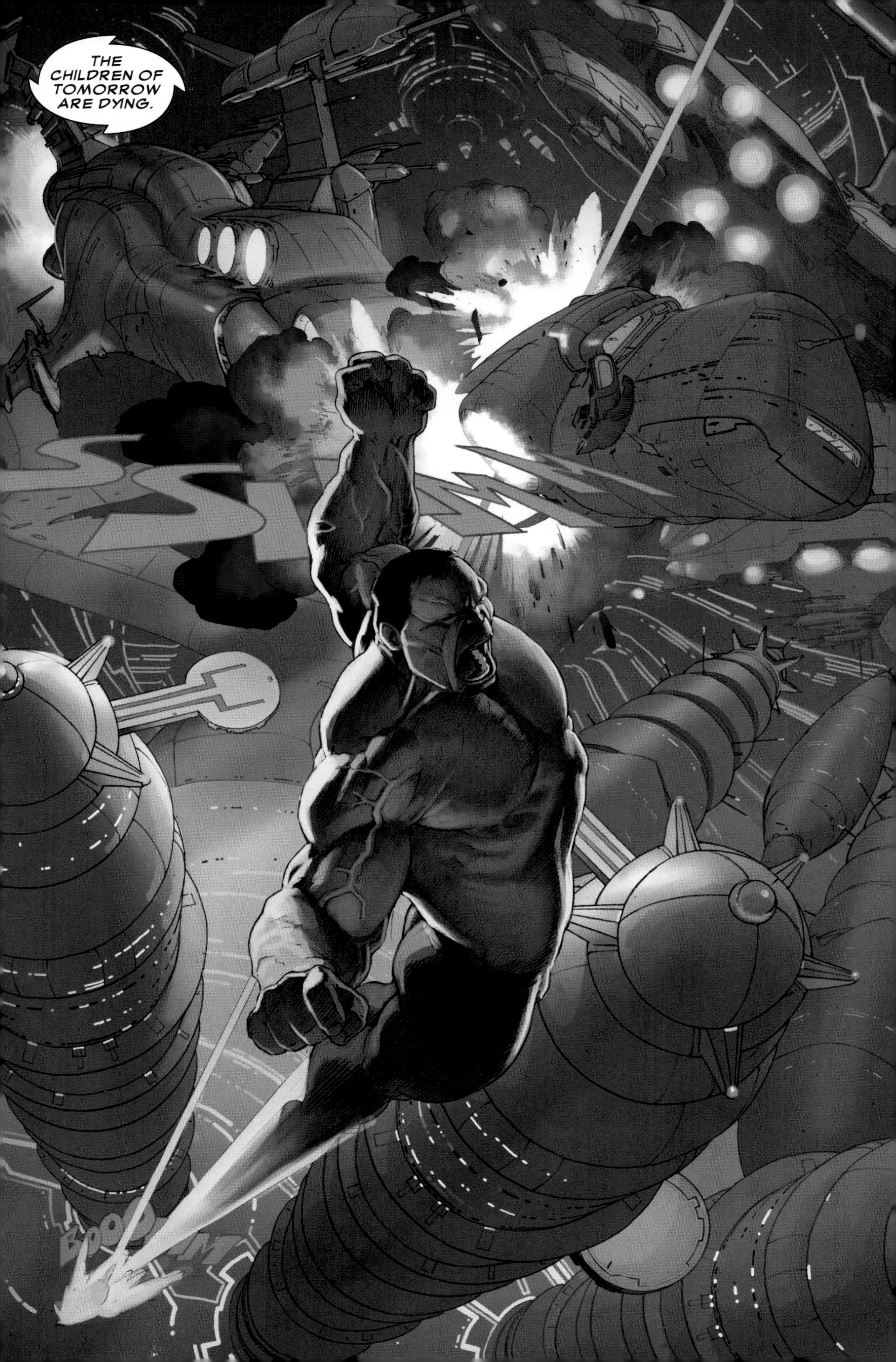
THE CHILDREN OF TOMORROW ARE DYING.

8

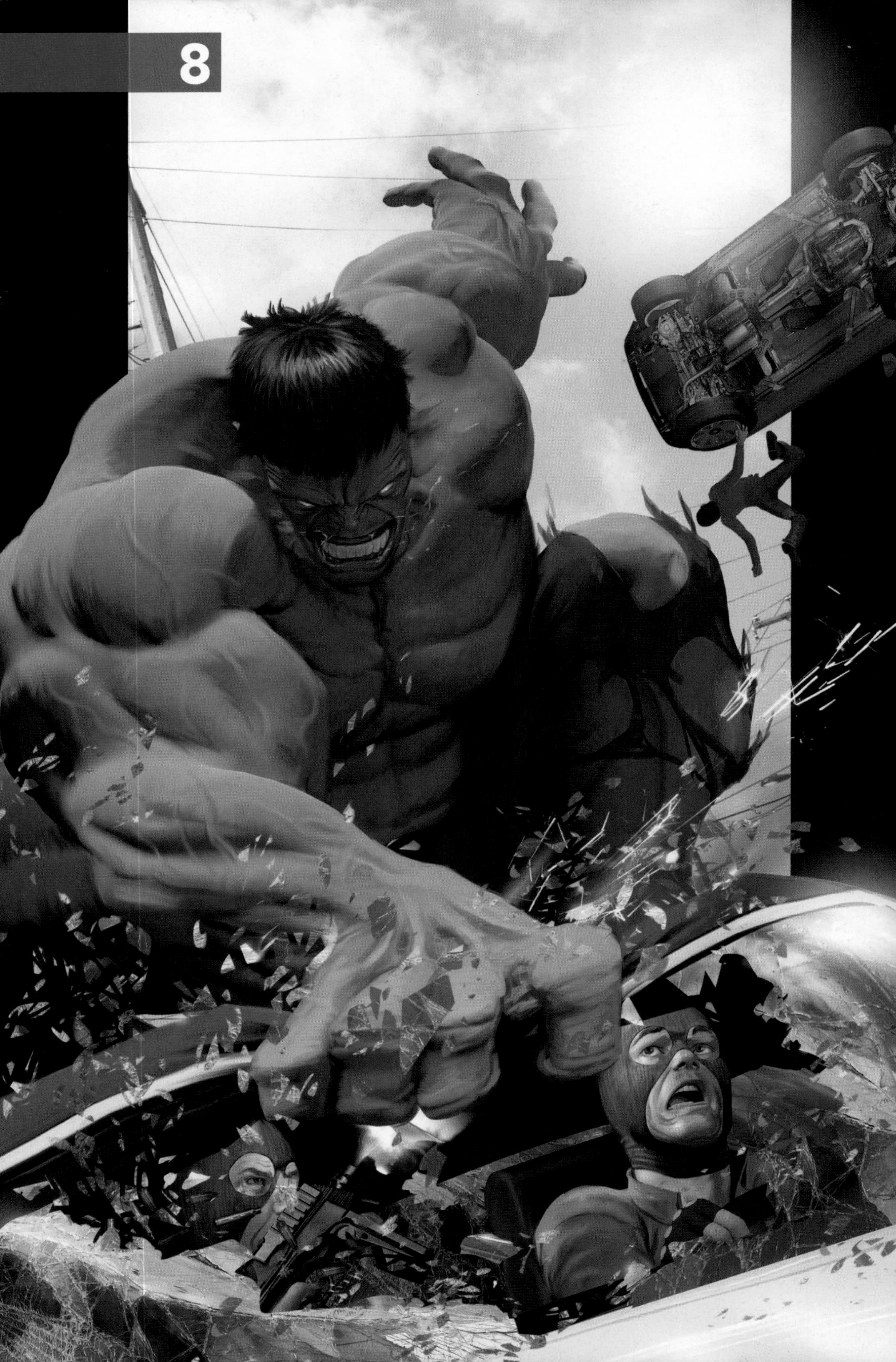

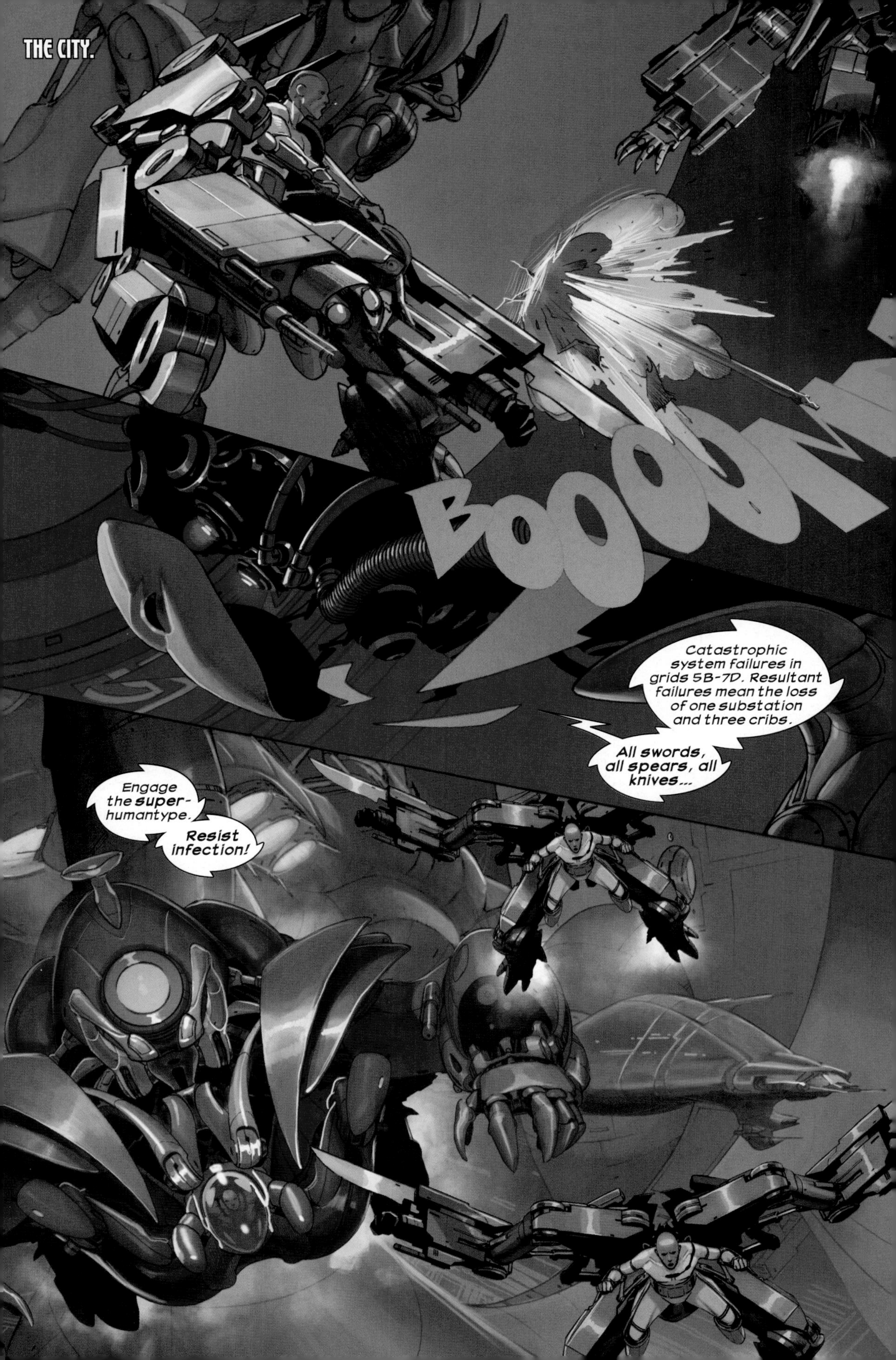
THE CITY.
BOOOOOM
Catastrophic system failures in grids 5B-7D. Resultant failures mean the loss of one substation and three cribs.
All swords, all spears, all knives...
Engage the super-humantype.
Resist infection!

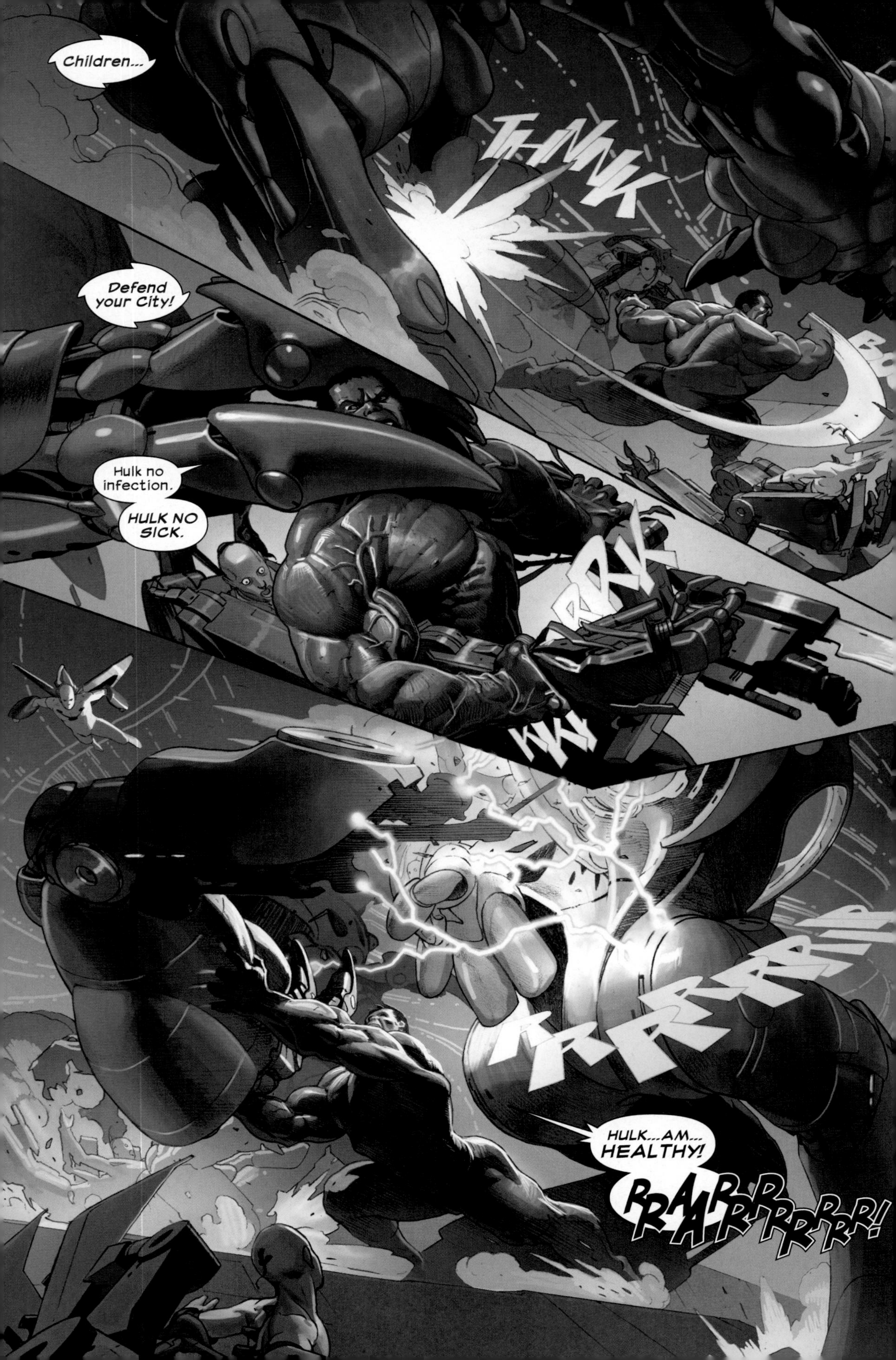
Children...
THNNK
Defend your City!
Hulk no infection.
HULK NO SICK.
KRRK
HULK...AM... HEALTHY!
RRAARRRRRRR!

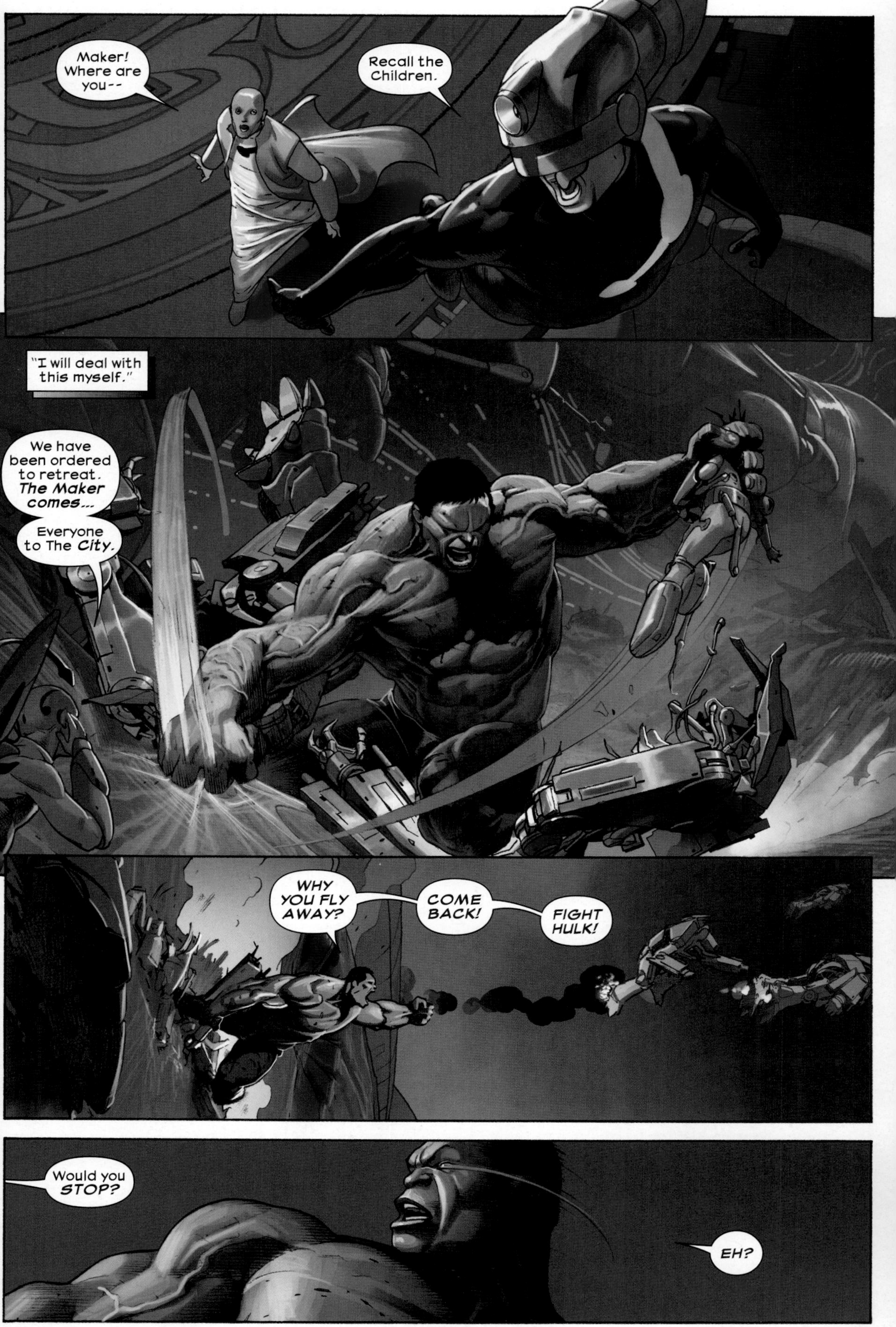
Maker! Where are you--
Recall the Children.
"I will deal with this myself."
We have been ordered to retreat. *The Maker comes...*
Everyone to The *City*.
WHY YOU FLY AWAY?
COME BACK!
FIGHT HULK!
Would you *STOP?*
EH?

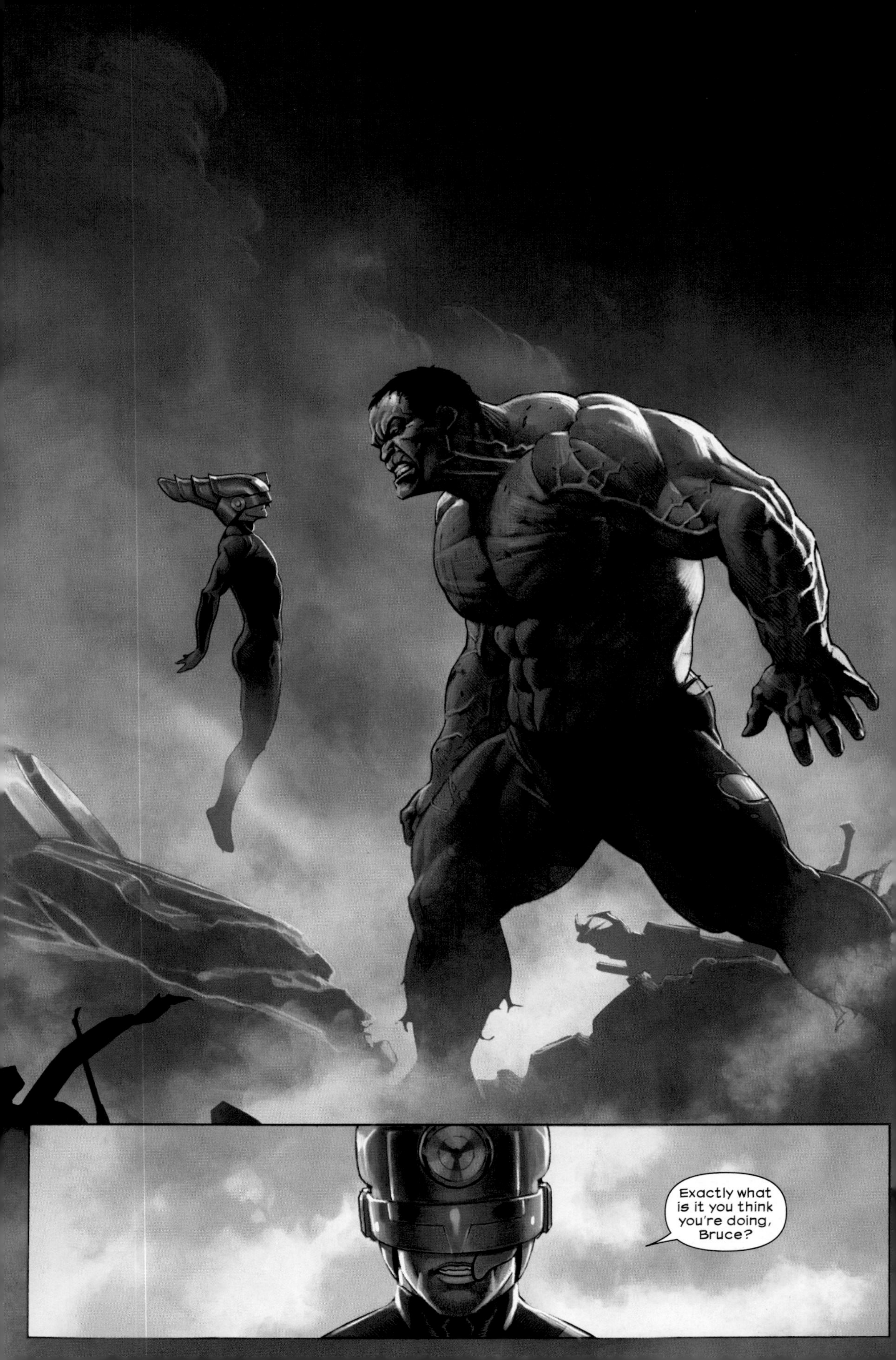
Exactly what is it you think you're doing, Bruce?

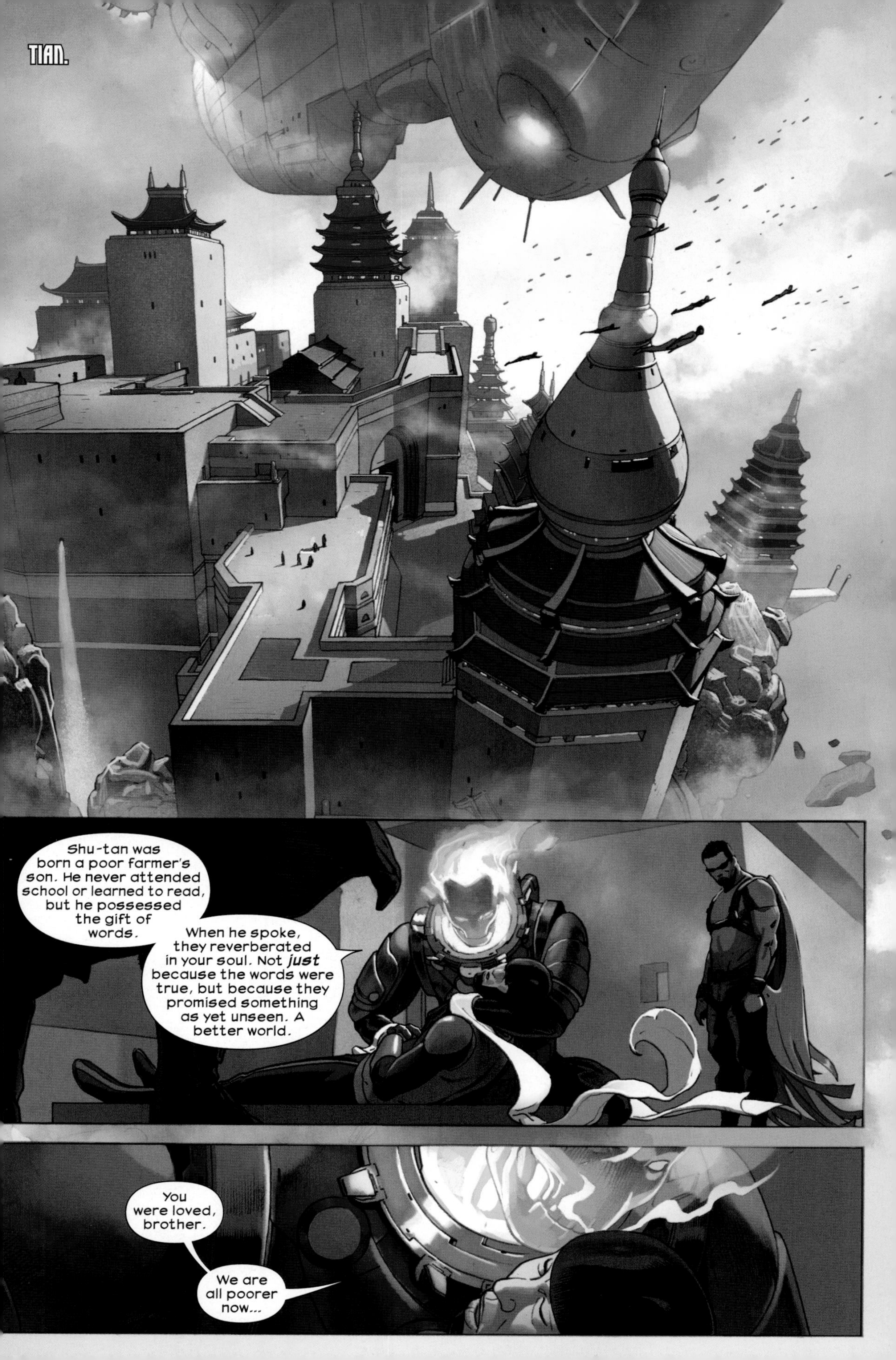
TIAN.
Shu-tan was born a poor farmer's son. He never attended school or learned to read, but he possessed the gift of words.
When he spoke, they reverberated in your soul. Not *just* because the words were true, but because they promised something as yet unseen. A better world.
You were loved, brother.
We are all poorer now...

Only you could account what comes next.

Opdeck says that even if we throw everything off the boat, we're only going to be able to carry eight, maybe nine, thousand of The *People* out of the zone.

Sure. Assuming The Children don't engage us, as well.

Good news on that front...

Helicarrier would make a pretty nice coffin.

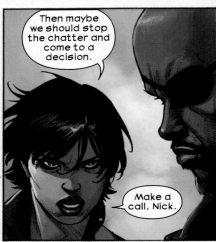

Then maybe we should stop the chatter and come to a decision.

Make a call, Nick.

Help him up, Sam.

Xorn, you need to quickly decide who among your People should come with us.

There will be no need for that, General.

These *animals* will not make it to Tian.

I'm sorry, sir...but you don't understand what they are capable of.

It is you who doesn't understand, Sam Wilson.

My brother is *all-consuming...*

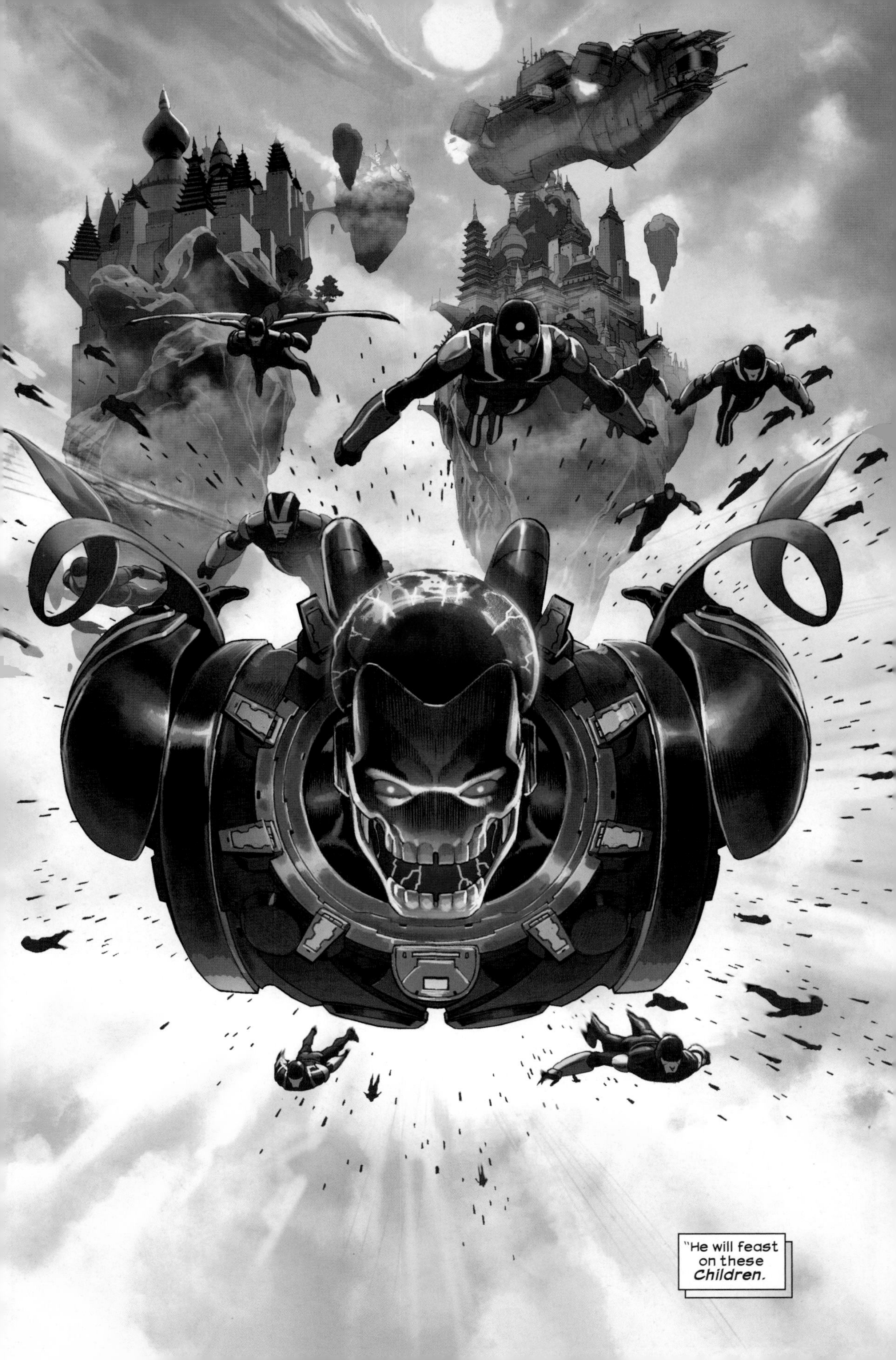
"He will feast on these *Children*.

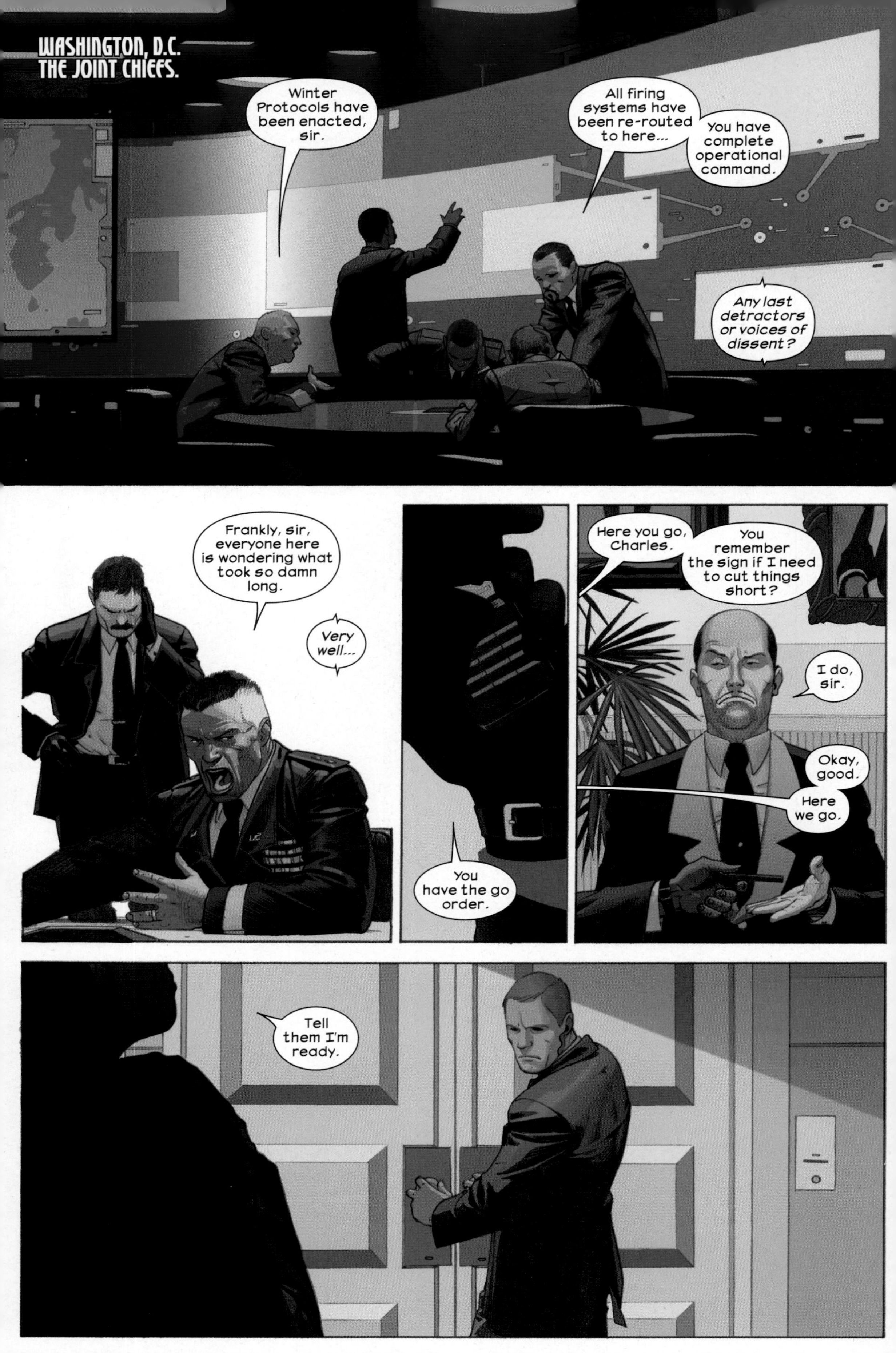
WASHINGTON, D.C.
THE JOINT CHIEFS.
Winter Protocols have been enacted, sir.
All firing systems have been re-routed to here...
You have complete operational command.
Any last detractors or voices of dissent?
Frankly, sir, everyone here is wondering what took so damn long.
Very well...
You have the go order.
Here you go, Charles.
You remember the sign if I need to cut things short?
I do, sir.
Okay, good.
Here we go.
Tell them I'm ready.

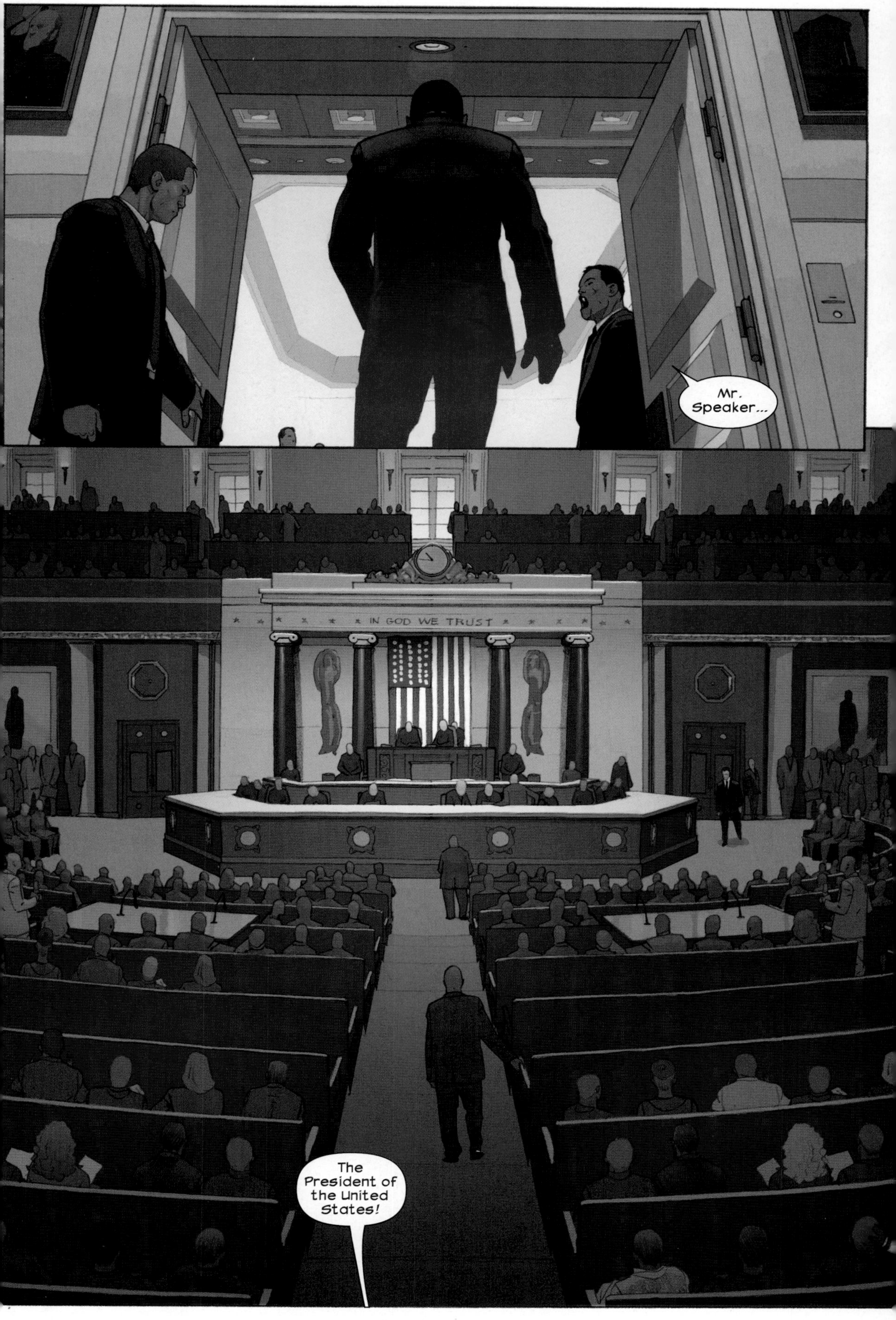
Mr. Speaker...
IN GOD WE TRUST
The President of the United States!

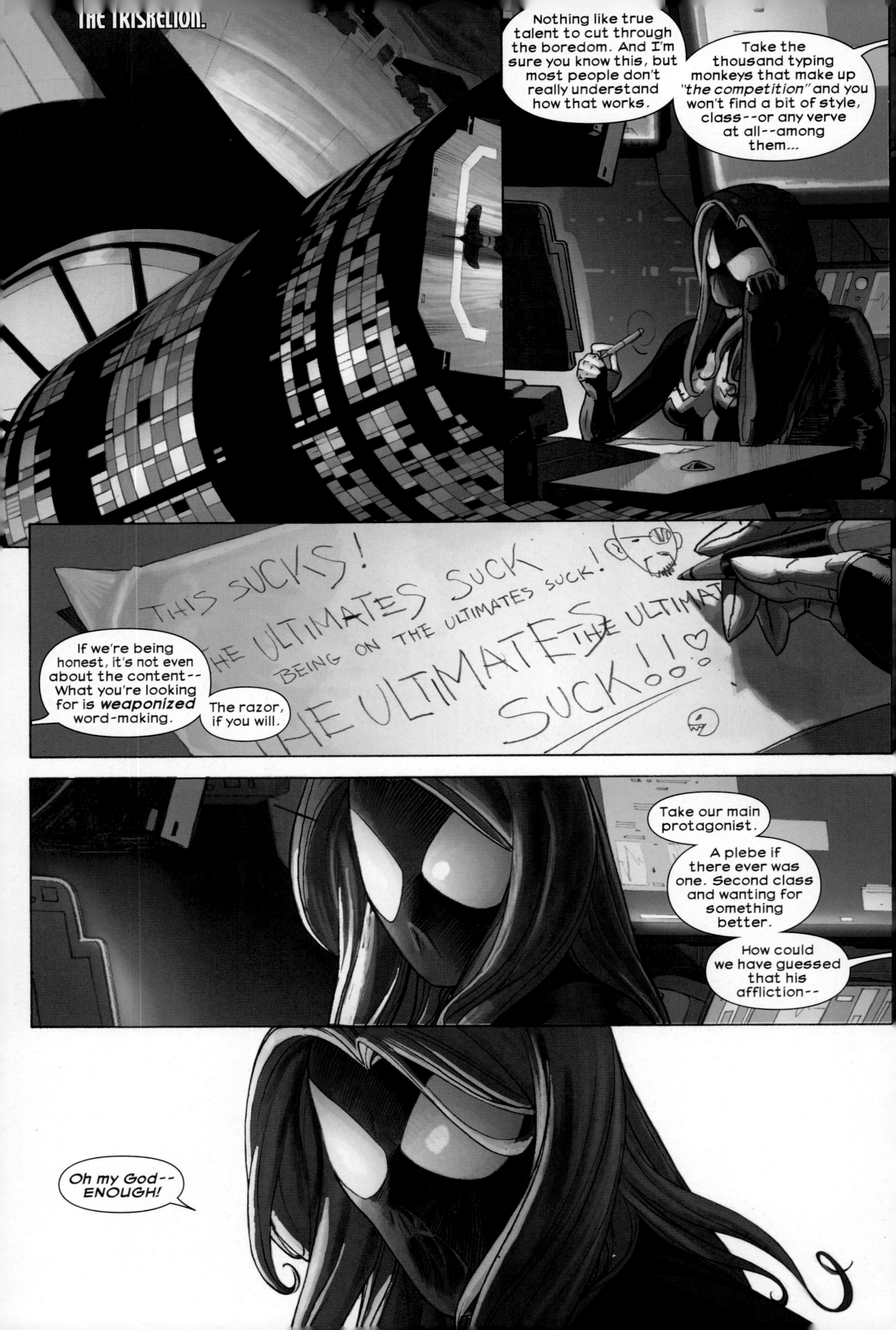
THE TRISKELION.
Nothing like true talent to cut through the boredom. And I'm sure you know this, but most people don't really understand how that works.
Take the thousand typing monkeys that make up *"the competition"* and you won't find a bit of style, class--or any verve at all--among them...
THIS SUCKS!
THE ULTIMATES SUCK
BEING ON THE ULTIMATES SUCK!
THE ULTIMATES
SUCK!!!
If we're being honest, it's not even about the content--What you're looking for is ***weaponized*** word-making.
The razor, if you will.
Take our main protagonist.
A plebe if there ever was one. Second class and wanting for something better.
How could we have guessed that his affliction--
Oh my God--ENOUGH!

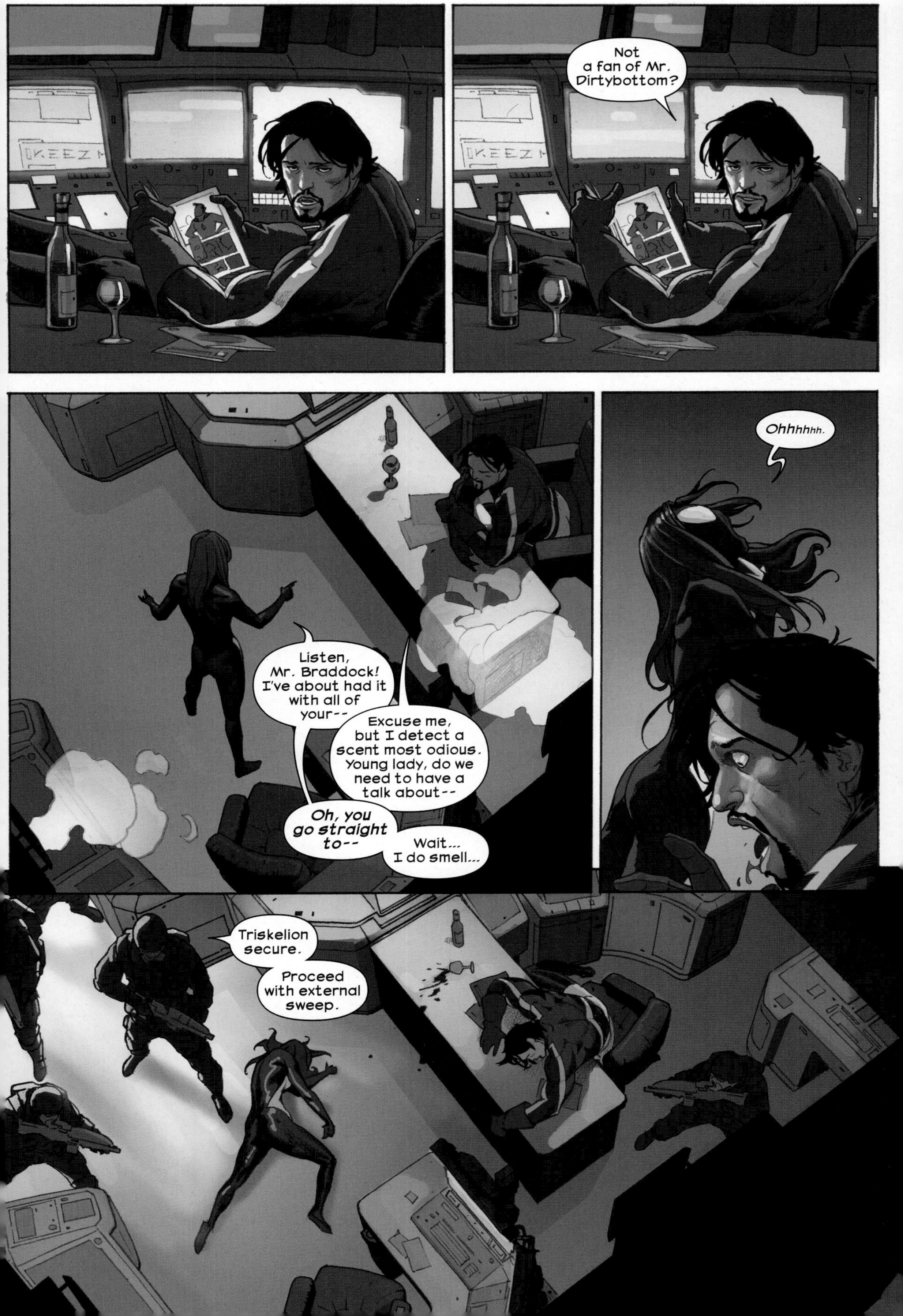
Not a fan of Mr. Dirtybottom?
Ohhhhhh.
Listen, Mr. Braddock! I've about had it with all of your--
Excuse me, but I detect a scent most odious. Young lady, do we need to have a talk about--
Oh, you go straight to--
Wait... I do smell...
Triskelion secure.
Proceed with external sweep.

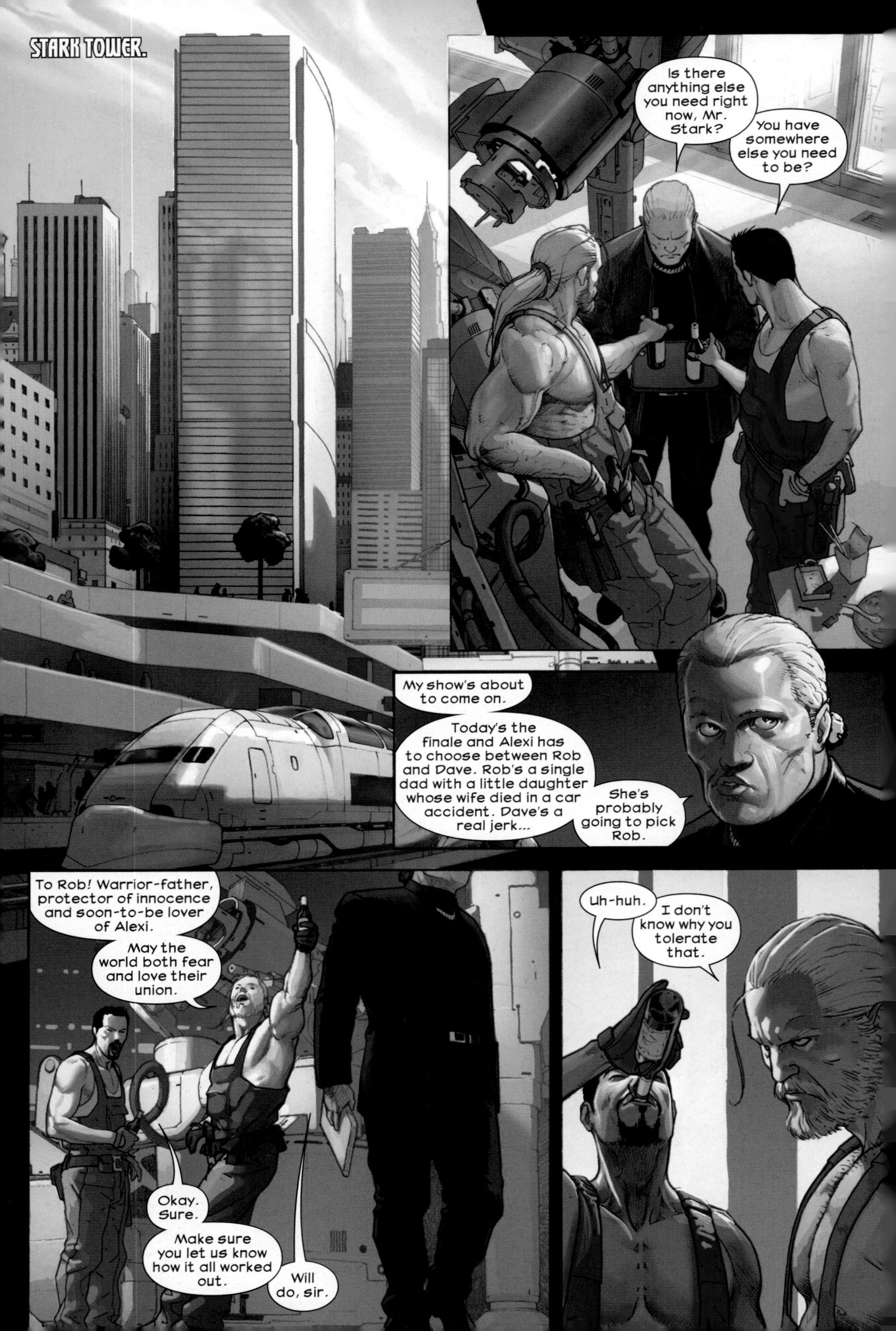
STARK TOWER.
Is there anything else you need right now, Mr. Stark?
You have somewhere else you need to be?
My show's about to come on.
Today's the finale and Alexi has to choose between Rob and Dave. Rob's a single dad with a little daughter whose wife died in a car accident. Dave's a real jerk...
She's probably going to pick Rob.
To Rob! Warrior-father, protector of innocence and soon-to-be lover of Alexi.
May the world both fear and love their union.
Okay. Sure.
Make sure you let us know how it all worked out.
Will do, sir.
Uh-huh.
I don't know why you tolerate that.

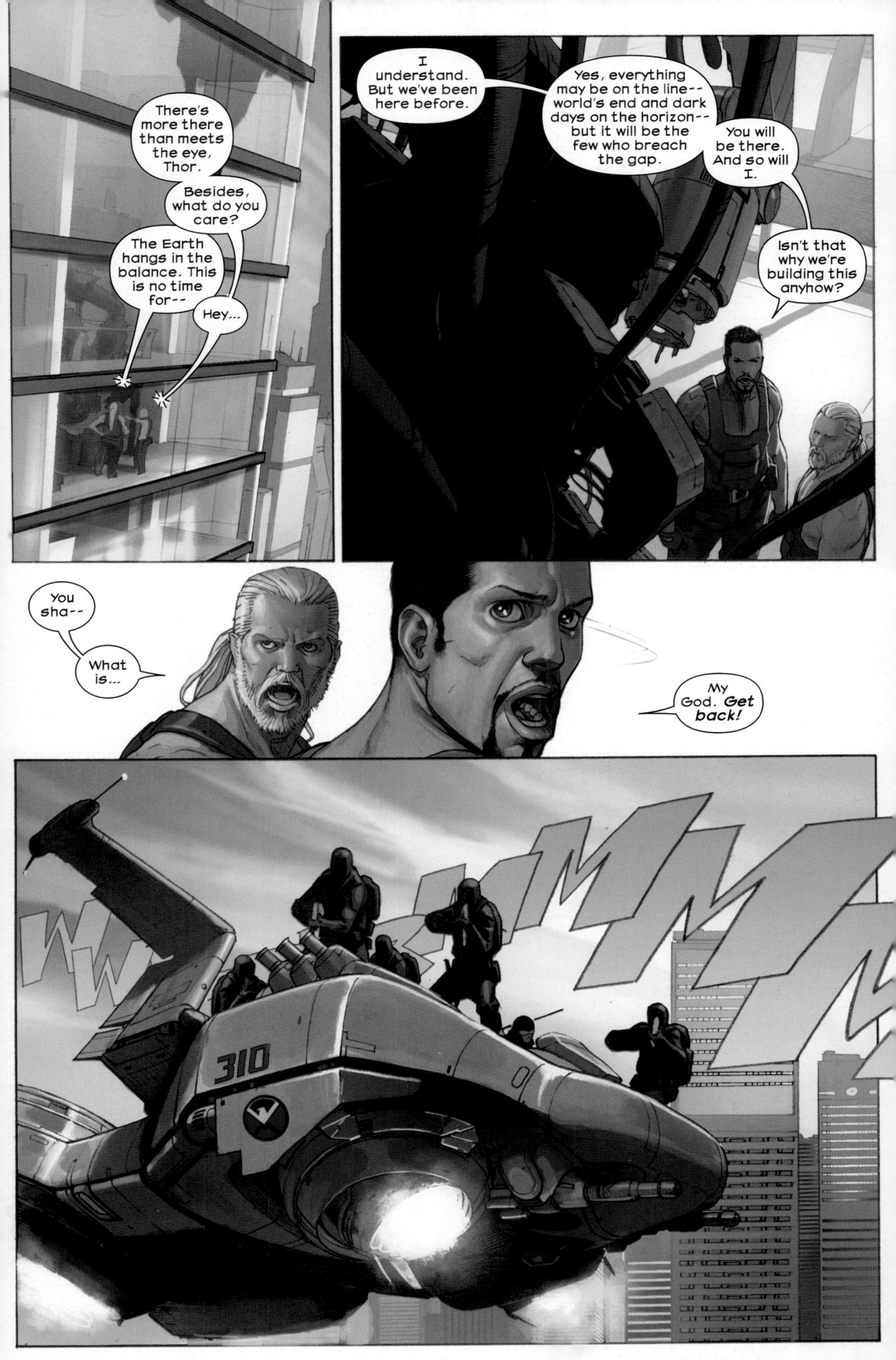
There's more there than meets the eye, Thor.
Besides, what do you care?
The Earth hangs in the balance. This is no time for--
Hey...
I understand. But we've been here before.
Yes, everything may be on the line-- world's end and dark days on the horizon-- but it will be the few who breach the gap.
You will be there. And so will I.
Isn't that why we're building this anyhow?
You sha--
What is...
My God. **Get back!**
310

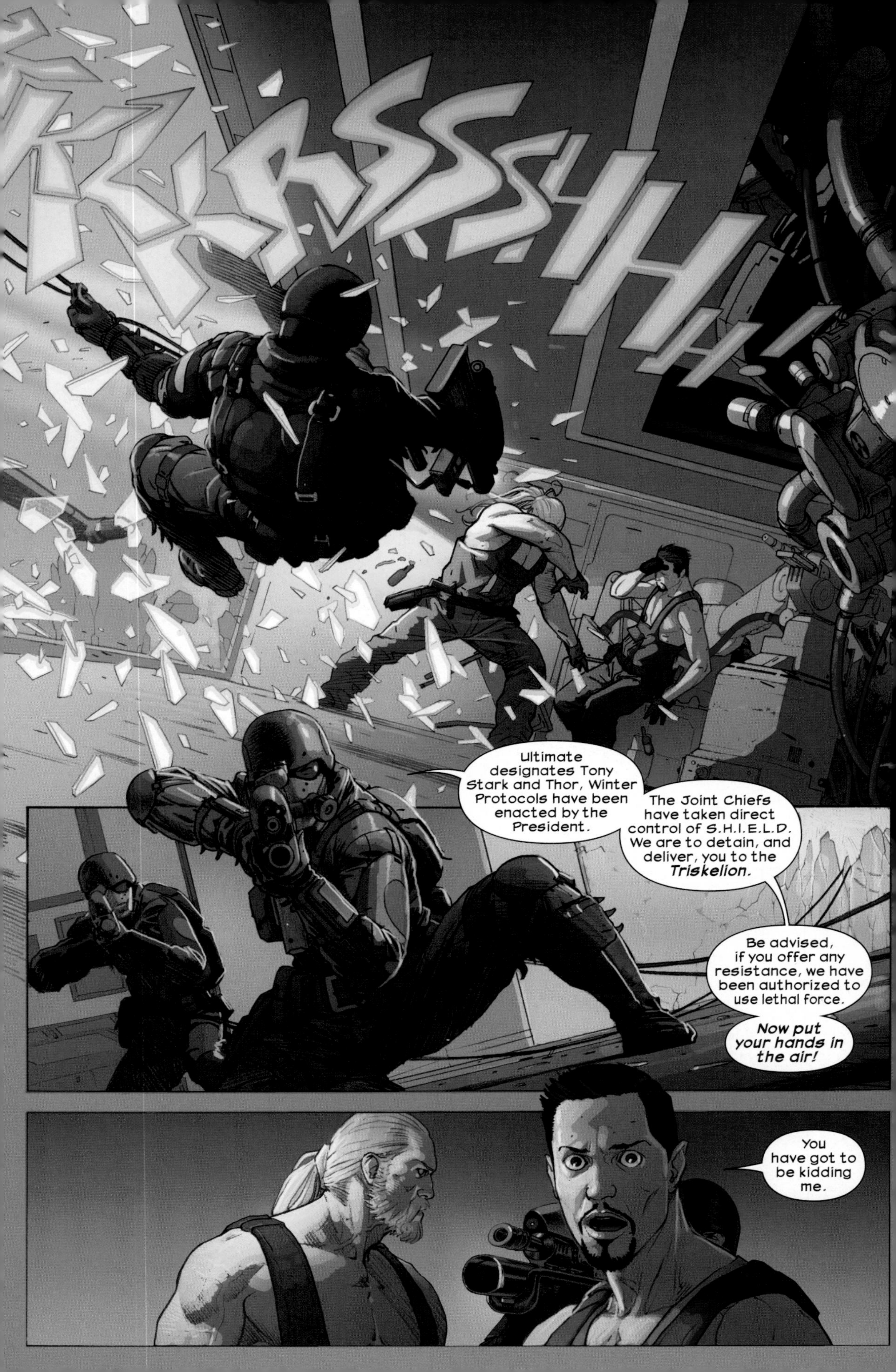
Ultimate designates Tony Stark and Thor, Winter Protocols have been enacted by the President.
The Joint Chiefs have taken direct control of S.H.I.E.L.D. We are to detain, and deliver, you to the *Triskelion.*
Be advised, if you offer any resistance, we have been authorized to use lethal force.
Now put your hands in the air!
You have got to be kidding me.

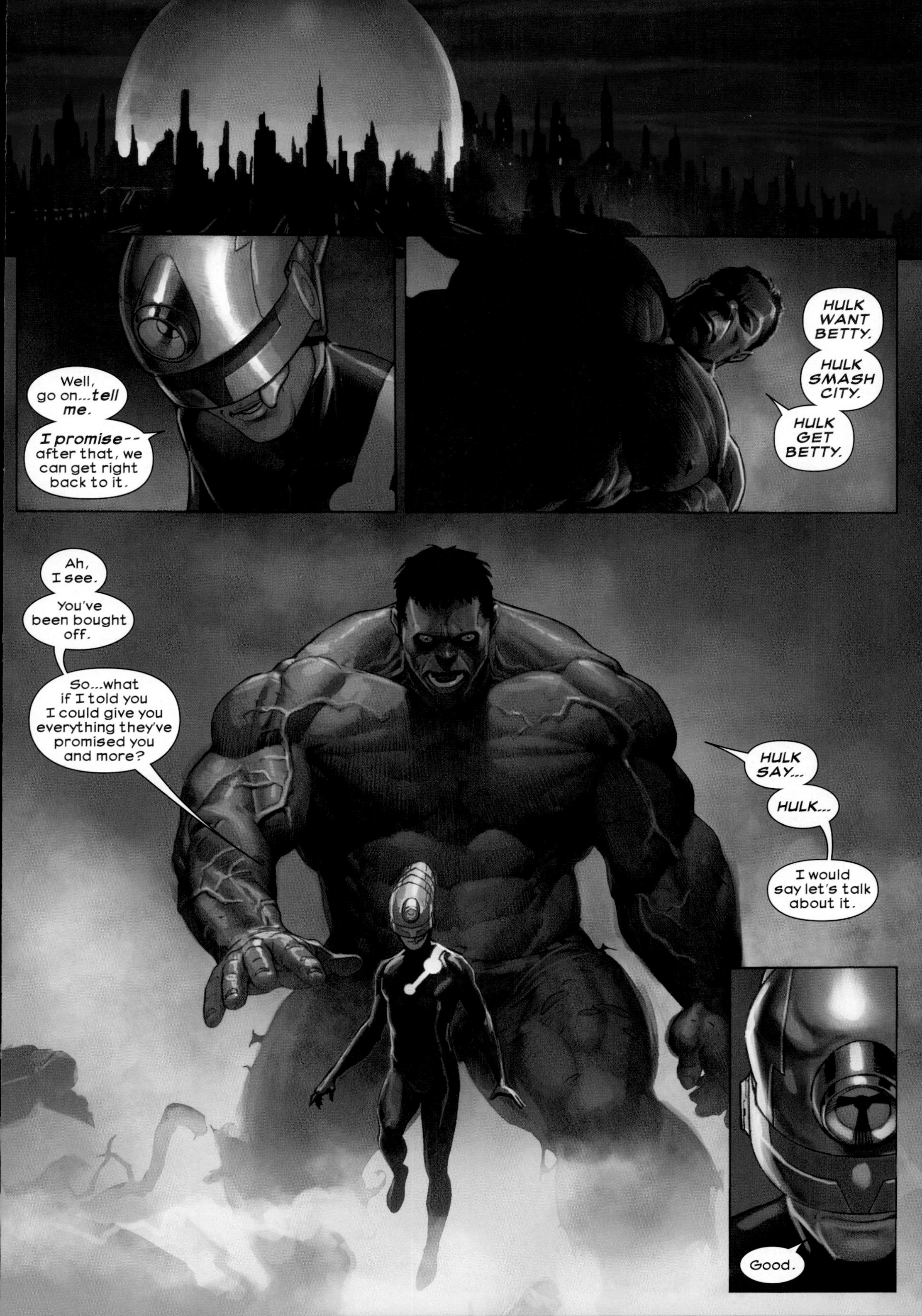

Well, go on...*tell me.*
I promise-- after that, we can get right back to it.
HULK WANT BETTY.
HULK SMASH CITY.
HULK GET BETTY.
Ah, I see.
You've been bought off.
So...what if I told you I could give you everything they've promised you and more?
HULK SAY...
HULK...
I would say let's talk about it.
Good.

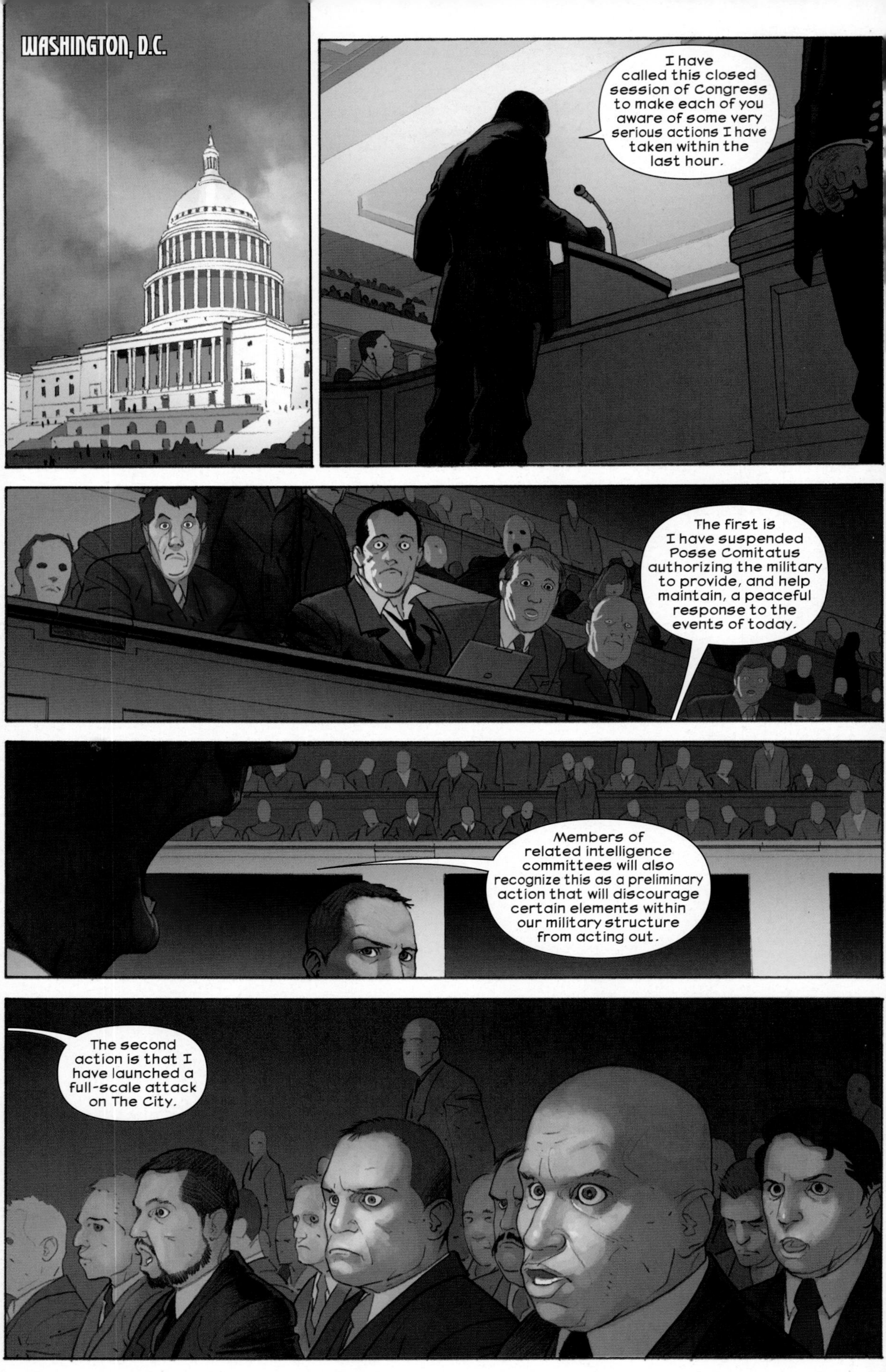
WASHINGTON, D.C.
I have called this closed session of Congress to make each of you aware of some very serious actions I have taken within the last hour.
The first is I have suspended Posse Comitatus authorizing the military to provide, and help maintain, a peaceful response to the events of today.
Members of related intelligence committees will also recognize this as a preliminary action that will discourage certain elements within our military structure from acting out.
The second action is that I have launched a full-scale attack on The City.

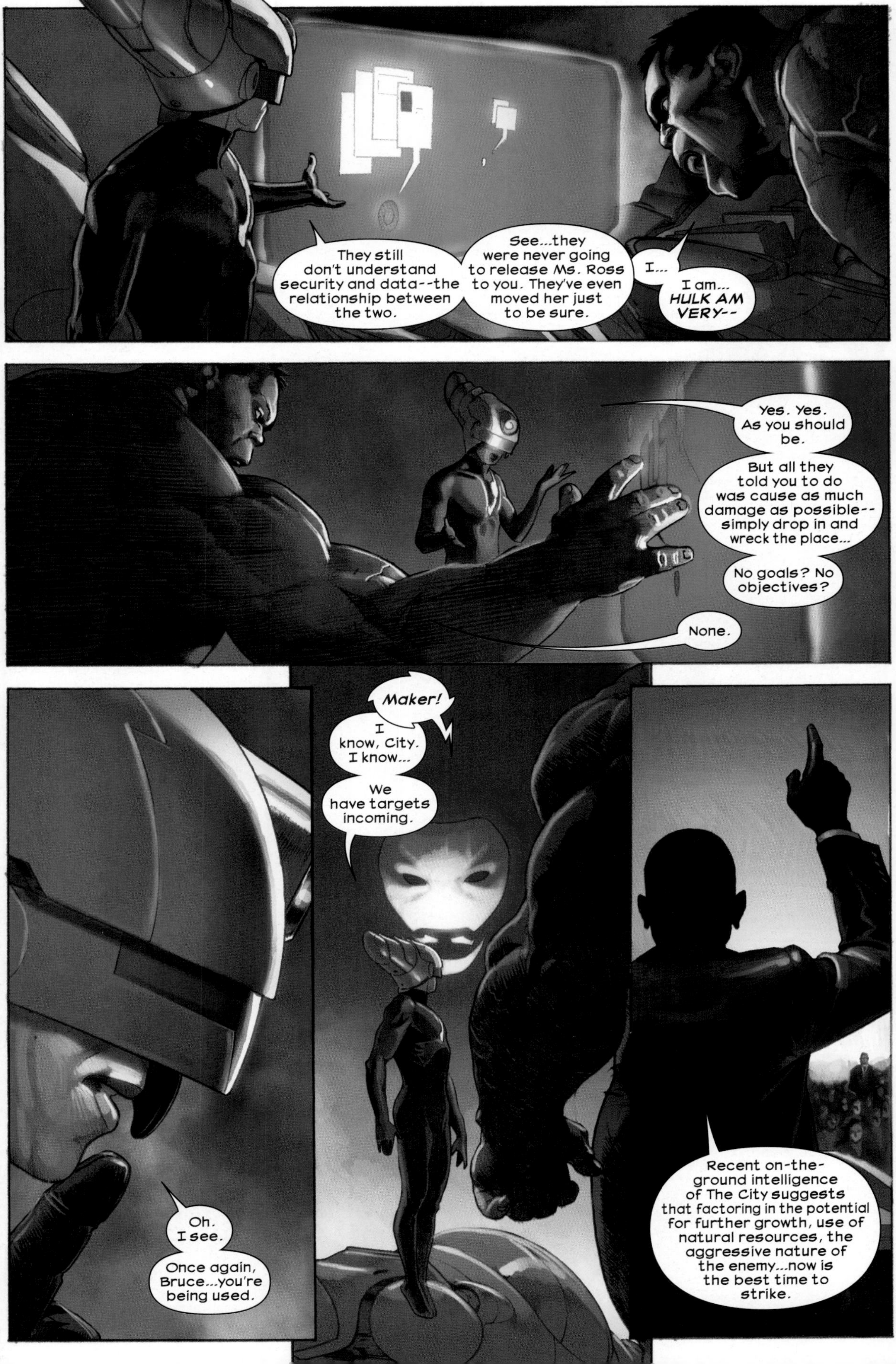

They still don't understand security and data--the relationship between the two.
See...they were never going to release Ms. Ross to you. They've even moved her just to be sure.
I...
I am... *HULK AM VERY--*
Yes. Yes. As you should be.
But all they told you to do was cause as much damage as possible--simply drop in and wreck the place...
No goals? No objectives?
None.
Oh. I see.
Once again, Bruce...you're being used.
Maker!
I know, City. I know...
We have targets incoming.
Recent on-the-ground intelligence of The City suggests that factoring in the potential for further growth, use of natural resources, the aggressive nature of the enemy...now is the best time to strike.

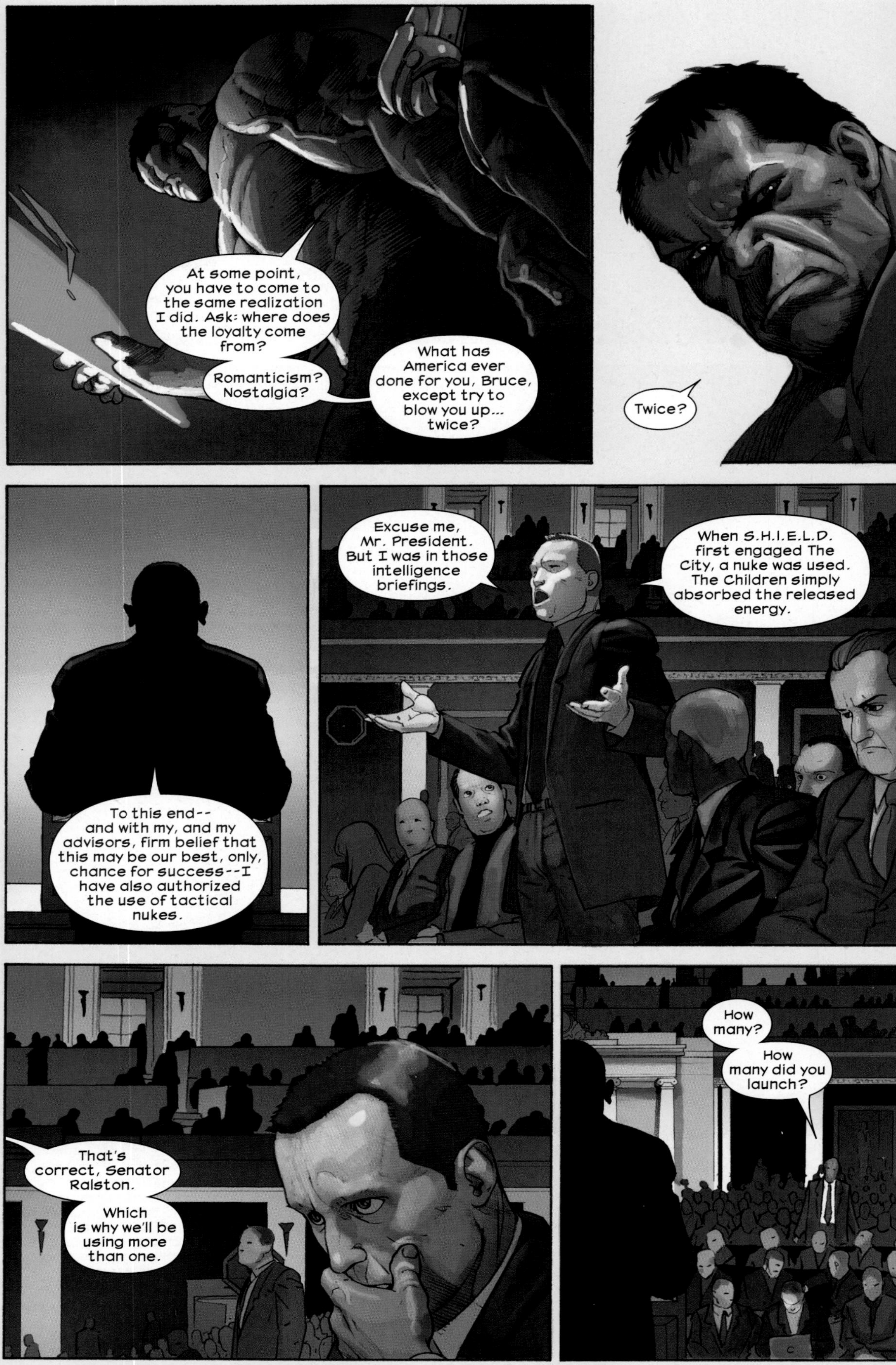
At some point, you have to come to the same realization I did. Ask: where does the loyalty come from?
Romanticism? Nostalgia?
What has America ever done for you, Bruce, except try to blow you up... twice?
Twice?
To this end--and with my, and my advisors, firm belief that this may be our best, only, chance for success--I have also authorized the use of tactical nukes.
Excuse me, Mr. President. But I was in those intelligence briefings.
When S.H.I.E.L.D. first engaged The City, a nuke was used. The Children simply absorbed the released energy.
That's correct, Senator Ralston.
Which is why we'll be using more than one.
How many?
How many did you launch?

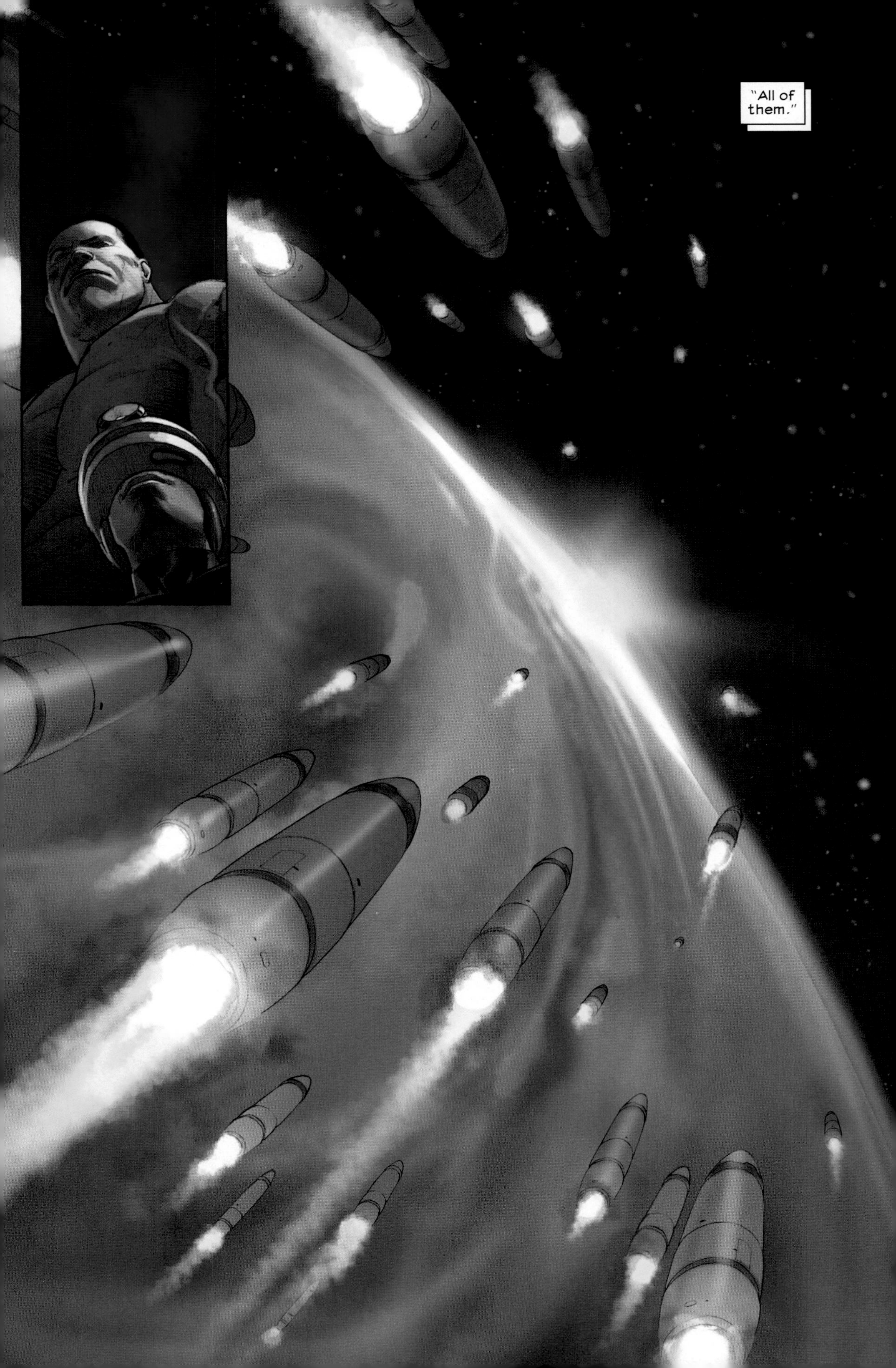
"All of them."

9

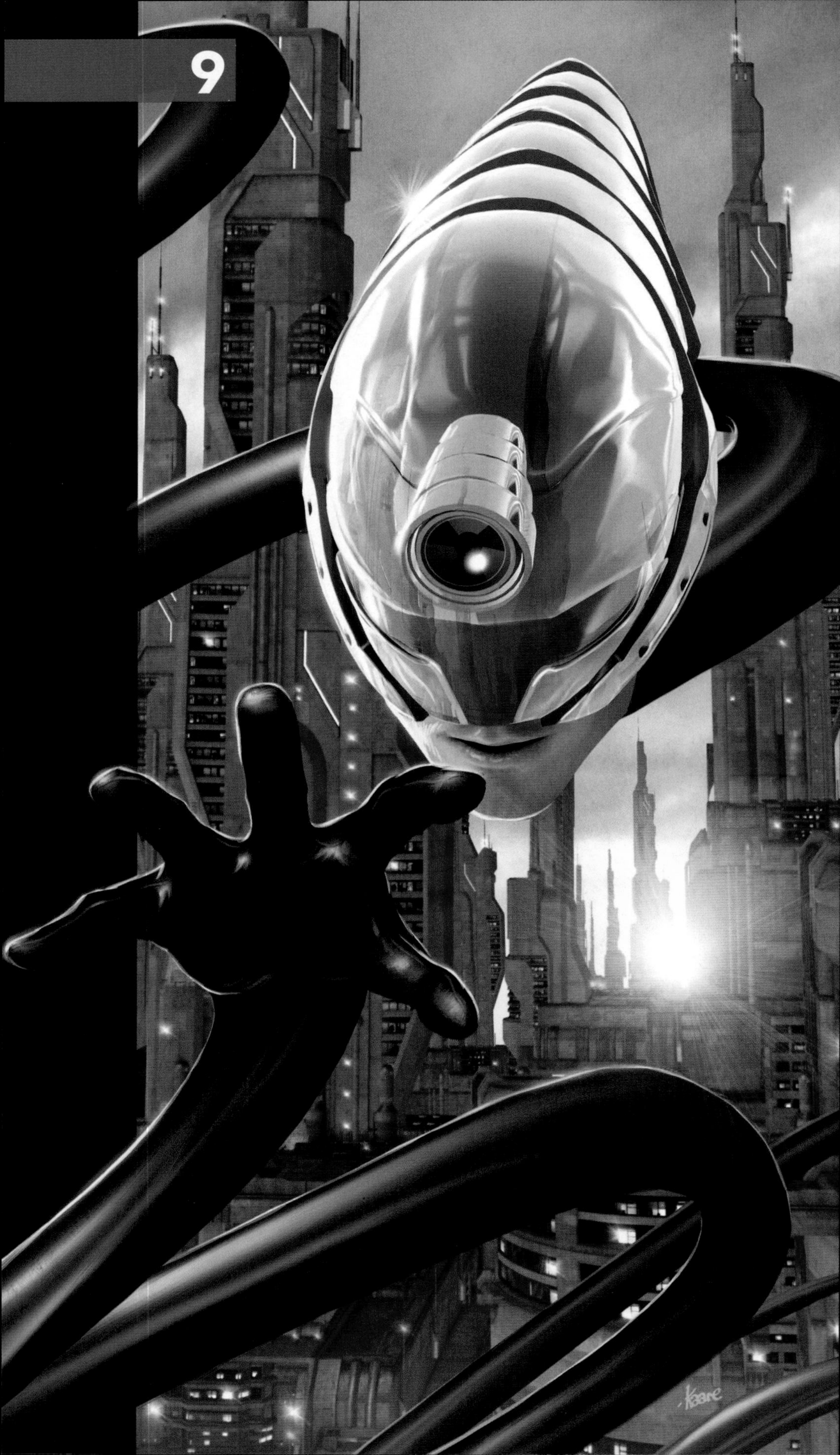
Kaare

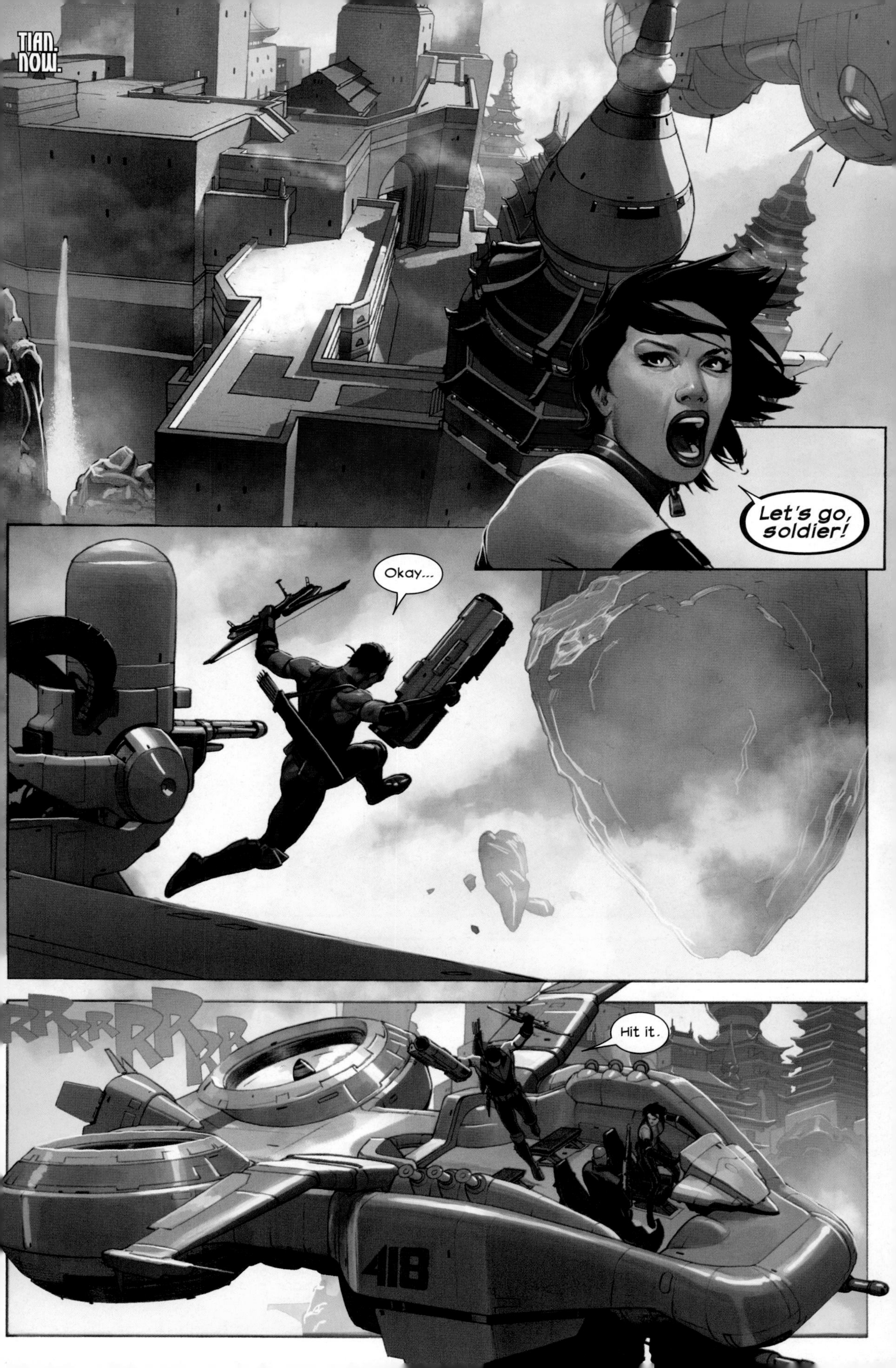
TIAN. NOW.
Let's go, soldier!
Okay...
RRRRRRRRR
Hit it.
418

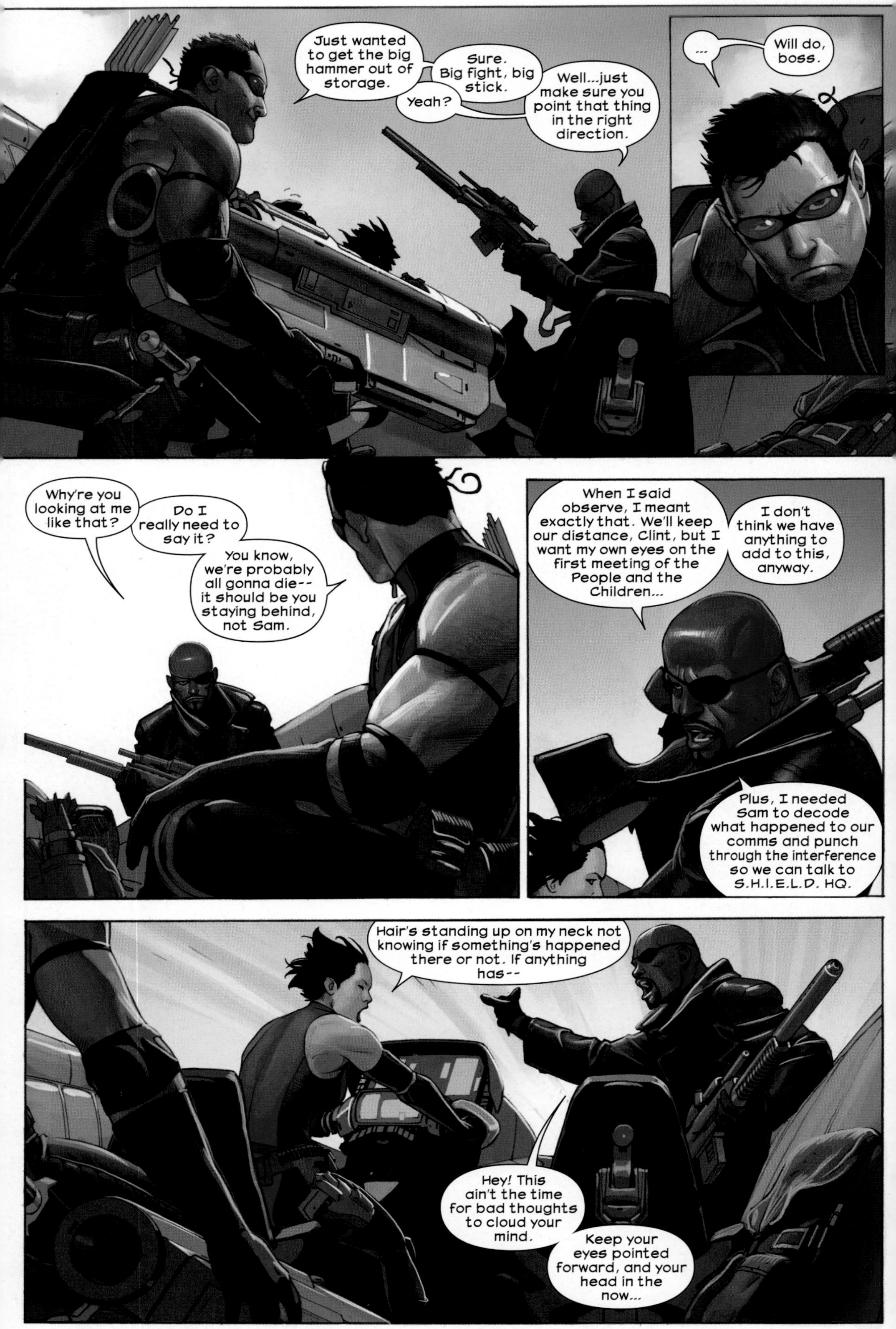

Just wanted to get the big hammer out of storage.
Sure. Big fight, big stick.
Yeah?
Well...just make sure you point that thing in the right direction.
...
Will do, boss.
Why're you looking at me like that?
Do I really need to say it?
You know, we're probably all gonna die-- it should be you staying behind, not Sam.
When I said observe, I meant exactly that. We'll keep our distance, Clint, but I want my own eyes on the first meeting of the People and the Children...
I don't think we have anything to add to this, anyway.
Plus, I needed Sam to decode what happened to our comms and punch through the interference so we can talk to S.H.I.E.L.D. HQ.
Hair's standing up on my neck not knowing if something's happened there or not. If anything has--
Hey! This ain't the time for bad thoughts to cloud your mind.
Keep your eyes pointed forward, and your head in the now...

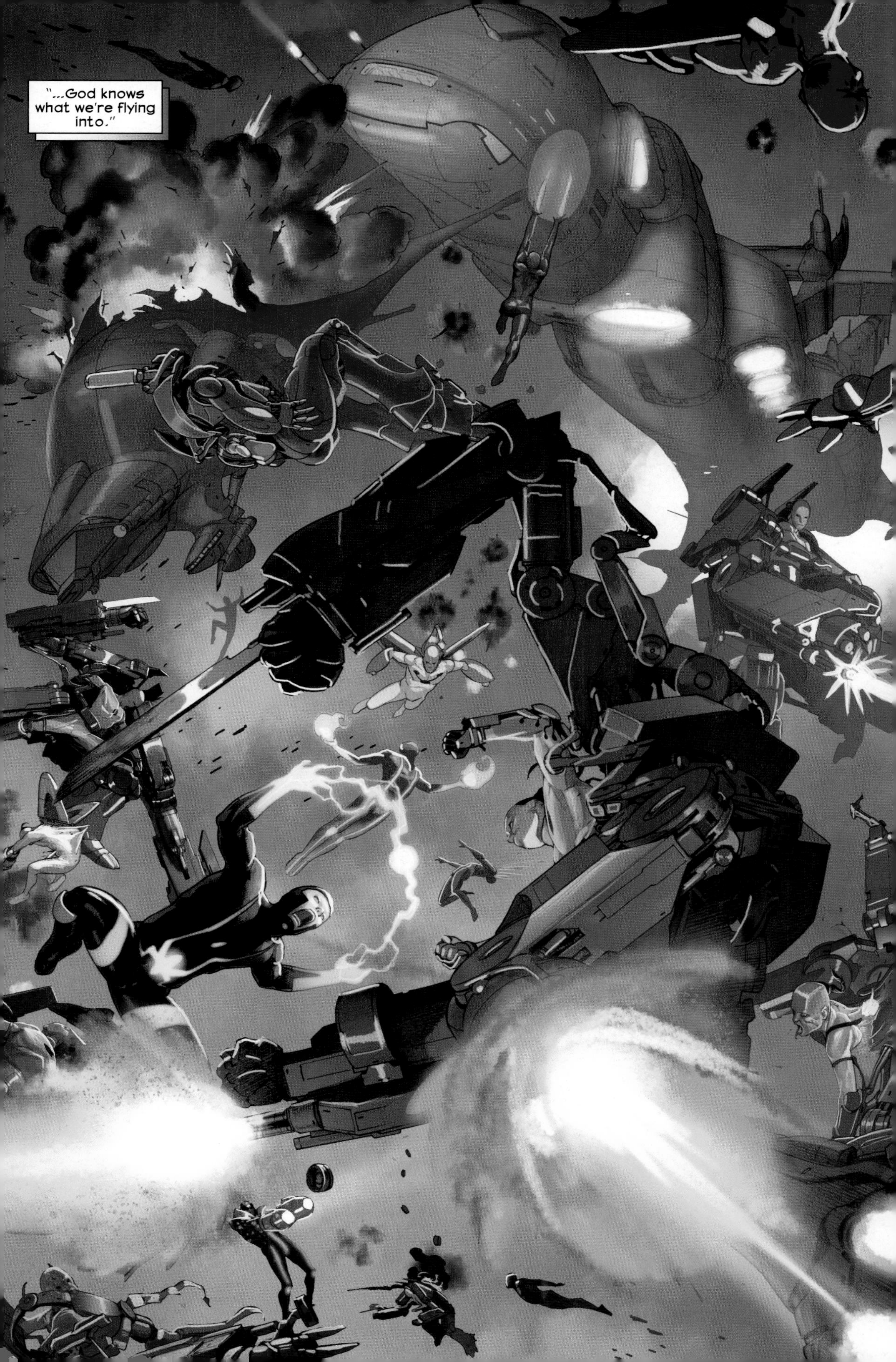
"...God knows what we're flying into."

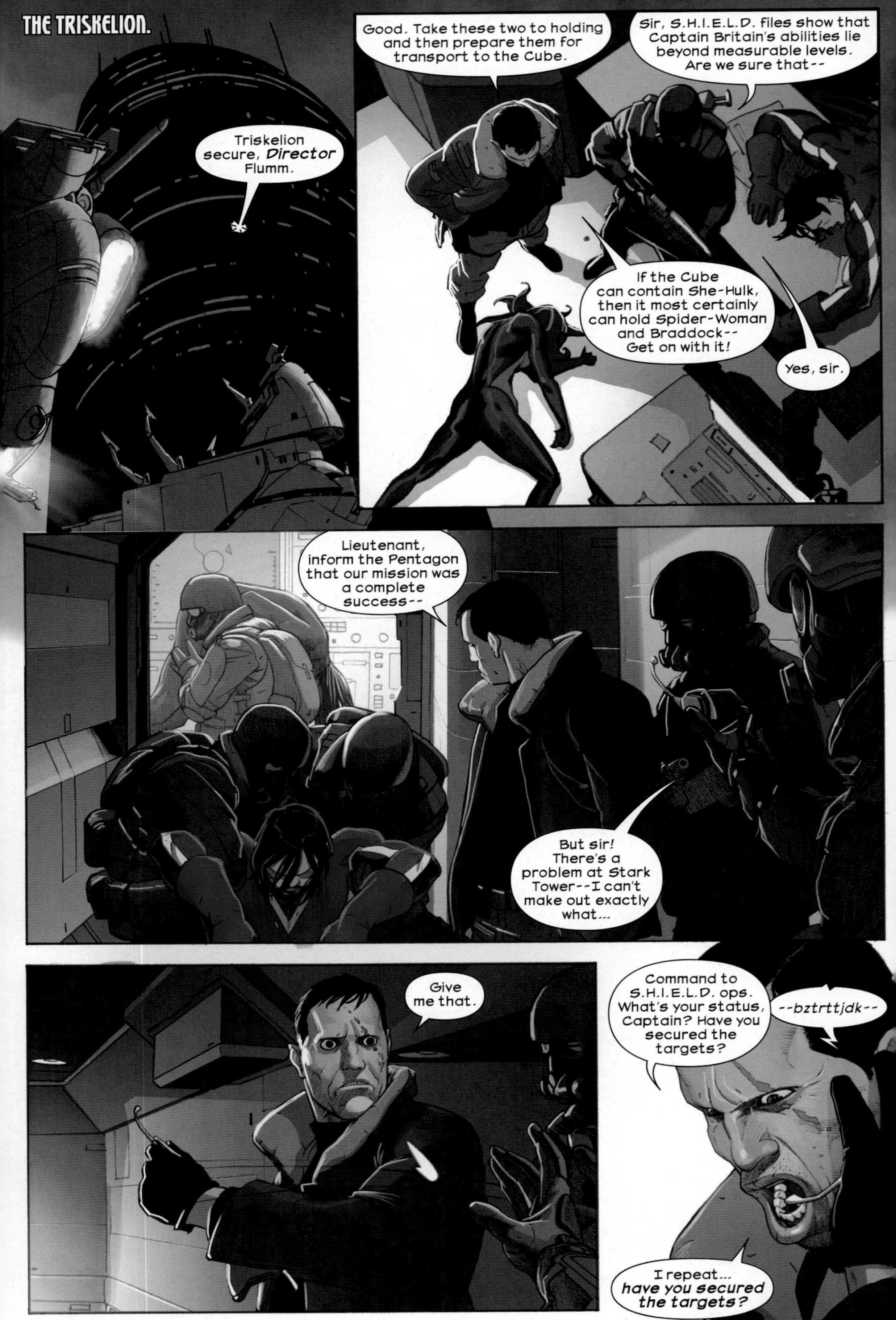
THE TRISKELION.
Triskelion secure, *Director* Flumm.
Good. Take these two to holding and then prepare them for transport to the Cube.
Sir, S.H.I.E.L.D. files show that Captain Britain's abilities lie beyond measurable levels. Are we sure that--
If the Cube can contain She-Hulk, then it most certainly can hold Spider-Woman and Braddock-- Get on with it!
Yes, sir.
Lieutenant, inform the Pentagon that our mission was a complete success--
But sir! There's a problem at Stark Tower--I can't make out exactly what...
Give me that.
Command to S.H.I.E.L.D. ops. What's your status, Captain? Have you secured the targets?
--bztrttjdk--
I repeat... *have you secured the targets?*

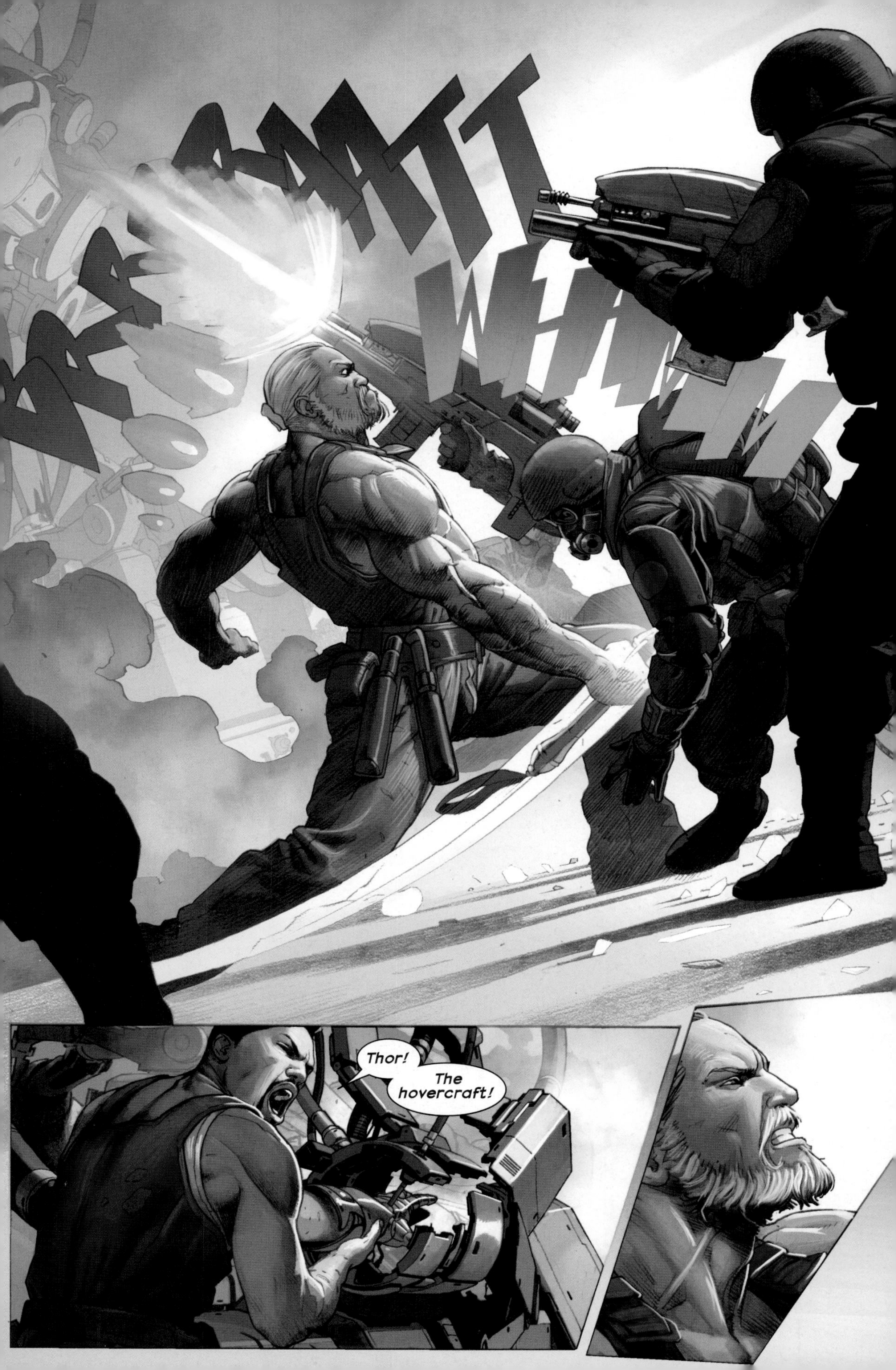
Thor!
The hovercraft!

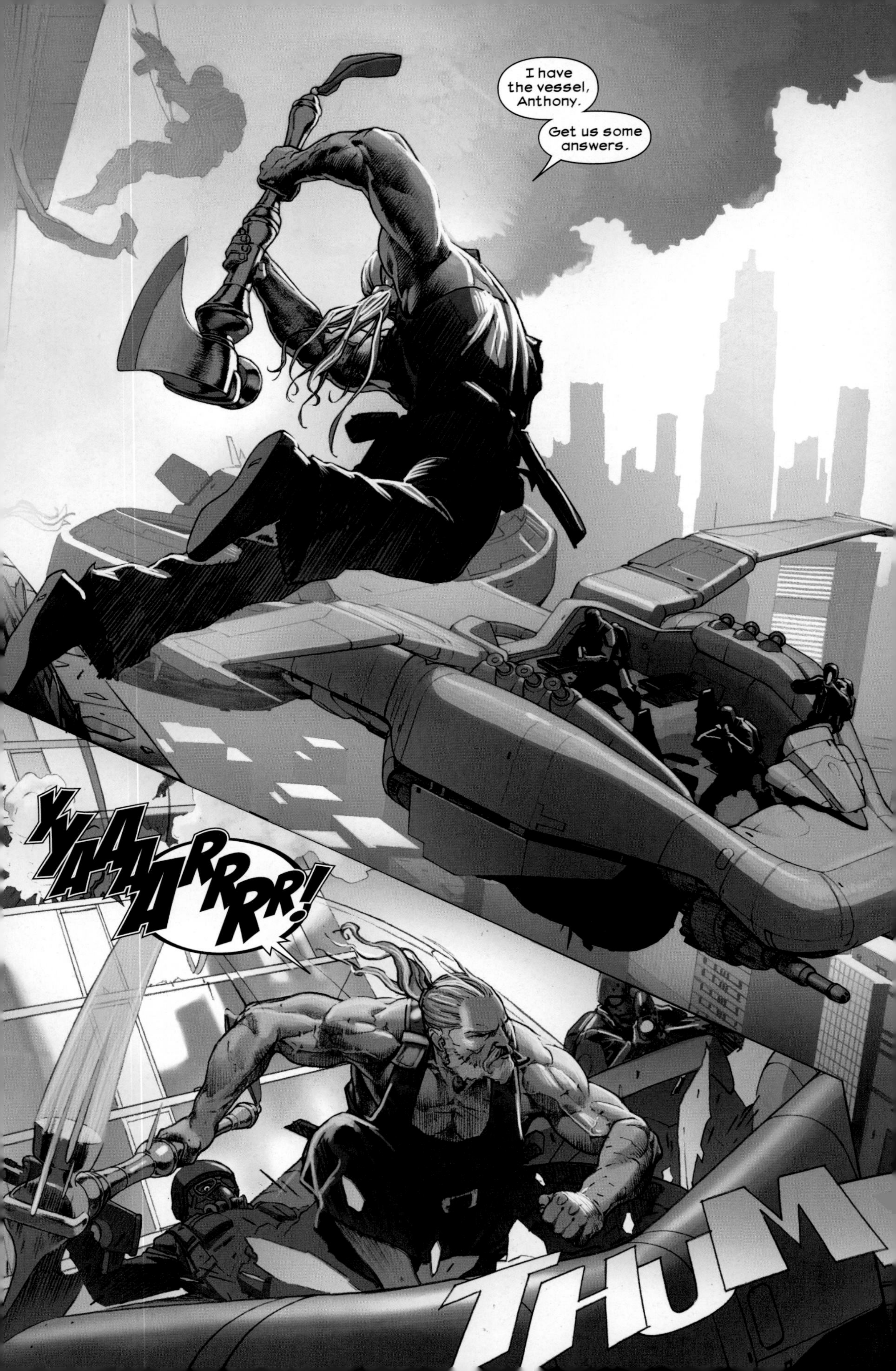
I have the vessel, Anthony.
Get us some answers.
YYAAARRRRR!
THUM

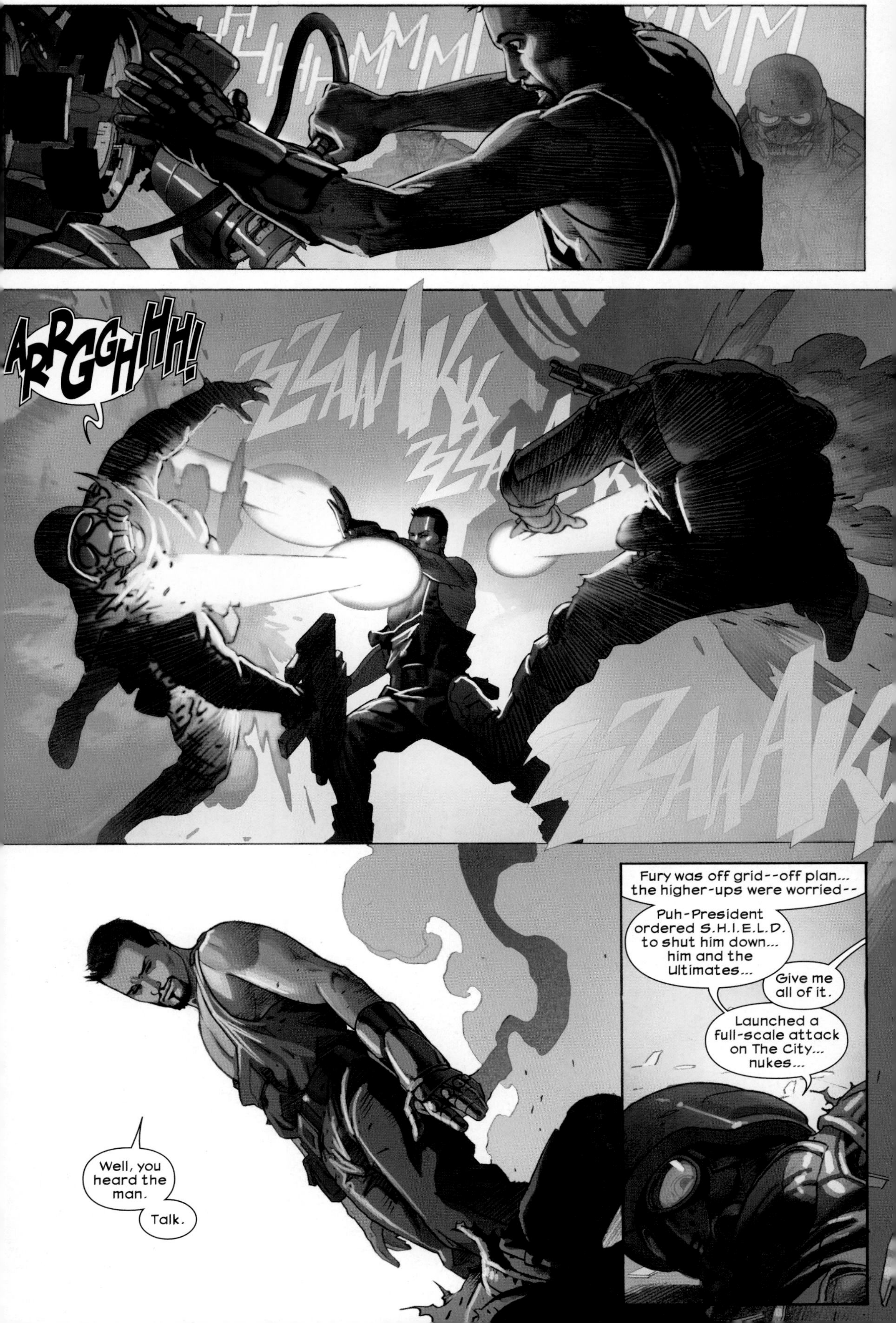
HHHHHMMMMMMMM
ARRGGHHHH!
ZZAAAKK
ZZAAAK
ZZAAAK!
Fury was off grid--off plan... the higher-ups were worried--
Puh-President ordered S.H.I.E.L.D. to shut him down... him and the Ultimates...
Give me all of it.
Launched a full-scale attack on The City... nukes...
Well, you heard the man.
Talk.

Oh...

Okay. You can pass out now.

Uhhhh.

The hovercraft was stubborn, but has now submitted.

Did you find out anything?

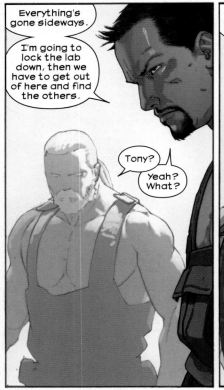

Everything's gone sideways.

I'm going to lock the lab down, then we have to get out of here and find the others.

Tony?

Yeah? What?

Did you get hit...are you...

No. Why?

You're bleeding.

Huh.

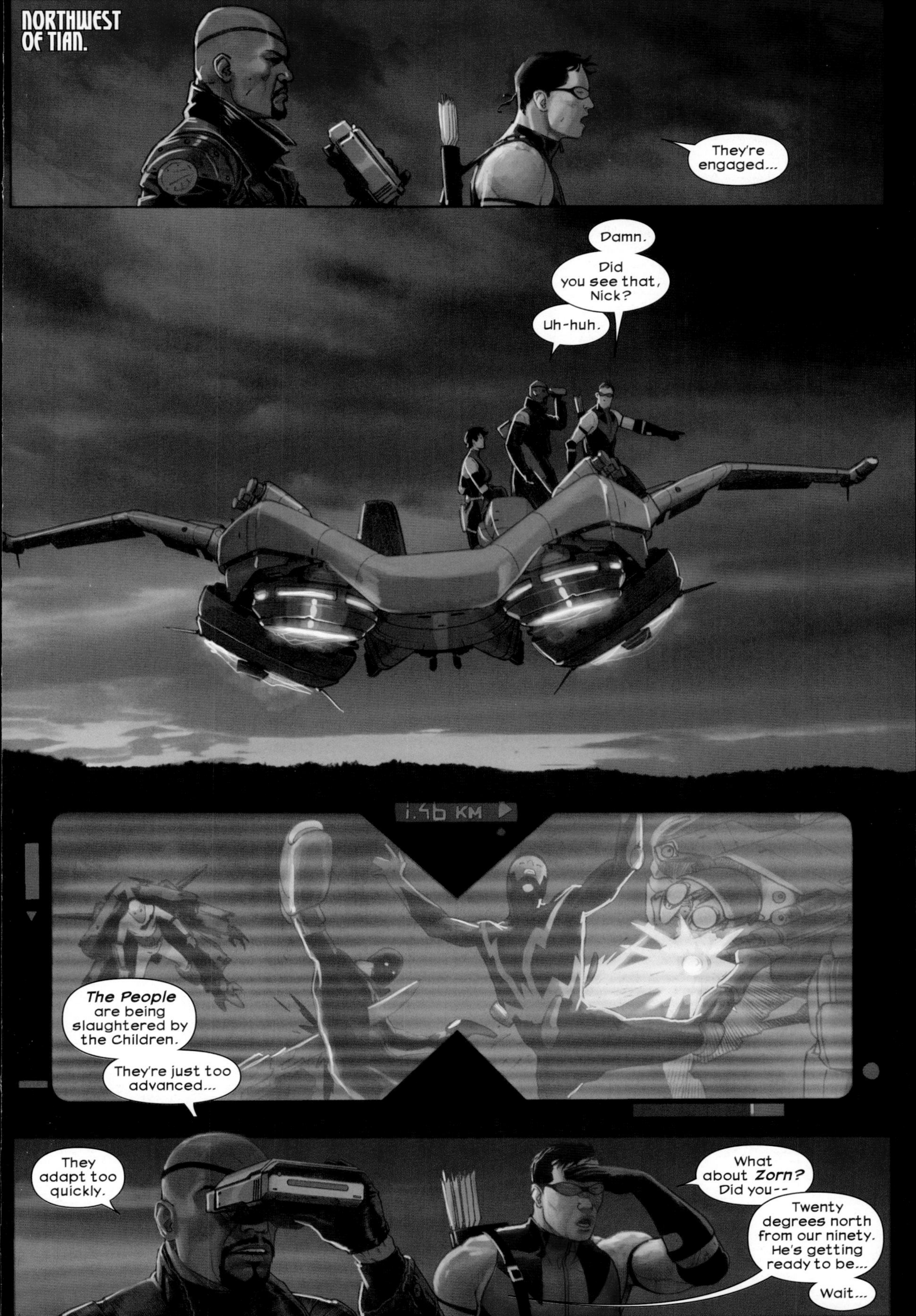
NORTHWEST OF TIAN.
They're engaged...
Damn.
Did you see that, Nick?
Uh-huh.
1.46 KM
The People are being slaughtered by the Children.
They're just too advanced...
They adapt too quickly.
What about Zorn? Did you--
Twenty degrees north from our ninety. He's getting ready to be...
Wait...

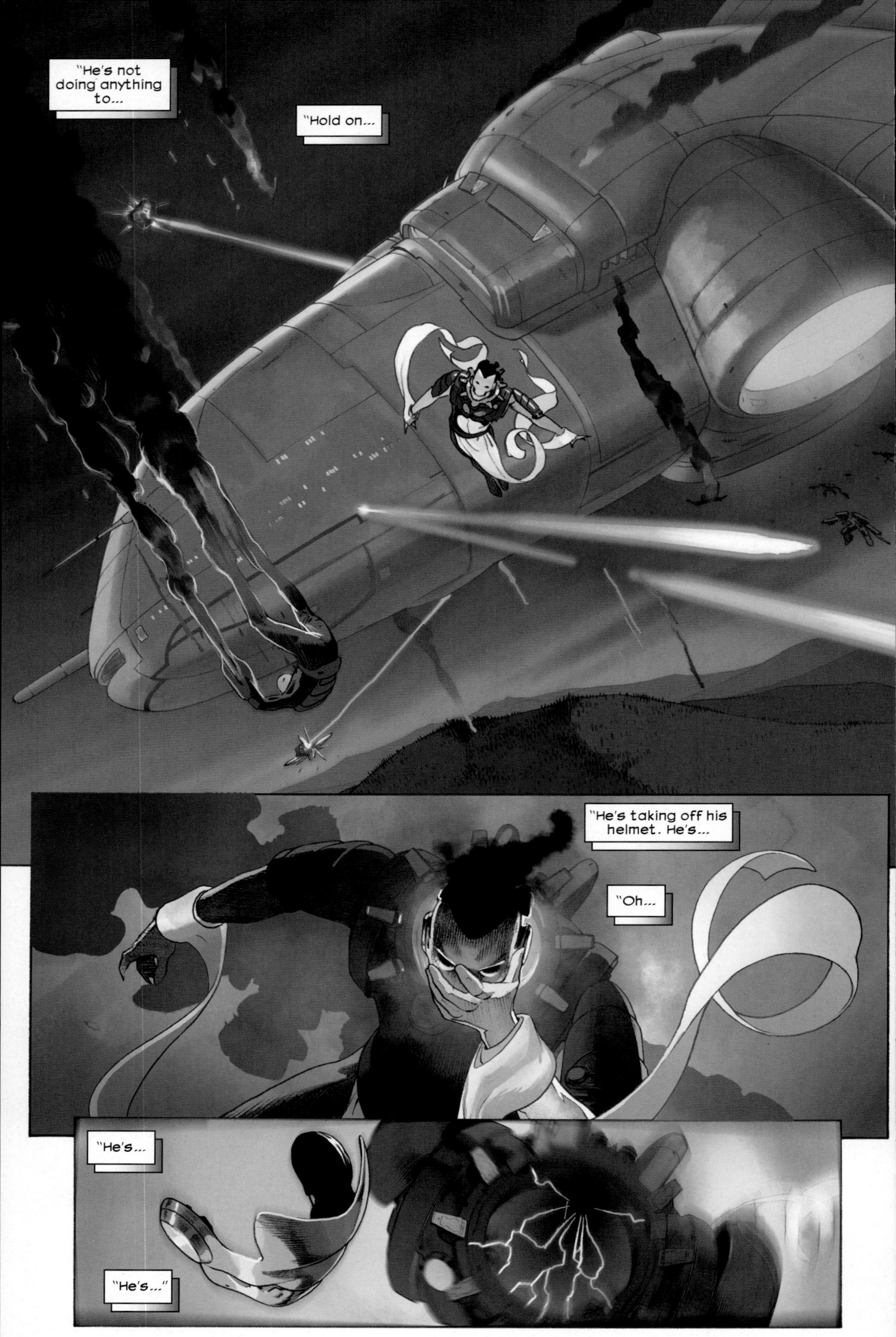
"He's not doing anything to...
"Hold on...
"He's taking off his helmet. He's...
"Oh...
"He's...
"He's..."

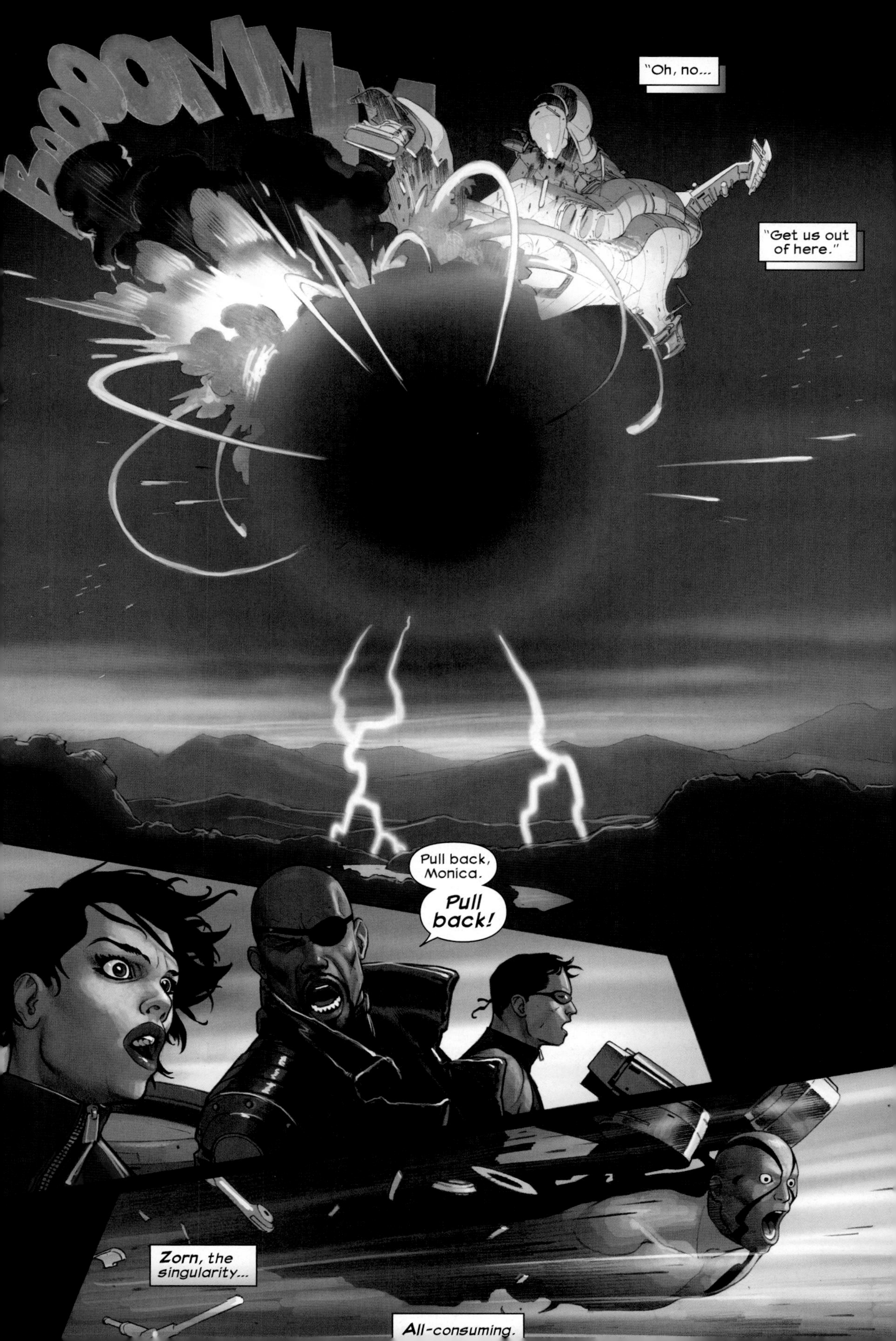
"Oh, no...
"Get us out of here."
Pull back, Monica.
Pull back!
Zorn, the singularity...
All-consuming.

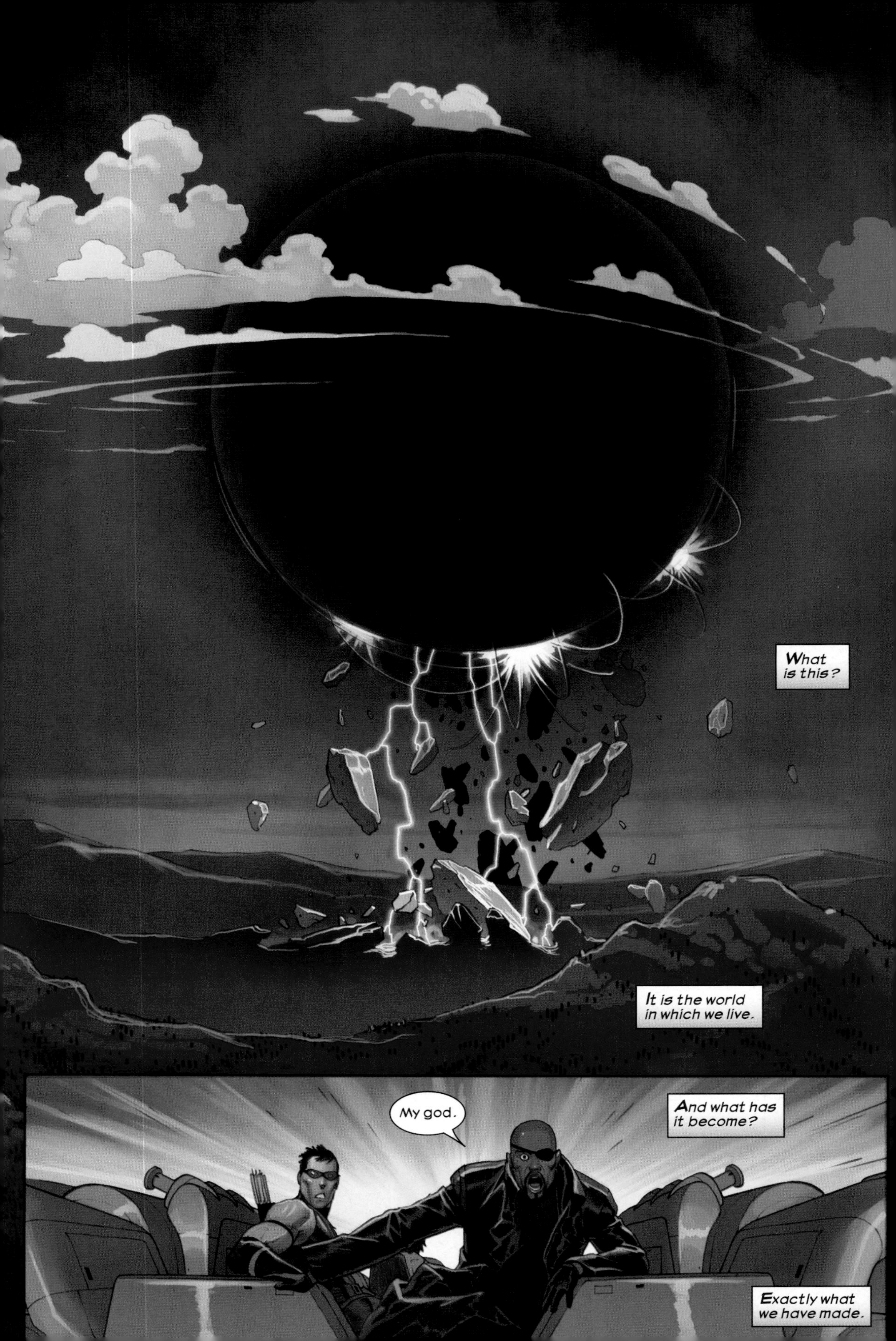
What is this?
It is the world in which we live.
My god.
And what has it become?
Exactly what we have made.

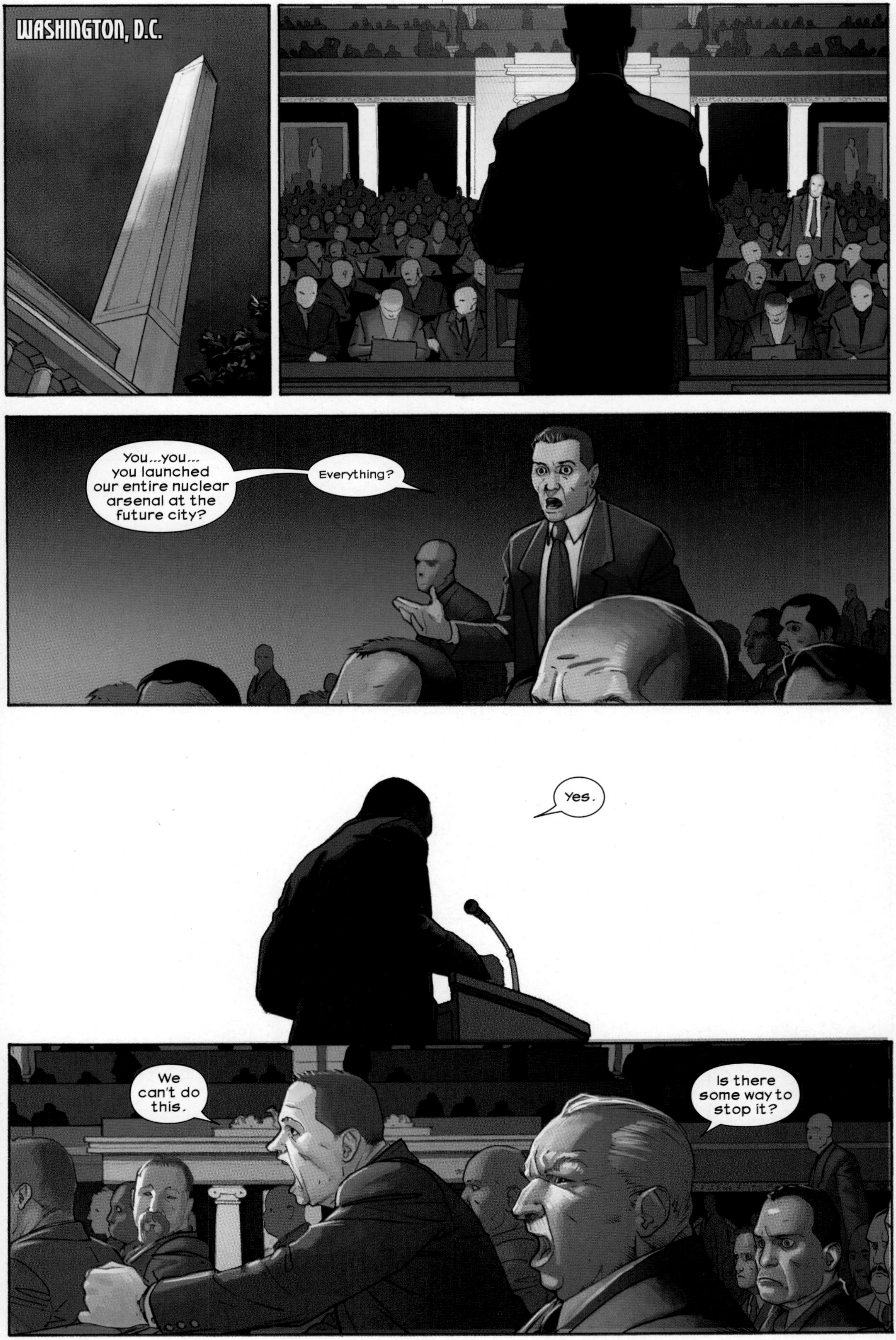
WASHINGTON, D.C.
You...you... you launched our entire nuclear arsenal at the future city?
Everything?
Yes.
We can't do this.
Is there some way to stop it?

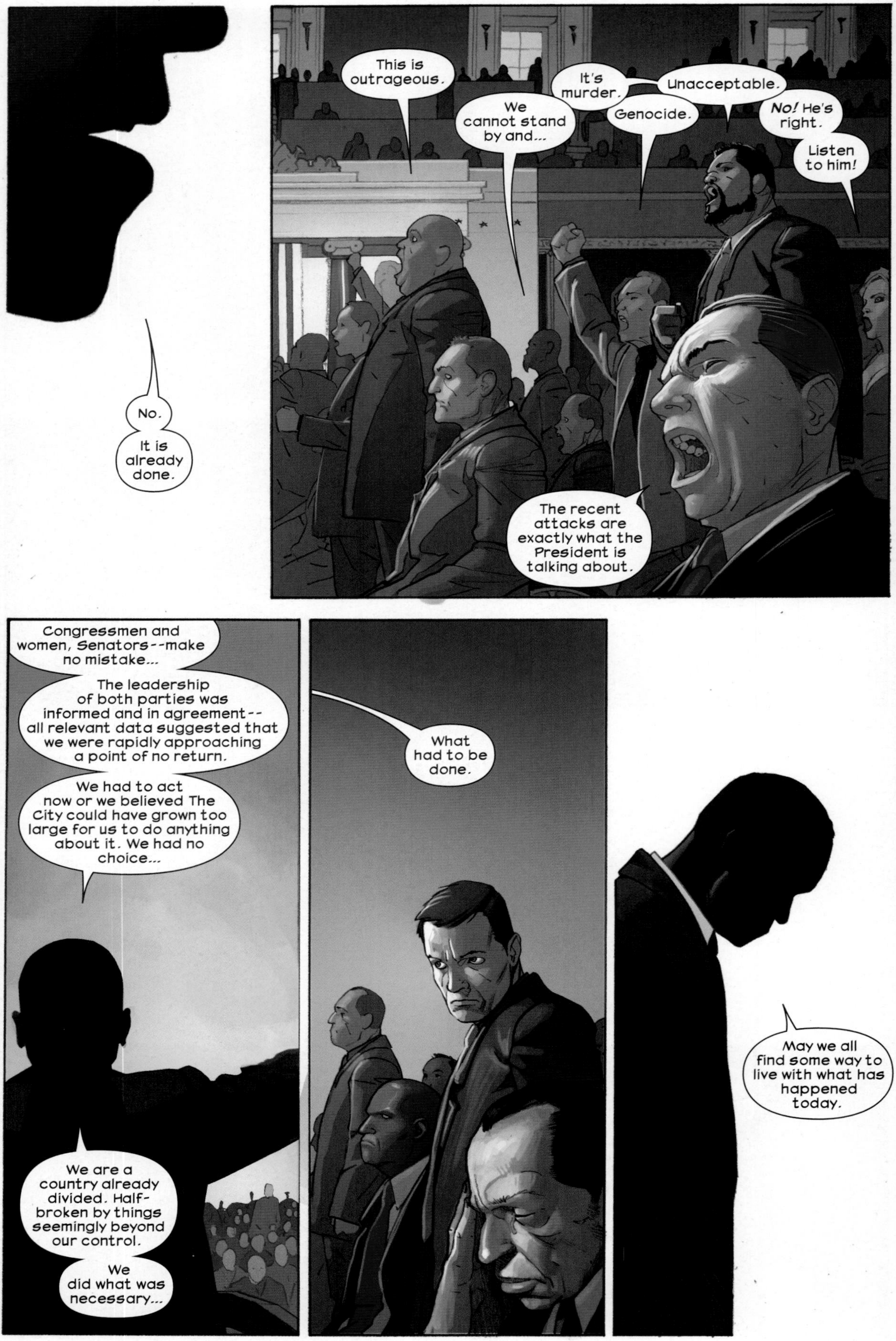
This is outrageous.
We cannot stand by and...
It's murder.
Unacceptable.
Genocide.
No! He's right.
Listen to him!
The recent attacks are exactly what the President is talking about.
No.
It is already done.
Congressmen and women, Senators--make no mistake...
The leadership of both parties was informed and in agreement--all relevant data suggested that we were rapidly approaching a point of no return.
We had to act now or we believed The City could have grown too large for us to do anything about it. We had no choice...
We are a country already divided. Half-broken by things seemingly beyond our control.
We did what was necessary...
What had to be done.
May we all find some way to live with what has happened today.

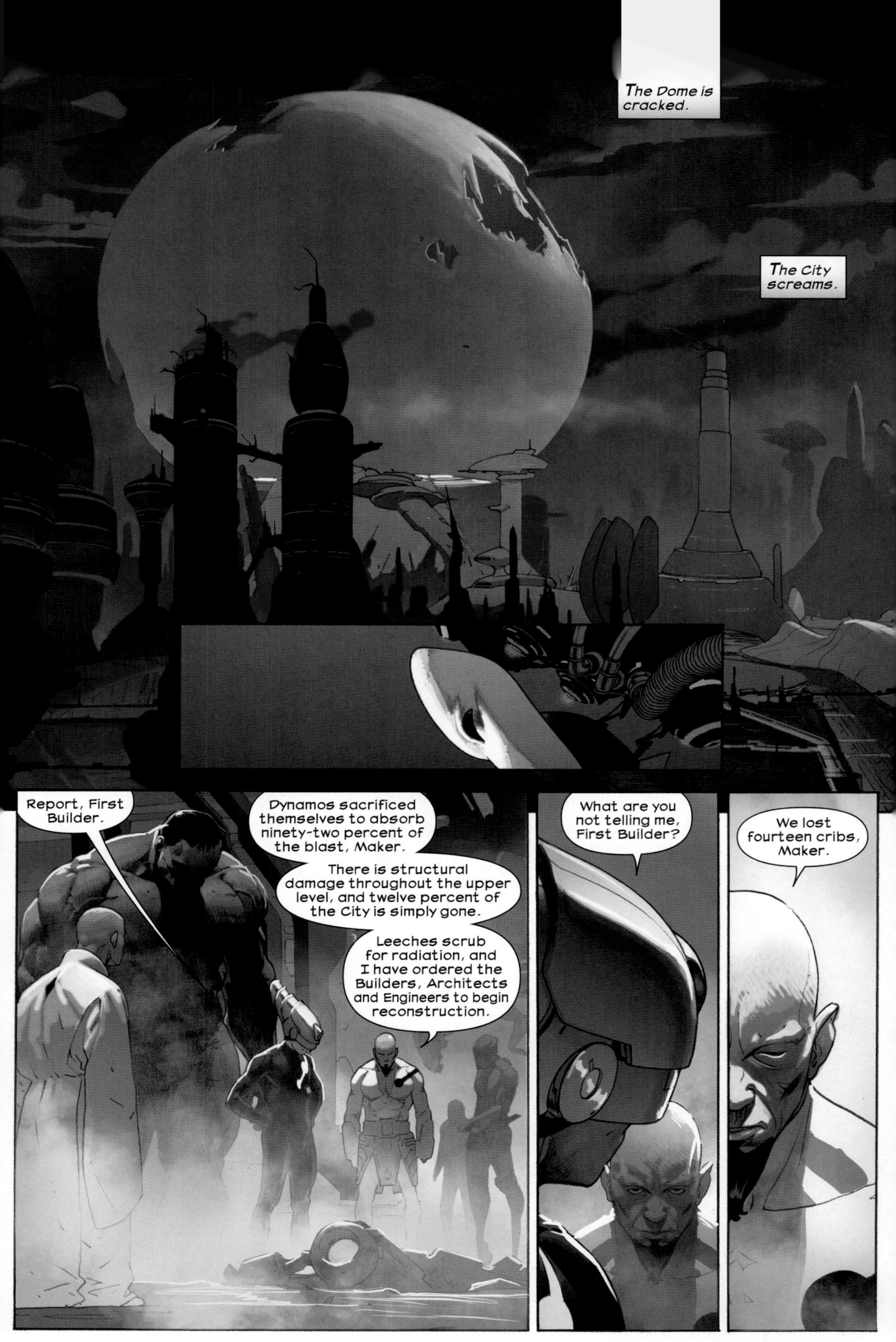
The Dome is cracked.
The City screams.
Report, First Builder.
Dynamos sacrificed themselves to absorb ninety-two percent of the blast, Maker.
There is structural damage throughout the upper level, and twelve percent of the City is simply gone.
Leeches scrub for radiation, and I have ordered the Builders, Architects and Engineers to begin reconstruction.
What are you not telling me, First Builder?
We lost fourteen cribs, Maker.

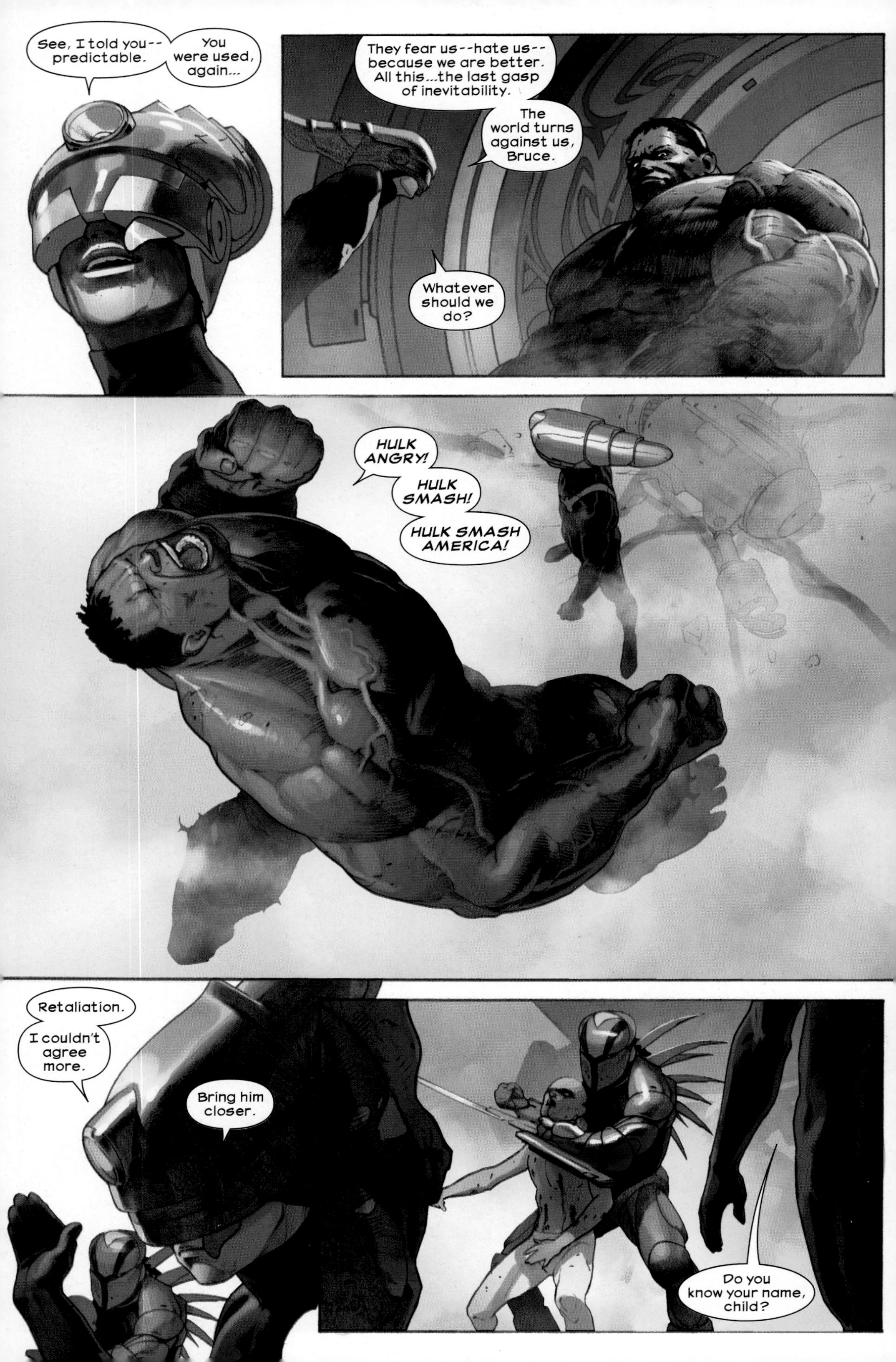
See, I told you--predictable.
You were used, again...
They fear us--hate us--because we are better. All this...the last gasp of inevitability.
The world turns against us, Bruce.
Whatever should we do?
HULK ANGRY!
HULK SMASH!
HULK SMASH AMERICA!
Retaliation.
I couldn't agree more.
Bring him closer.
Do you know your name, child?

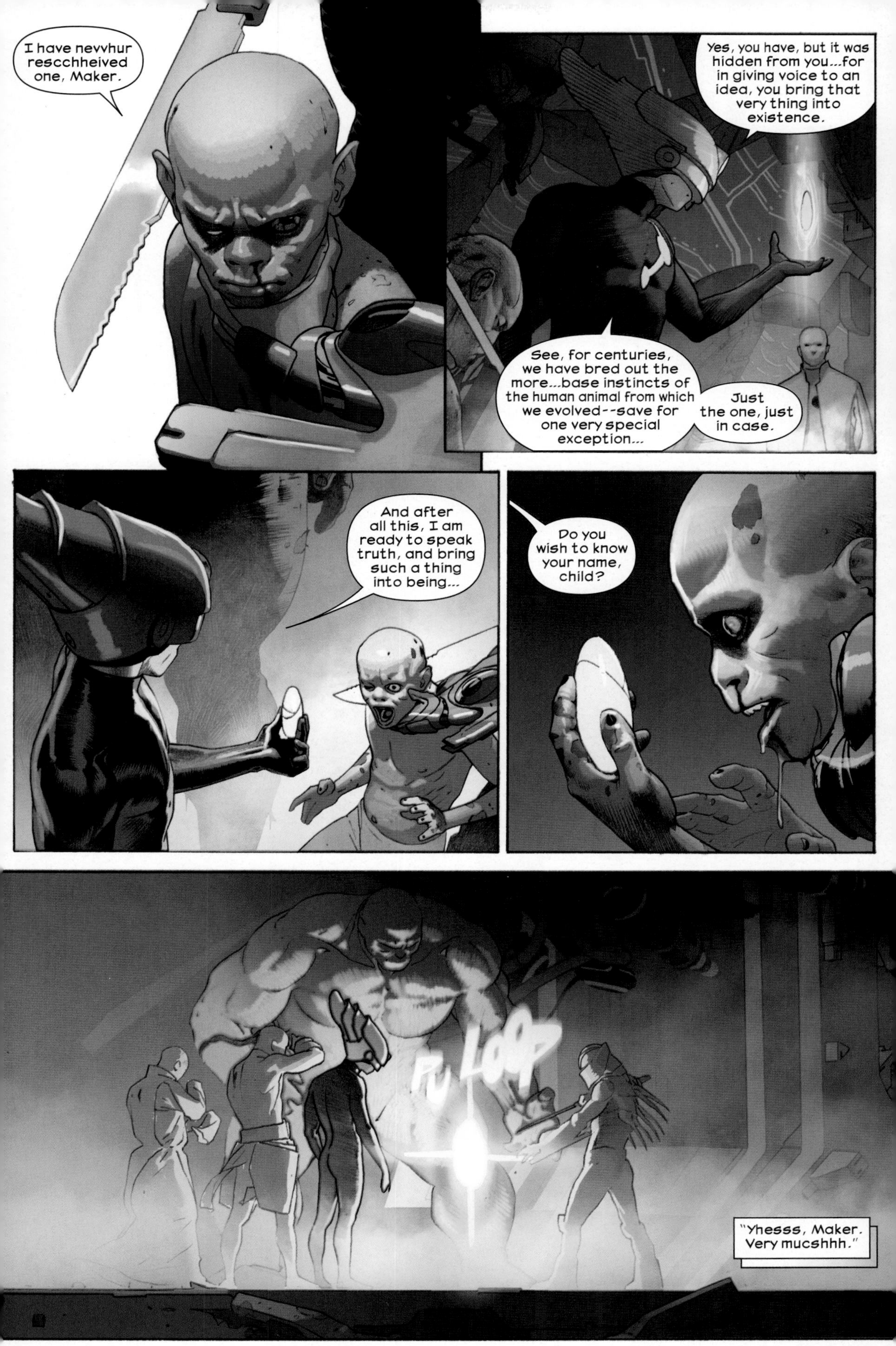
I have nevvhur rescchheived one, Maker.
Yes, you have, but it was hidden from you...for in giving voice to an idea, you bring that very thing into existence.
See, for centuries, we have bred out the more...base instincts of the human animal from which we evolved--save for one very special exception...
Just the one, just in case.
And after all this, I am ready to speak truth, and bring such a thing into being...
Do you wish to know your name, child?
PU LOOP
"Yhesss, Maker. Very mucshhh."

"You are *Death*, the first and last of a generation.

"Where there is life, you will end it.

"Where there was hope, it will die.

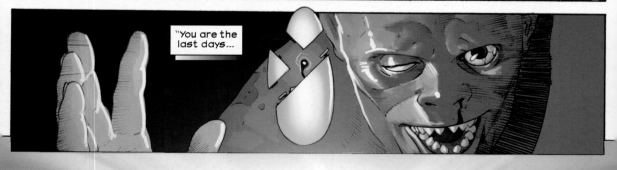

"You are the last days...

"The end of an era...

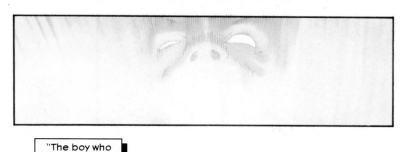

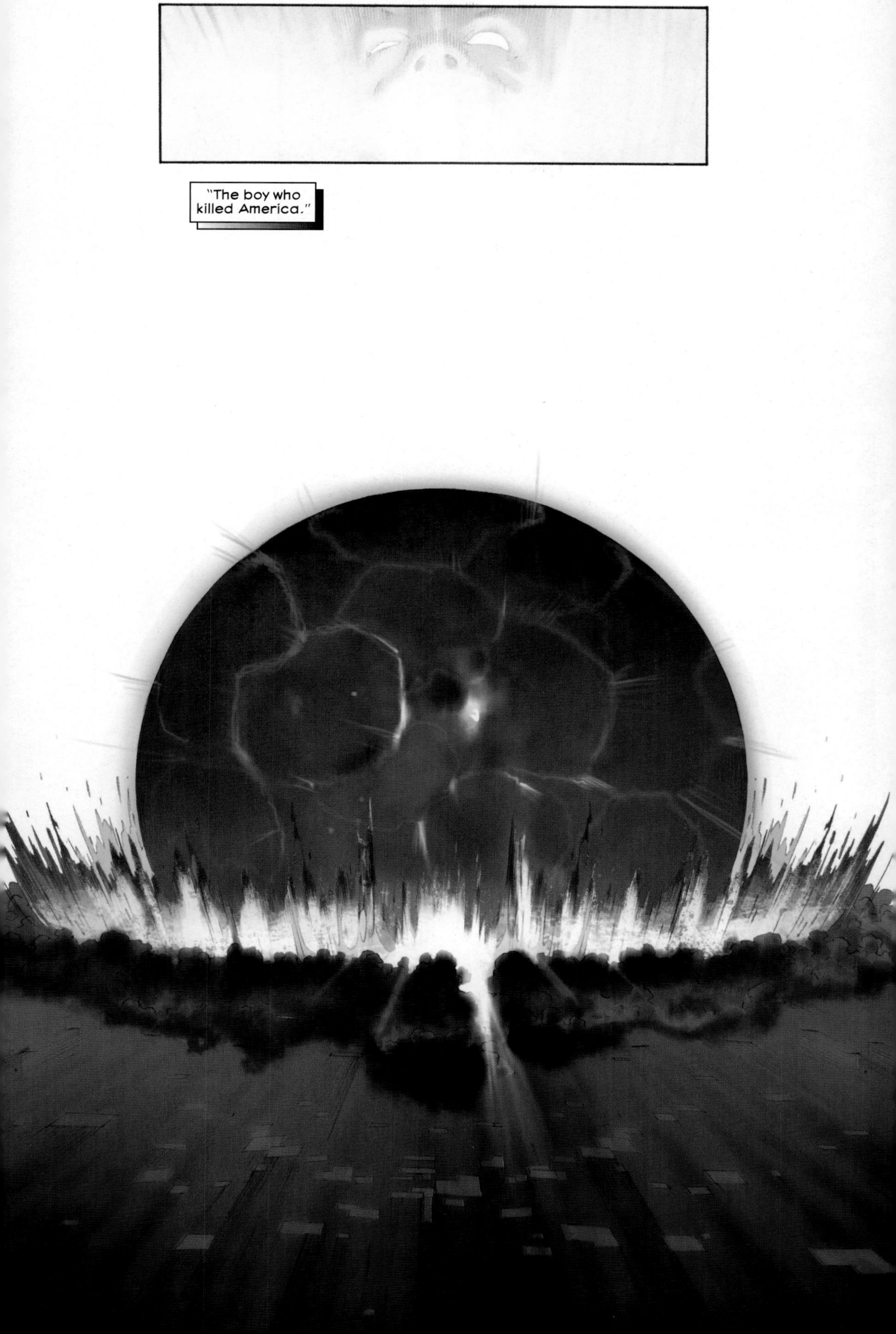
"The boy who killed America."

10

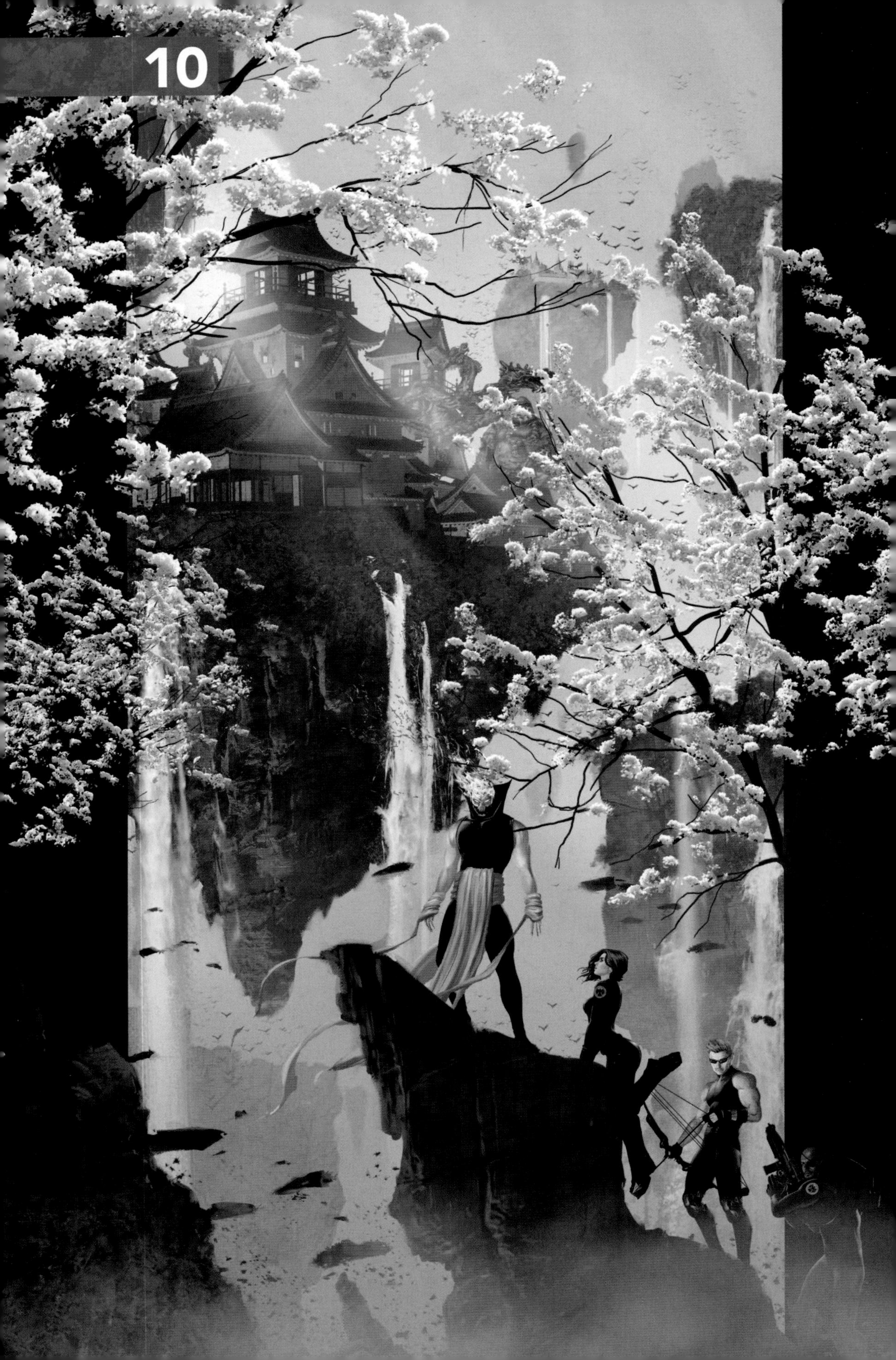

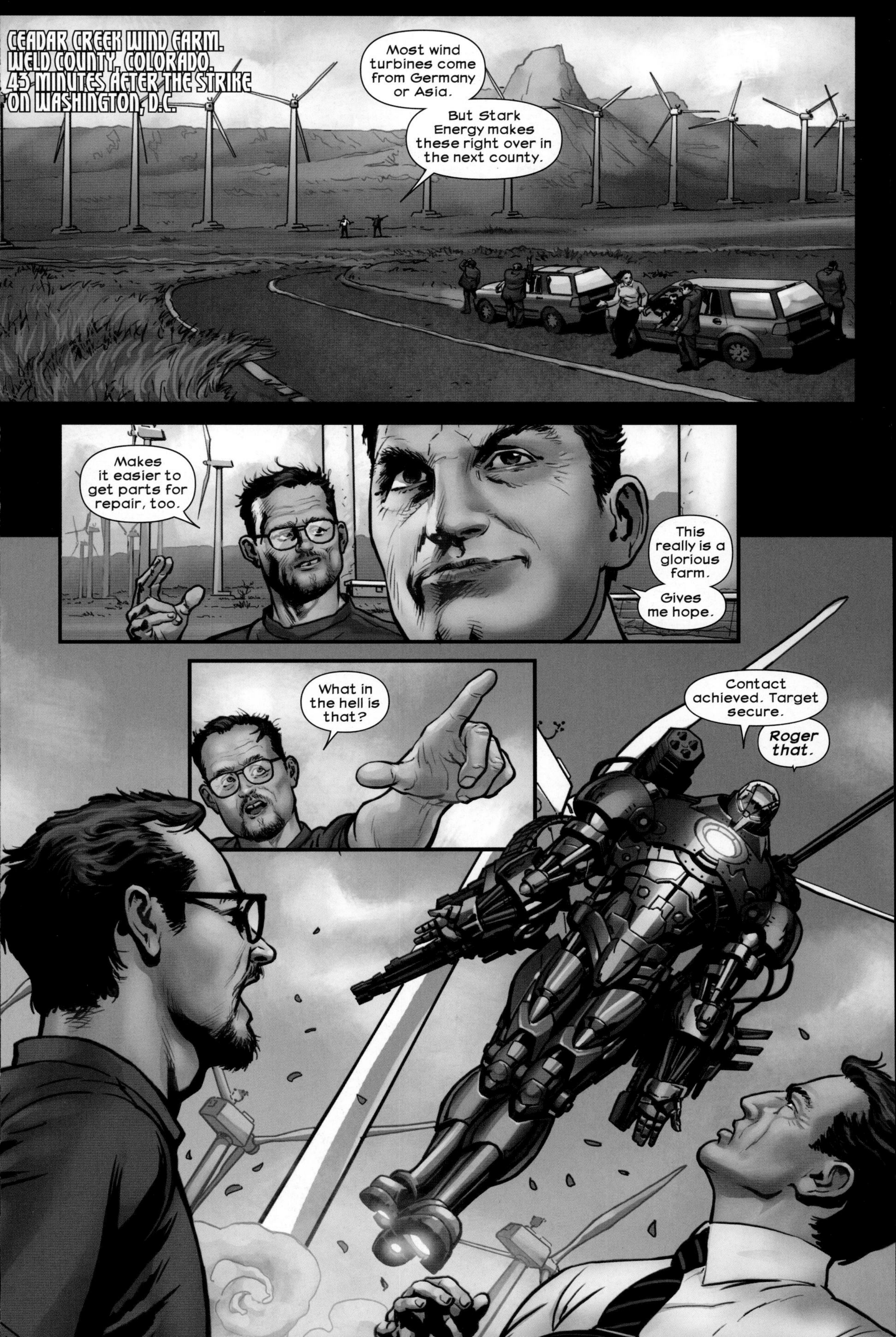
CEADAR CREEK WIND FARM.
WELD COUNTY, COLORADO.
43 MINUTES AFTER THE STRIKE ON WASHINGTON, D.C.
Most wind turbines come from Germany or Asia.
But Stark Energy makes these right over in the next county.
Makes it easier to get parts for repair, too.
This really is a glorious farm.
Gives me hope.
What in the hell is that?
Contact achieved. Target secure.
Roger that.

Secretary of Energy Howard? I am Sergeant Major James Rhodes, S.H.I.E.L.D. War Machine Brigade.

You. Farmer John. I need you to give us two hundred yards as fast as you can haul ass.

I know who you are, son, and this man is okay, he's with me.

Now calm down, tell me what seems to be the--

Sir, you need to come with me *immediately*.

I am under orders to escort you directly to the Southwest S.H.I.E.L.D. Helicarrier to take the oath of office and assume command.

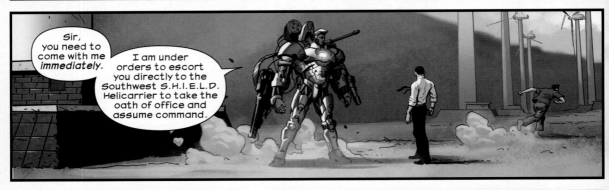

Excuse me?

There must be a mistake. I'm so far down the line of succession, surely --

There's been an *attack*, sir. On *Washington*. You'll be briefed en route.

Frankly, we weren't even sure you were still *alive*.

You are next in line to be *President of the United States*.

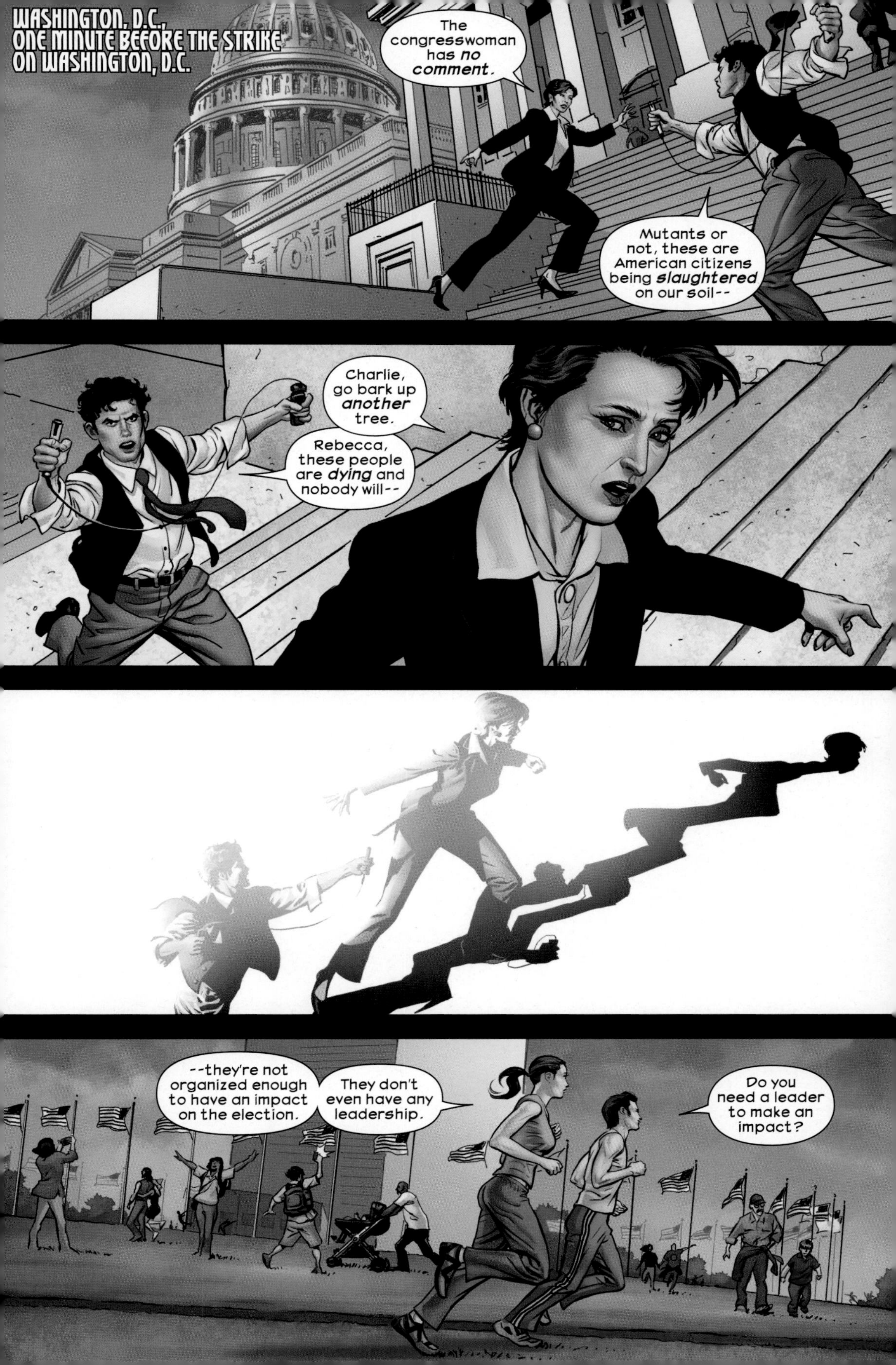
WASHINGTON, D.C., ONE MINUTE BEFORE THE STRIKE ON WASHINGTON, D.C.
The congresswoman has *no comment.*
Mutants or not, these are American citizens being *slaughtered* on our soil--
Charlie, go bark up *another* tree.
Rebecca, these people are *dying* and nobody will--
--they're not organized enough to have an impact on the election.
They don't even have any leadership.
Do you need a leader to make an impact?

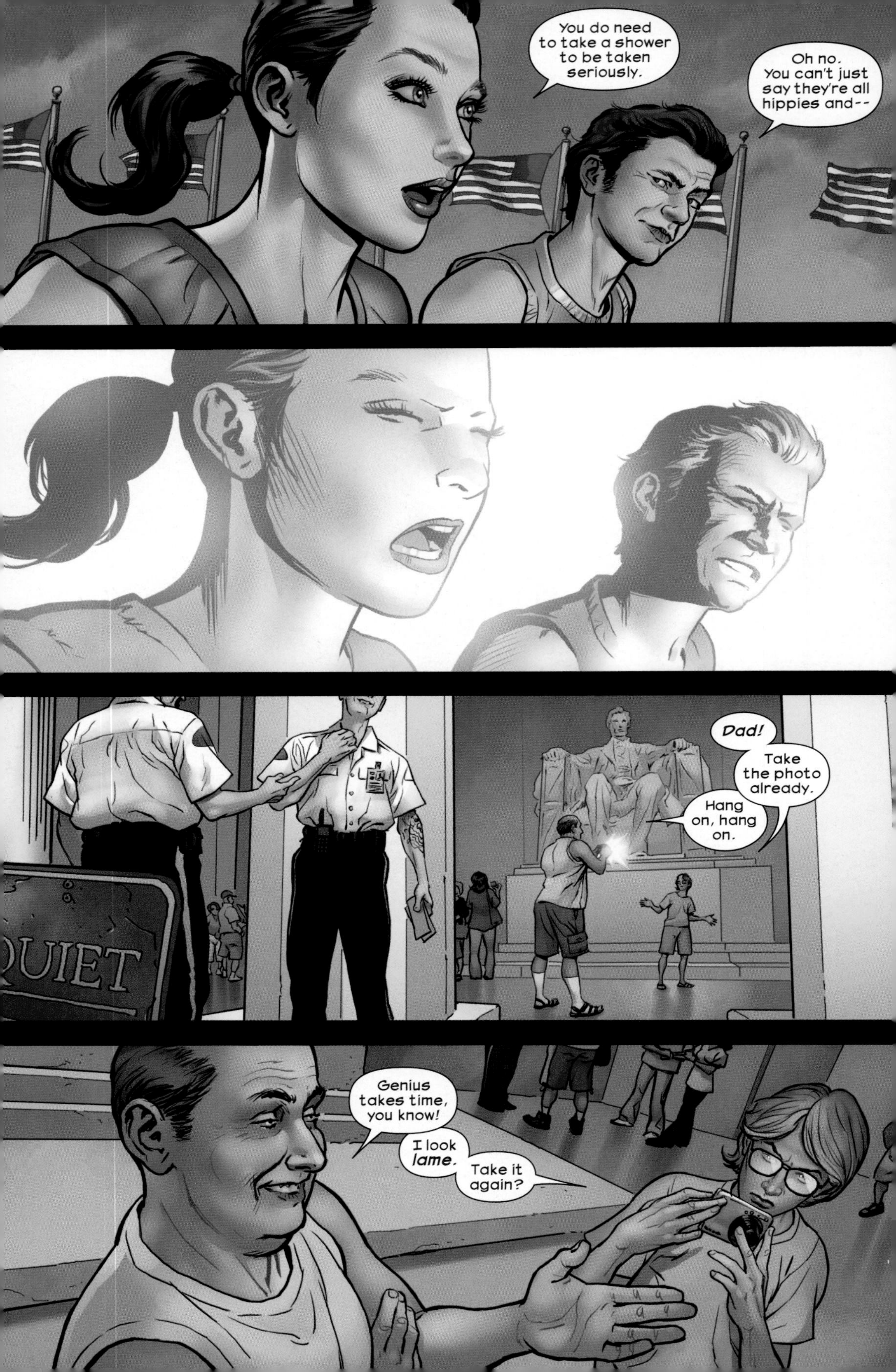
You do need to take a shower to be taken seriously.
Oh no. You can't just say they're all hippies and--
QUIET
Dad!
Take the photo already.
Hang on, hang on.
Genius takes time, you know!
I look *lame.*
Take it again?

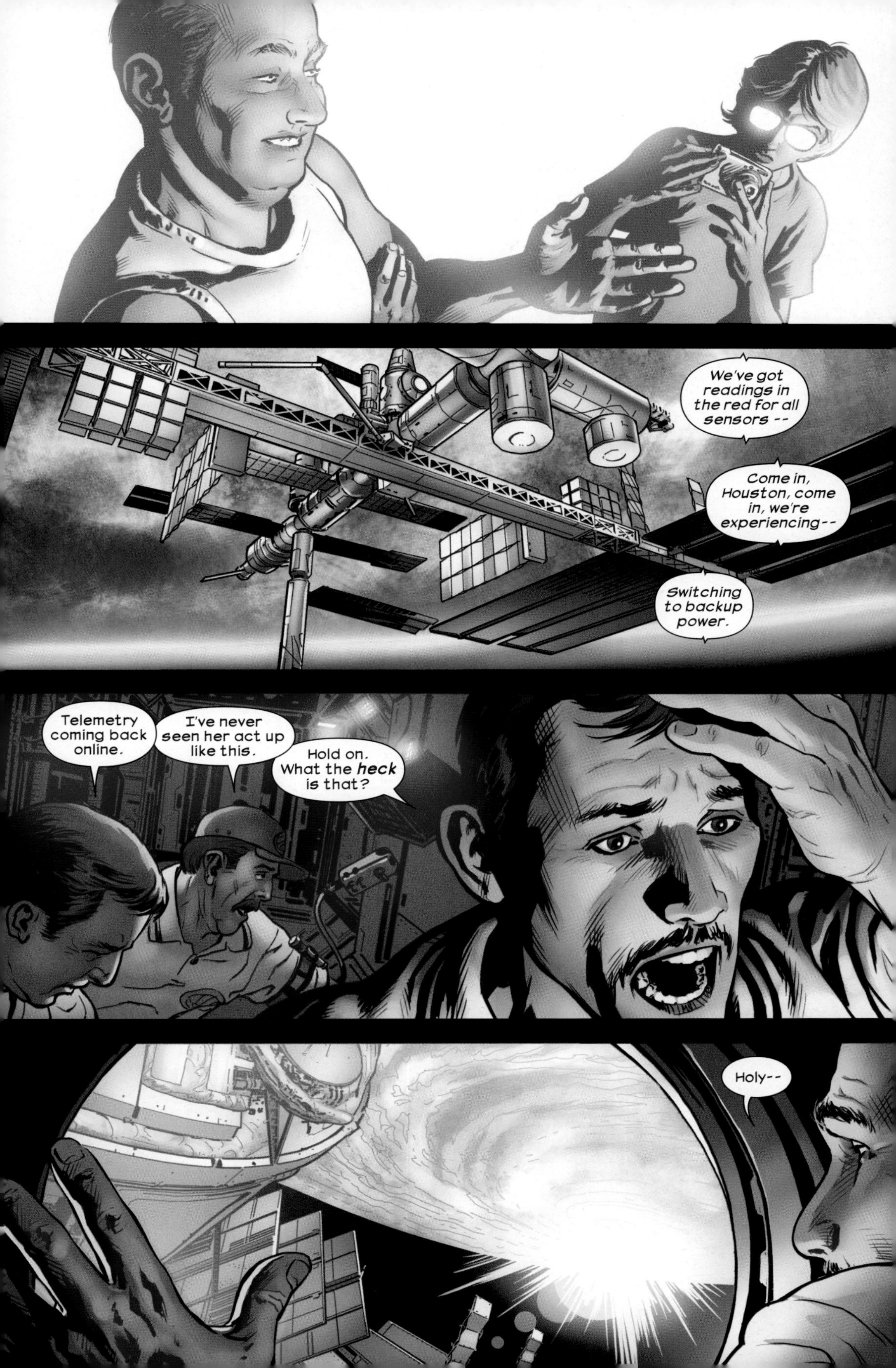
We've got readings in the red for all sensors --
Come in, Houston, come in, we're experiencing--
Switching to backup power.
Telemetry coming back online.
I've never seen her act up like this.
Hold on. What the heck is that?
Holy--

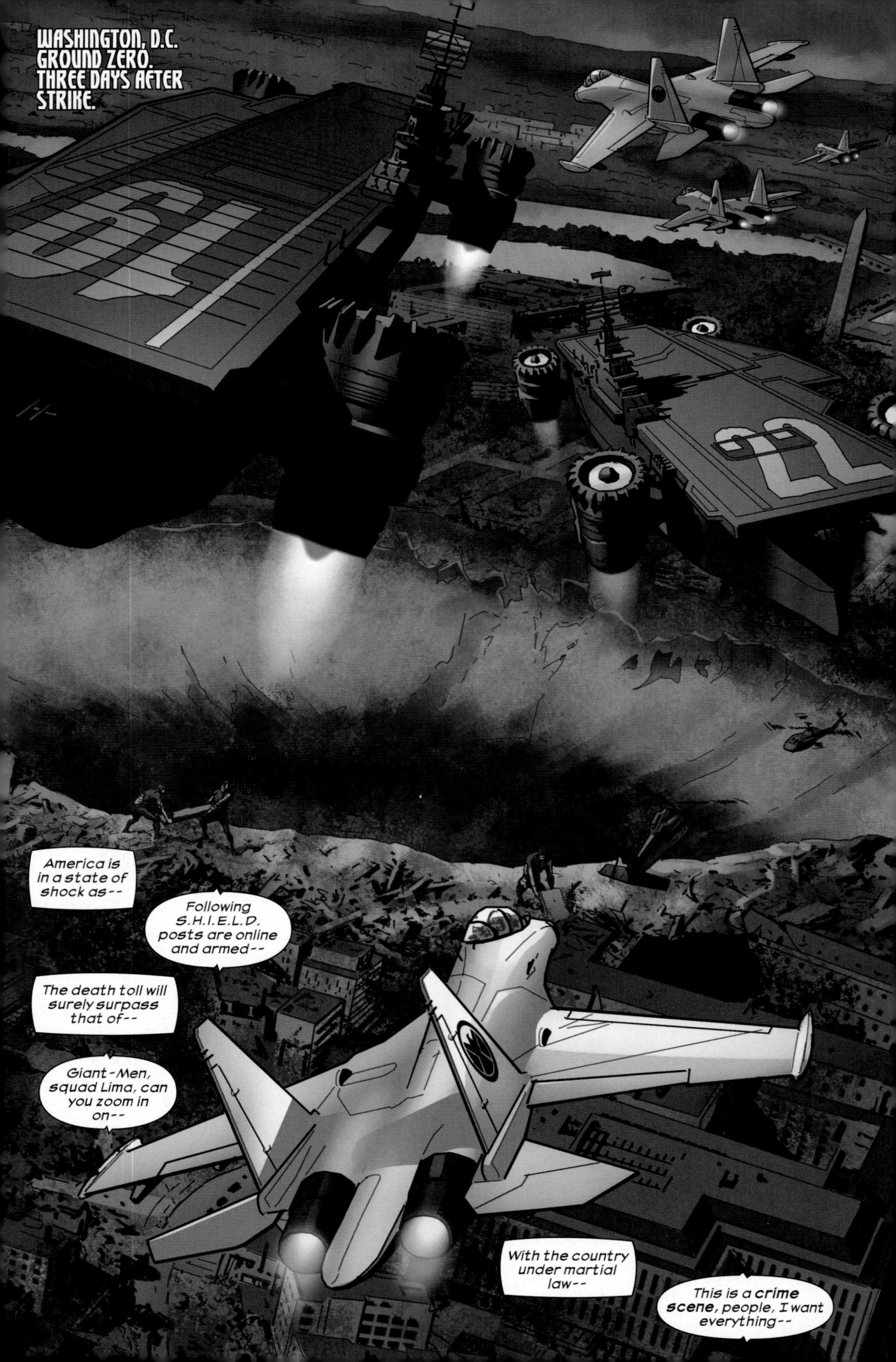
WASHINGTON, D.C. GROUND ZERO. THREE DAYS AFTER STRIKE.
America is in a state of shock as--
Following S.H.I.E.L.D. posts are online and armed--
The death toll will surely surpass that of--
Giant-Men, squad Lima, can you zoom in on--
With the country under martial law--
This is a **crime scene**, people, I want everything--

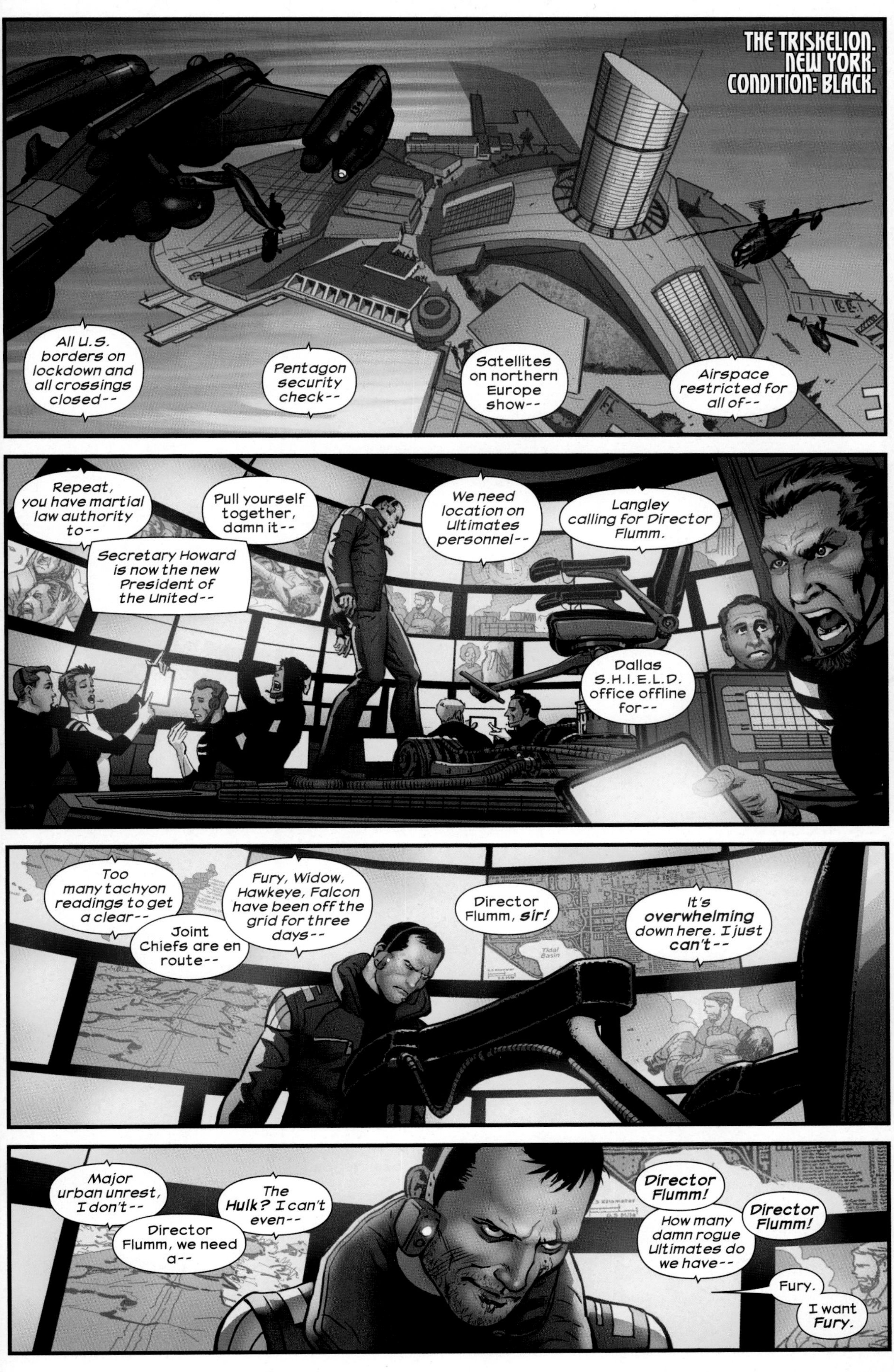
THE TRISKELION. NEW YORK. CONDITION: BLACK.
All U.S. borders on lockdown and all crossings closed--
Pentagon security check--
Satellites on northern Europe show--
Airspace restricted for all of--
Repeat, you have martial law authority to--
Secretary Howard is now the new President of the United--
Pull yourself together, damn it--
We need location on Ultimates personnel--
Langley calling for Director Flumm.
Dallas S.H.I.E.L.D. office offline for--
Too many tachyon readings to get a clear--
Joint Chiefs are en route--
Fury, Widow, Hawkeye, Falcon have been off the grid for three days--
Director Flumm, sir!
It's overwhelming down here. I just can't--
Major urban unrest, I don't--
Director Flumm, we need a--
The Hulk? I can't even--
Director Flumm!
How many damn rogue Ultimates do we have--
Director Flumm!
Fury.
I want Fury.

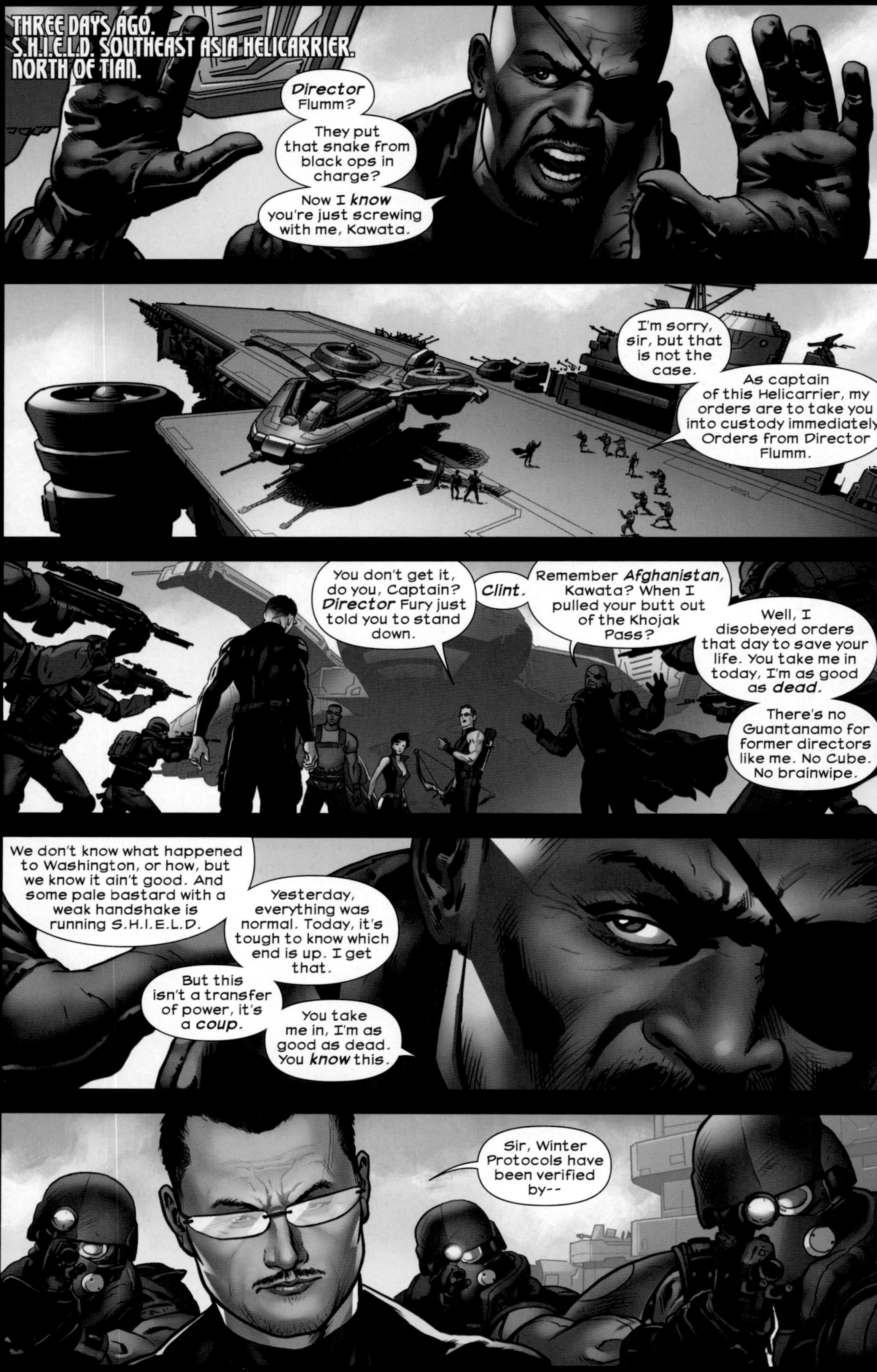
THREE DAYS AGO. S.H.I.E.L.D. SOUTHEAST ASIA HELICARRIER. NORTH OF TIAN.
Director Flumm?
They put that snake from black ops in charge?
Now I know you're just screwing with me, Kawata.
I'm sorry, sir, but that is not the case.
As captain of this Helicarrier, my orders are to take you into custody immediately. Orders from Director Flumm.
You don't get it, do you, Captain? Director Fury just told you to stand down.
Clint.
Remember Afghanistan, Kawata? When I pulled your butt out of the Khojak Pass?
Well, I disobeyed orders that day to save your life. You take me in today, I'm as good as dead.
There's no Guantanamo for former directors like me. No Cube. No brainwipe.
We don't know what happened to Washington, or how, but we know it ain't good. And some pale bastard with a weak handshake is running S.H.I.E.L.D.
Yesterday, everything was normal. Today, it's tough to know which end is up. I get that.
But this isn't a transfer of power, it's a coup.
You take me in, I'm as good as dead. You know this.
Sir, Winter Protocols have been verified by--

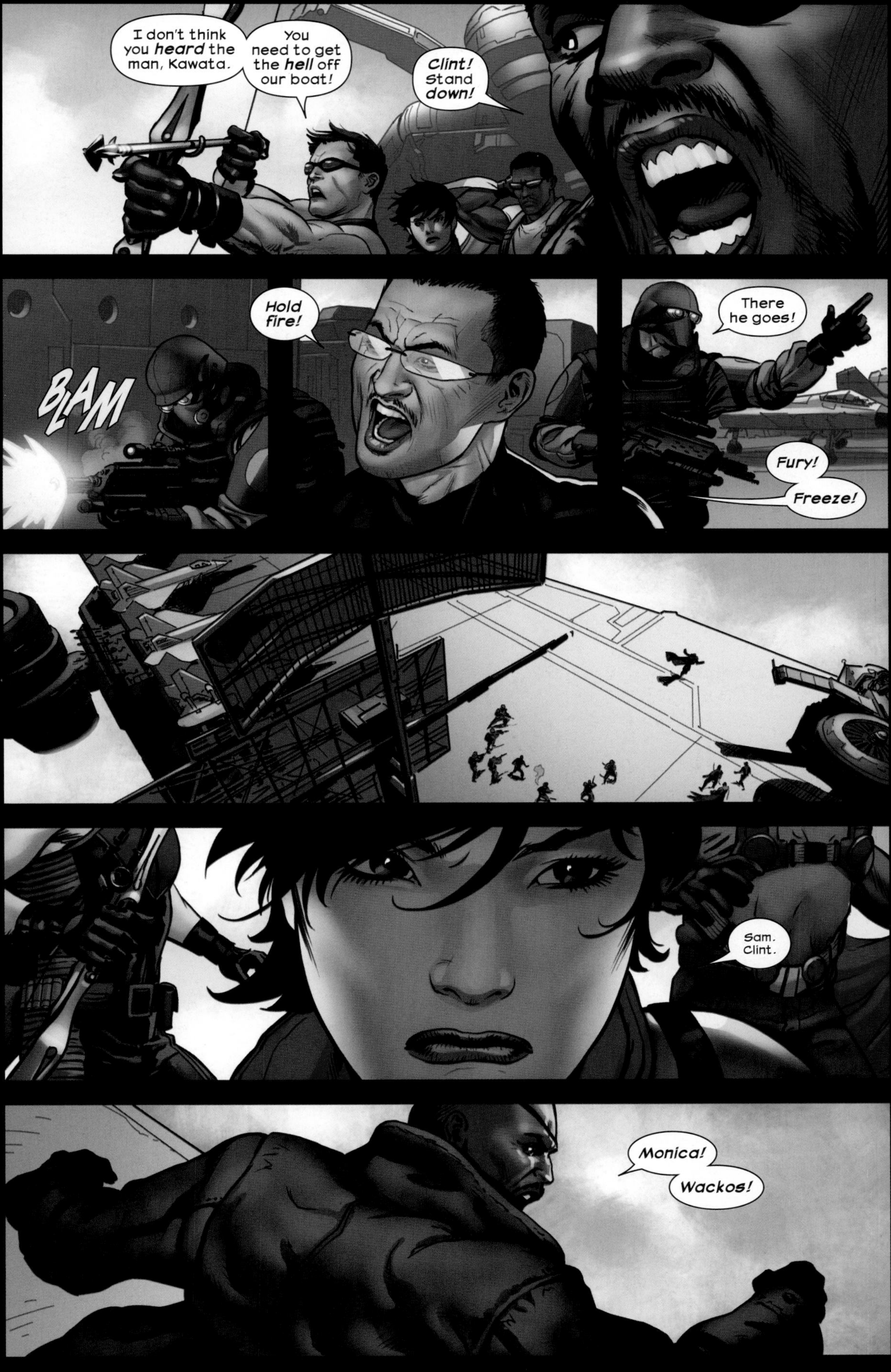
I don't think you *heard* the man, Kawata.
You need to get the *hell* off our boat!
Clint! Stand *down!*
BLAM
Hold fire!
There he goes!
Fury!
Freeze!
Sam. Clint.
Monica!
Wackos!

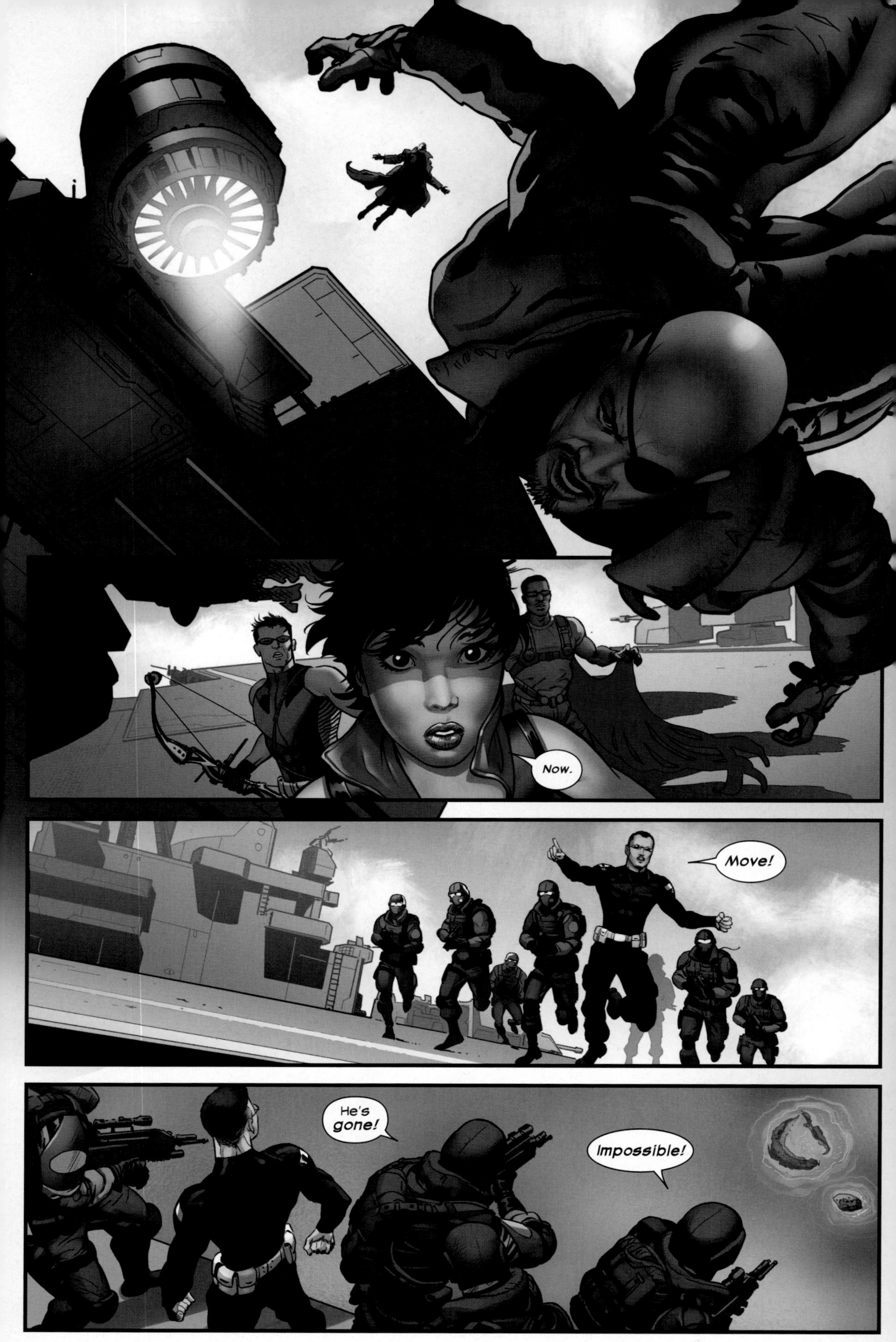

Now.
Move!
He's gone!
Impossible!

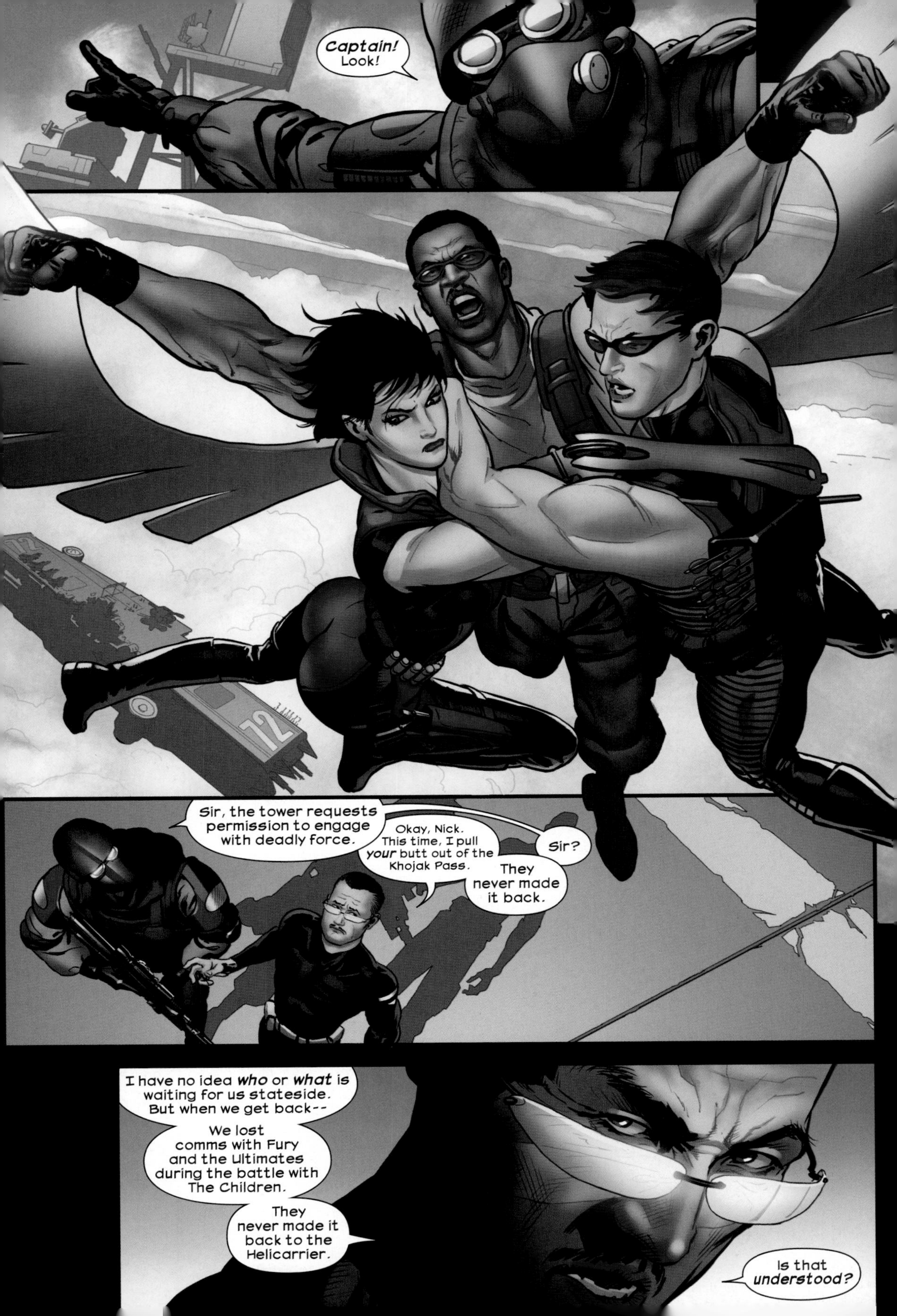

Captain! Look!
Sir, the tower requests permission to engage with deadly force.
Okay, Nick. This time, I pull your butt out of the Khojak Pass.
Sir?
They never made it back.
I have no idea who or what is waiting for us stateside. But when we get back--
We lost comms with Fury and the Ultimates during the battle with The Children.
They never made it back to the Helicarrier.
Is that understood?

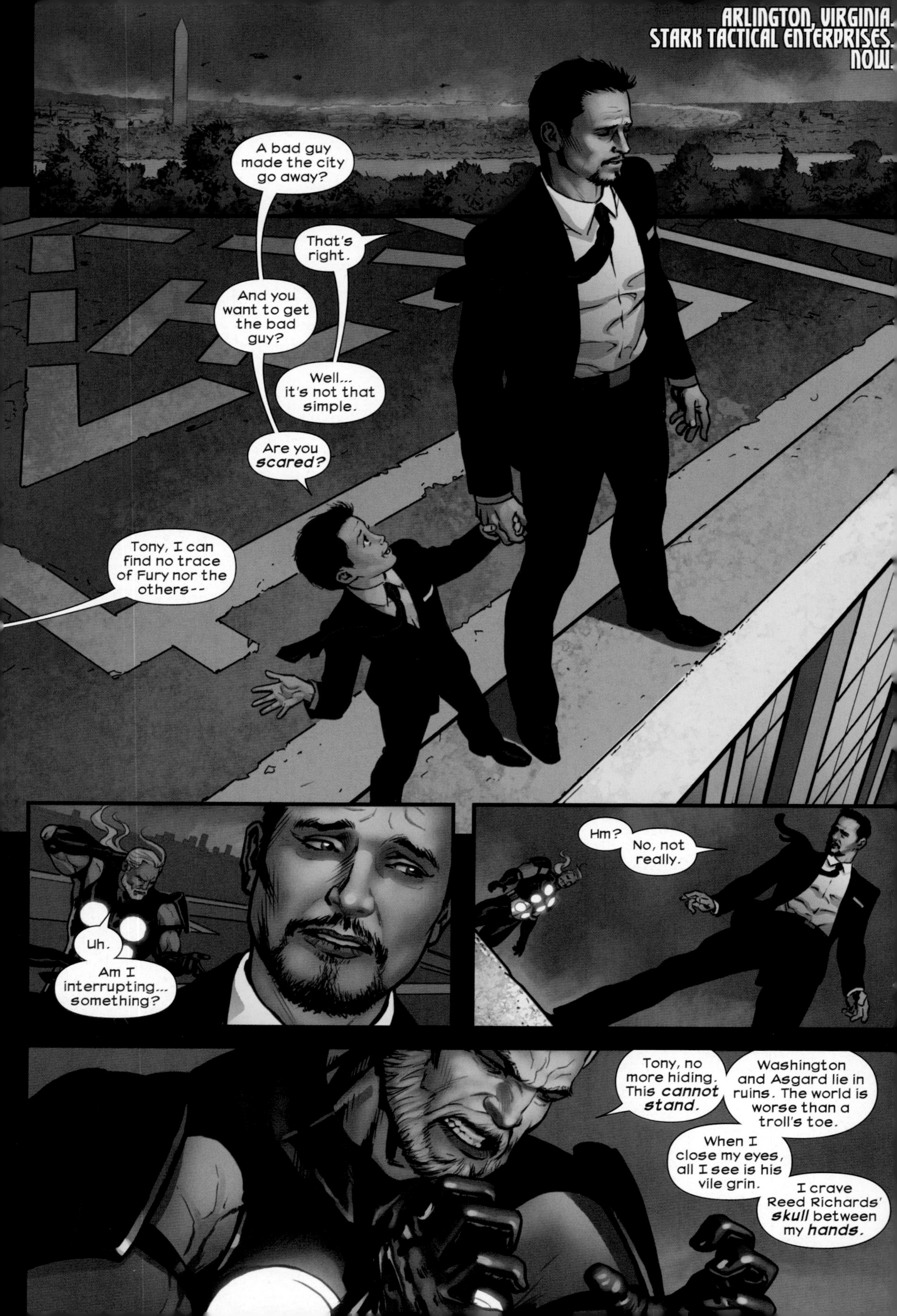

ARLINGTON, VIRGINIA. STARK TACTICAL ENTERPRISES. NOW.
A bad guy made the city go away?
That's right.
And you want to get the bad guy?
Well... it's not that simple.
Are you *scared?*
Tony, I can find no trace of Fury nor the others--
Uh.
Am I interrupting... something?
Hm?
No, not really.
Tony, no more hiding. This *cannot stand.*
Washington and Asgard lie in ruins. The world is worse than a troll's toe.
When I close my eyes, all I see is his vile grin.
I crave Reed Richards' *skull* between my *hands.*

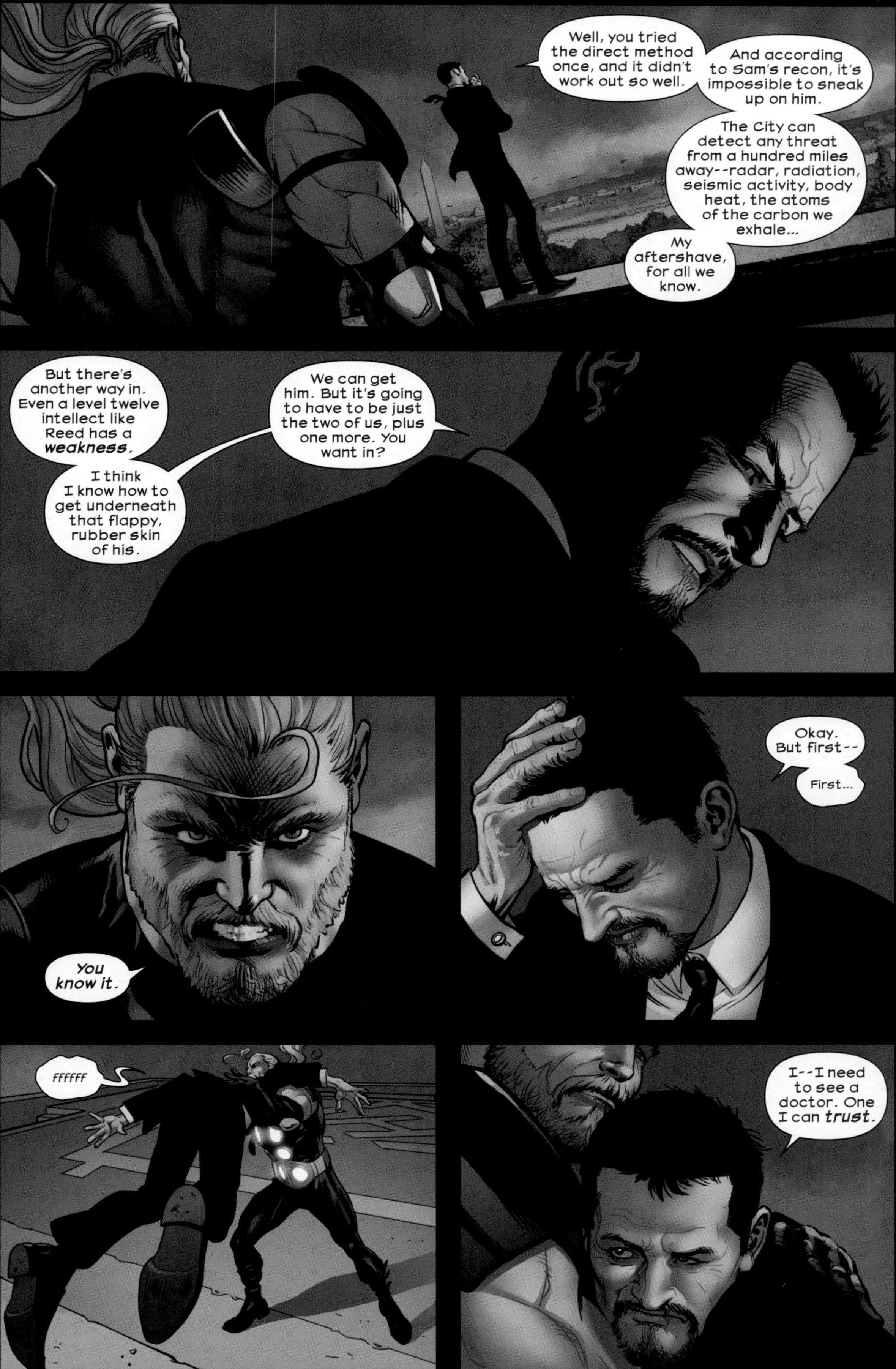
Well, you tried the direct method once, and it didn't work out so well.
And according to Sam's recon, it's impossible to sneak up on him.
The City can detect any threat from a hundred miles away--radar, radiation, seismic activity, body heat, the atoms of the carbon we exhale...
My aftershave, for all we know.
But there's another way in. Even a level twelve intellect like Reed has a *weakness*.
I think I know how to get underneath that flappy, rubber skin of his.
We can get him. But it's going to have to be just the two of us, plus one more. You want in?
You know it.
Okay. But first--
First...
FFFFFF
I--I need to see a doctor. One I can *trust*.

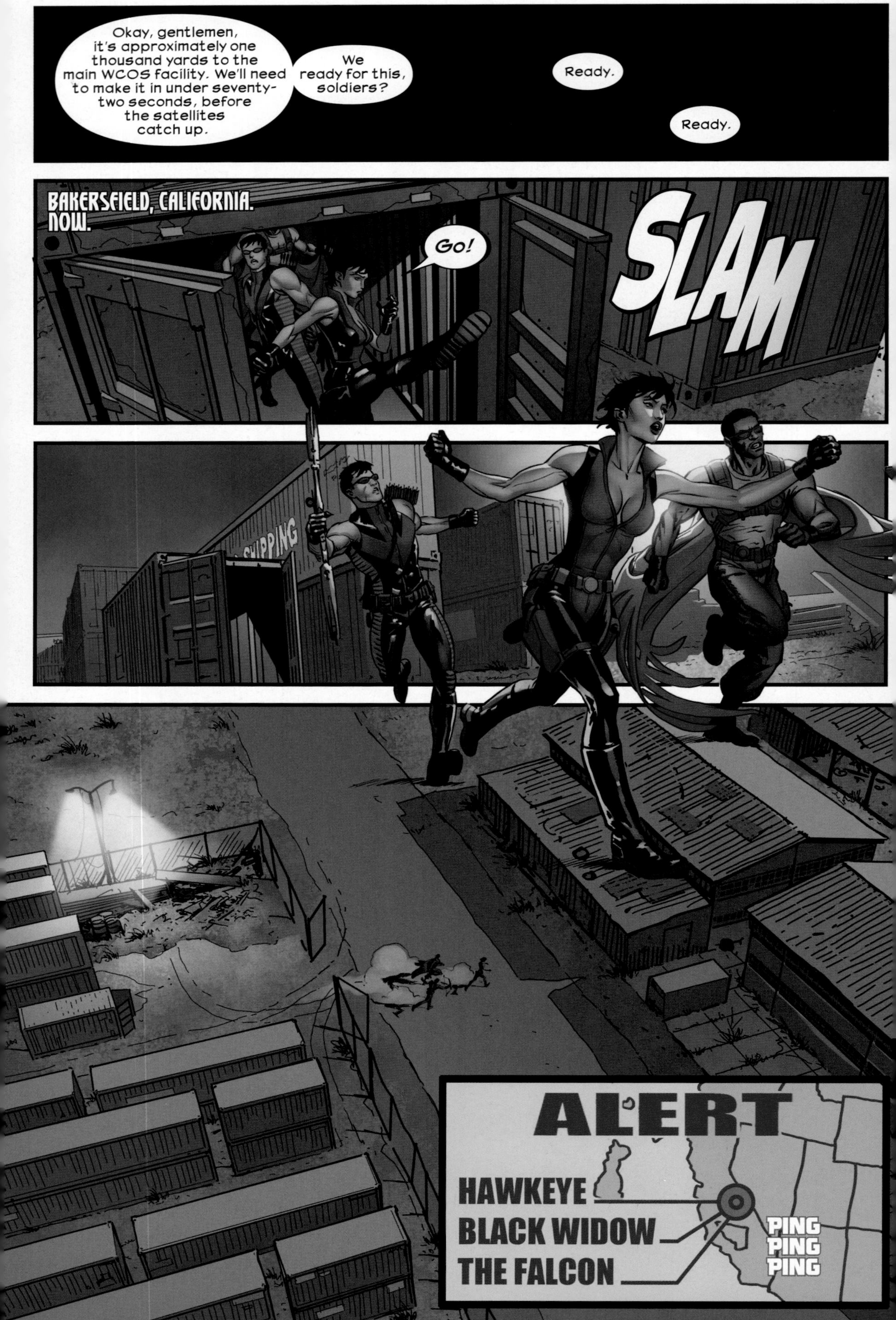

Okay, gentlemen, it's approximately one thousand yards to the main WCOS facility. We'll need to make it in under seventy-two seconds, before the satellites catch up.
We ready for this, soldiers?
Ready.
Ready.
BAKERSFIELD, CALIFORNIA. NOW.
Go!
SLAM
SHIPPING
ALERT
HAWKEYE
BLACK WIDOW
THE FALCON
PING PING PING

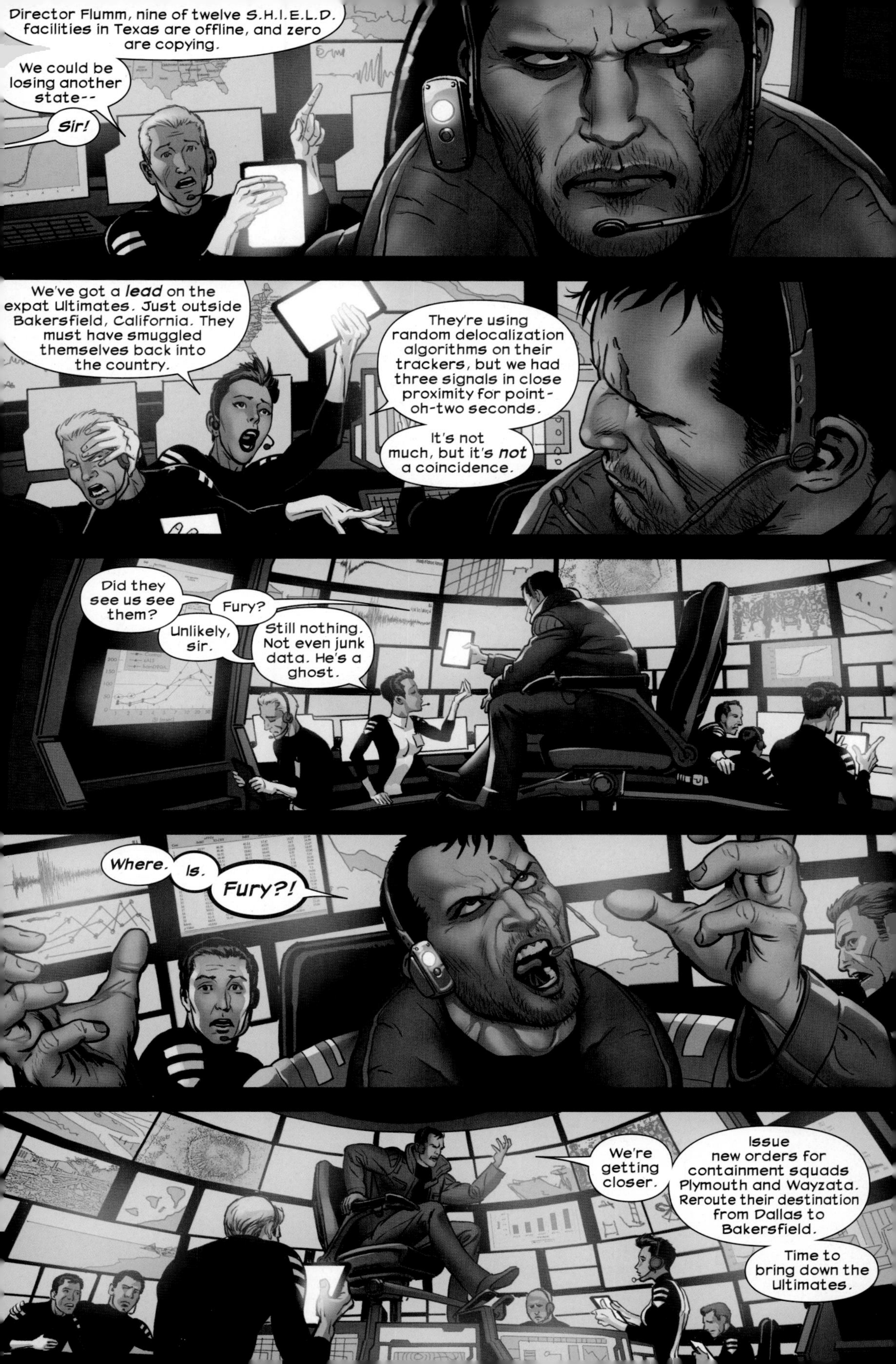
Director Flumm, nine of twelve S.H.I.E.L.D. facilities in Texas are offline, and zero are copying.
We could be losing another state--
Sir!
We've got a *lead* on the expat Ultimates. Just outside Bakersfield, California. They must have smuggled themselves back into the country.
They're using random delocalization algorithms on their trackers, but we had three signals in close proximity for point-oh-two seconds.
It's not much, but it's *not* a coincidence.
Did they see us see them?
Fury?
Unlikely, sir.
Still nothing. Not even junk data. He's a ghost.
Where.
Is.
Fury?!
We're getting closer.
Issue new orders for containment squads Plymouth and Wayzata. Reroute their destination from Dallas to Bakersfield.
Time to bring down the Ultimates.

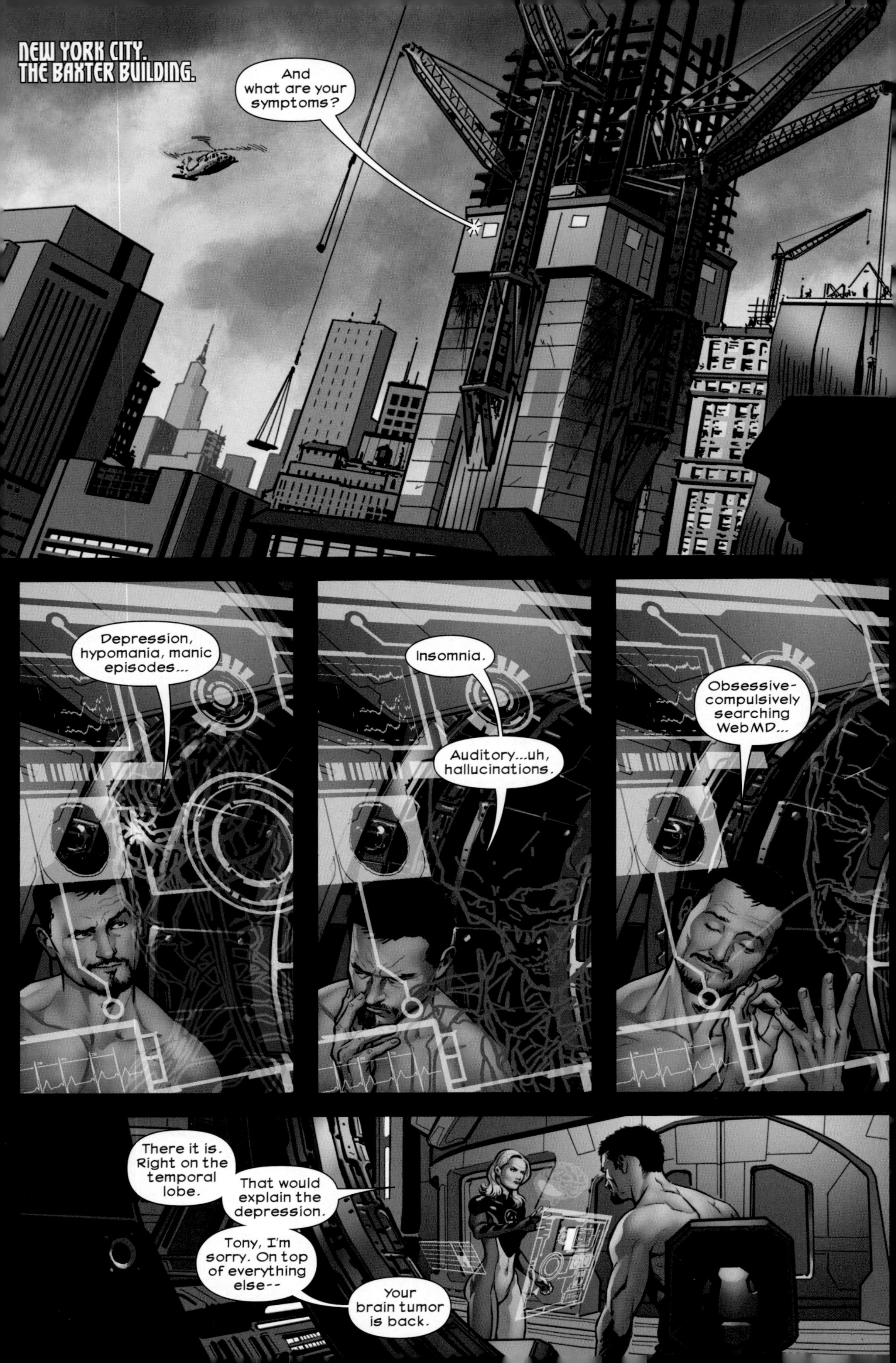
NEW YORK CITY.
THE BAXTER BUILDING.
And what are your symptoms?
Depression, hypomania, manic episodes...
Insomnia.
Auditory...uh, hallucinations.
Obsessive-compulsively searching WebMD...
There it is. Right on the temporal lobe.
That would explain the depression.
Tony, I'm sorry. On top of everything else--
Your brain tumor is back.

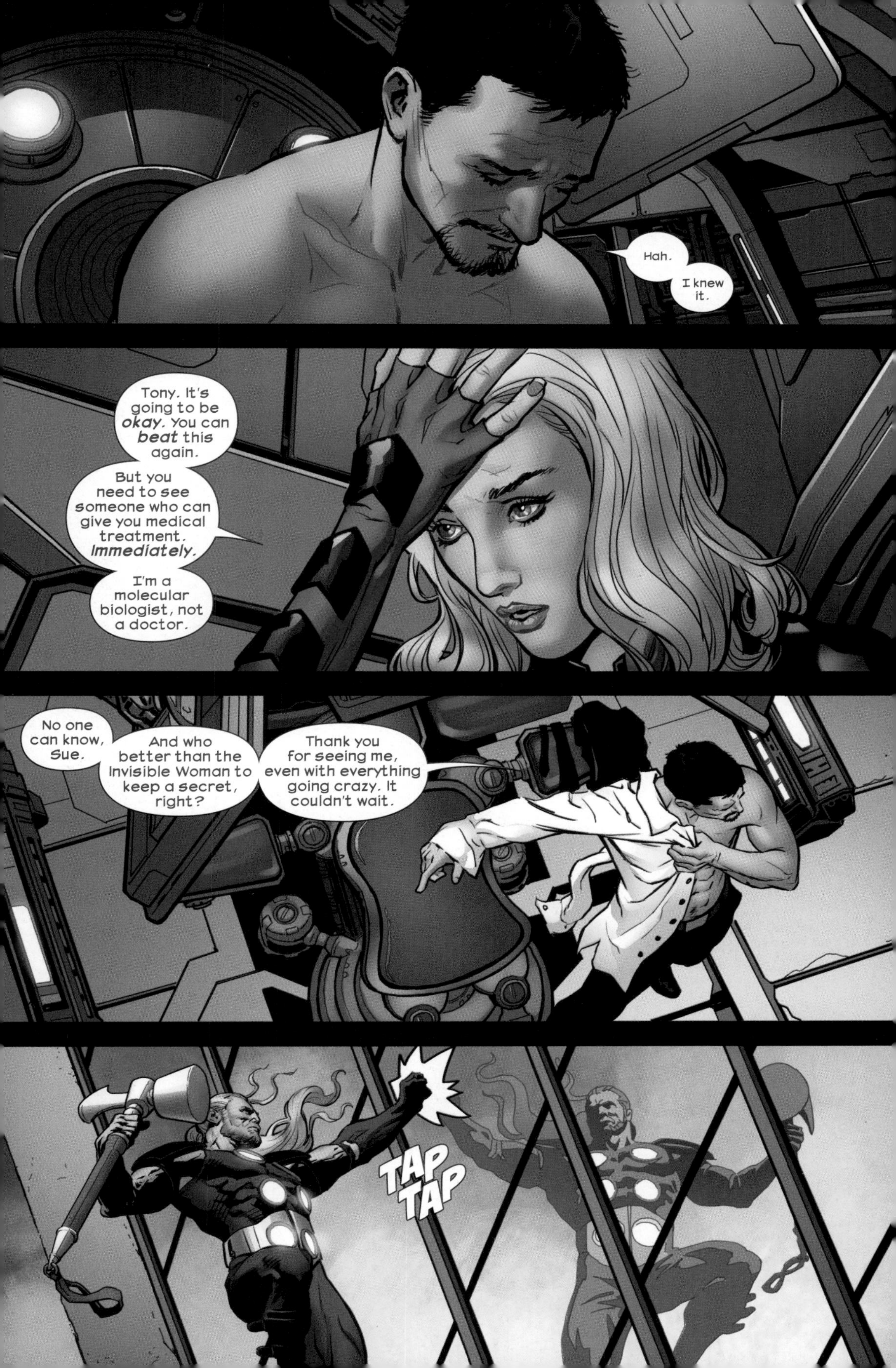
Hah.
I knew it.
Tony. It's going to be *okay.* You can *beat* this again.
But you need to see someone who can give you medical treatment. *Immediately.*
I'm a molecular biologist, not a doctor.
No one can know, Sue.
And who better than the Invisible Woman to keep a secret, right?
Thank you for seeing me, even with everything going crazy. It couldn't wait.
TAP TAP

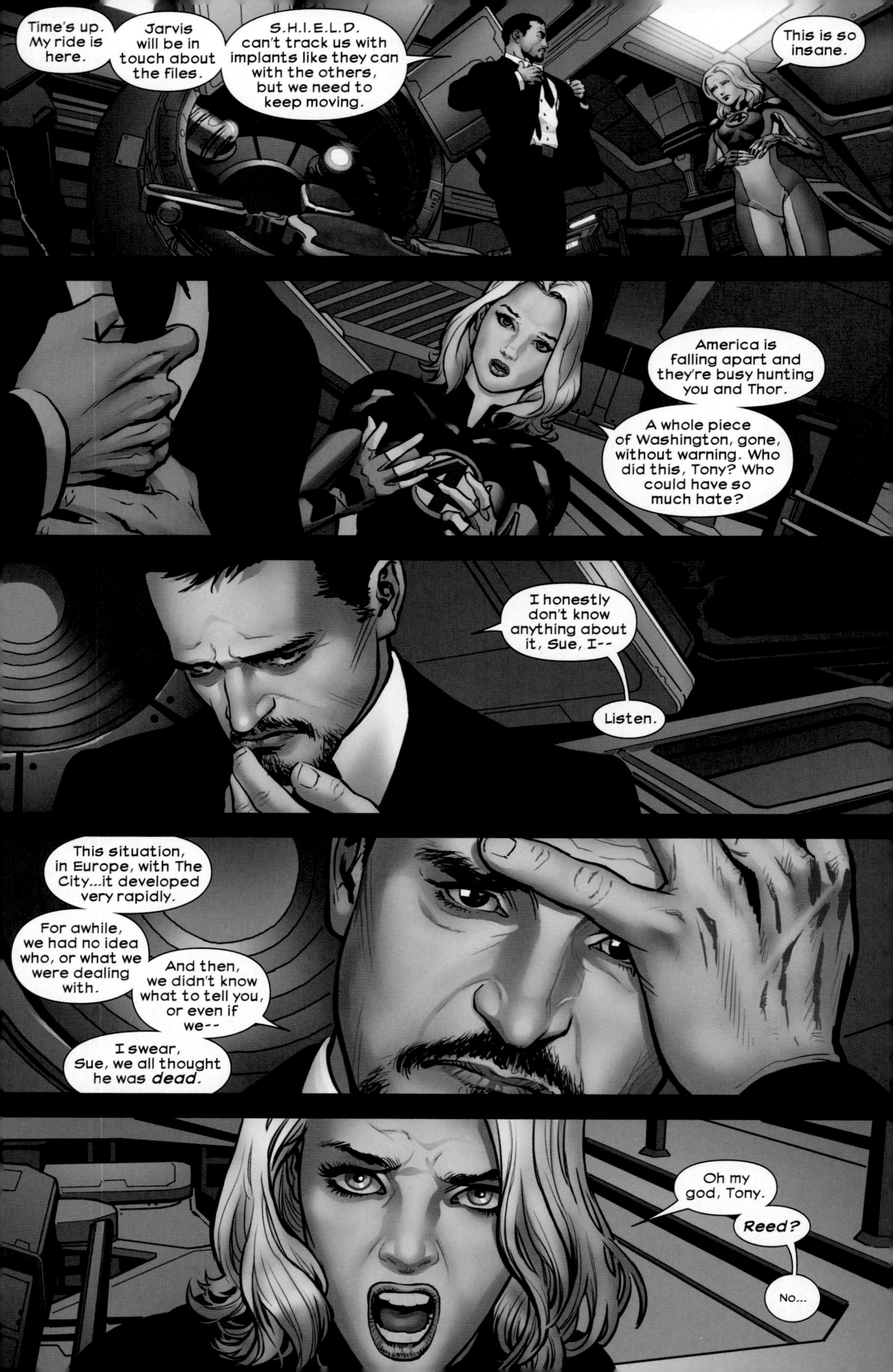

Time's up. My ride is here.
Jarvis will be in touch about the files.
S.H.I.E.L.D. can't track us with implants like they can with the others, but we need to keep moving.
This is so insane.
America is falling apart and they're busy hunting you and Thor.
A whole piece of Washington, gone, without warning. Who did this, Tony? Who could have so much hate?
I honestly don't know anything about it, Sue, I--
Listen.
This situation, in Europe, with The City...it developed very rapidly.
For awhile, we had no idea who, or what we were dealing with.
And then, we didn't know what to tell you, or even if we--
I swear, Sue, we all thought he was *dead.*
Oh my god, Tony.
Reed?
No...

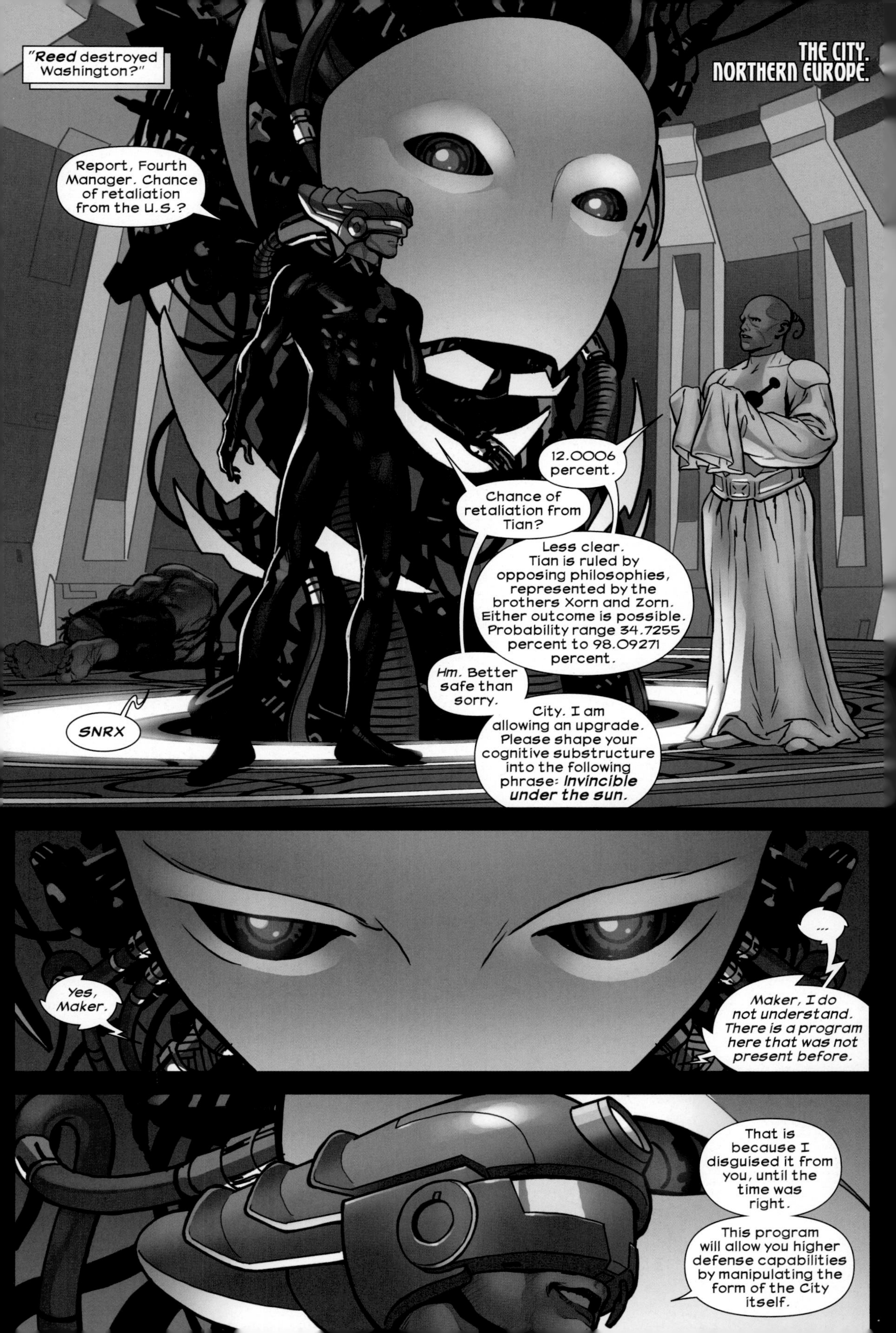
"Reed destroyed Washington?"
THE CITY. NORTHERN EUROPE.
Report, Fourth Manager. Chance of retaliation from the U.S.?
12.0006 percent.
Chance of retaliation from Tian?
Less clear. Tian is ruled by opposing philosophies, represented by the brothers Xorn and Zorn. Either outcome is possible. Probability range 34.7255 percent to 98.09271 percent.
Hm. Better safe than sorry.
SNRX
City. I am allowing an upgrade. Please shape your cognitive substructure into the following phrase: Invincible under the sun.
Yes, Maker.
...
Maker, I do not understand. There is a program here that was not present before.
That is because I disguised it from you, until the time was right.
This program will allow you higher defense capabilities by manipulating the form of the City itself.

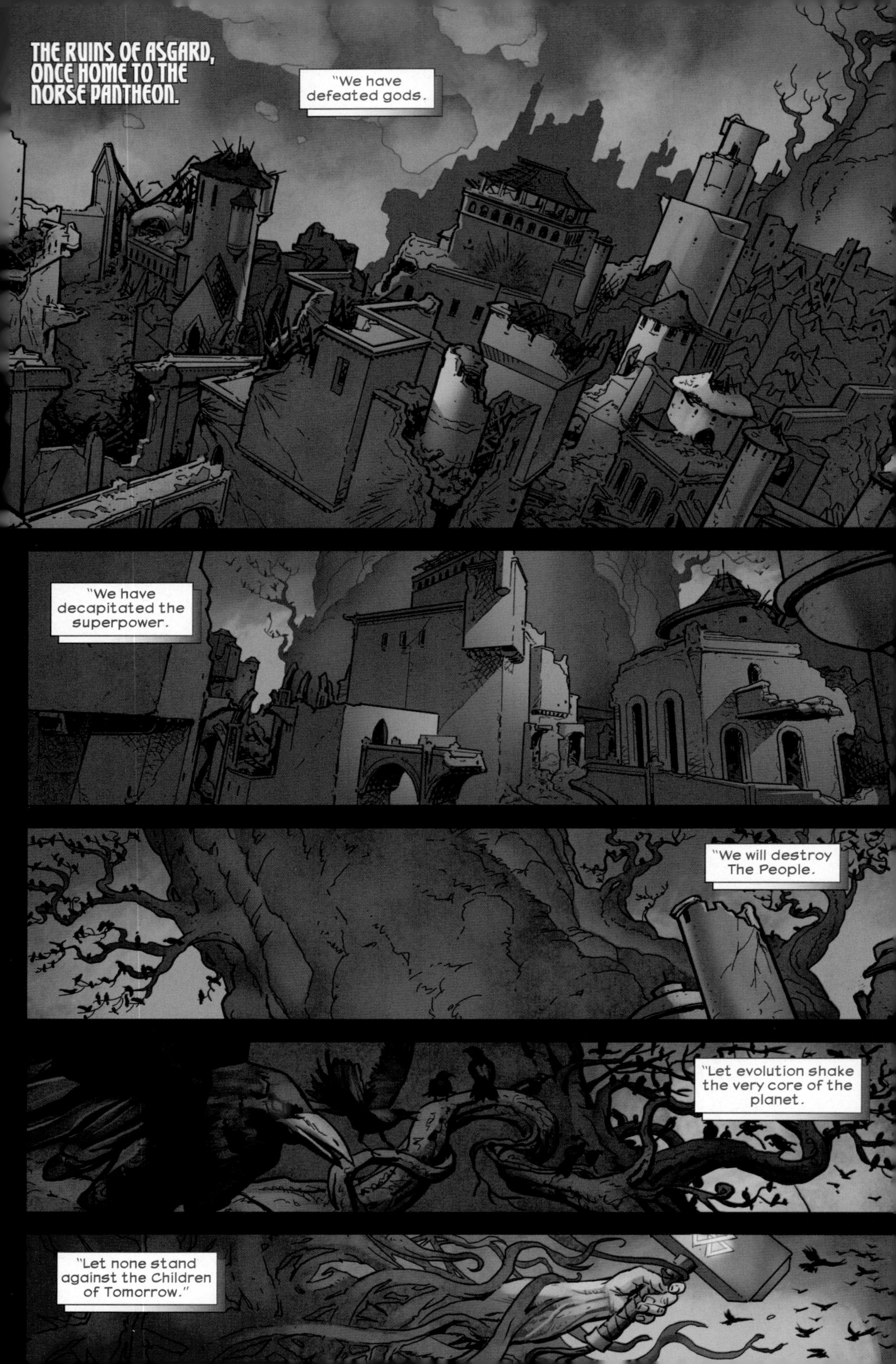
THE RUINS OF ASGARD, ONCE HOME TO THE NORSE PANTHEON.
"We have defeated gods.
"We have decapitated the superpower.
"We will destroy The People.
"Let evolution shake the very core of the planet.
"Let none stand against the Children of Tomorrow."

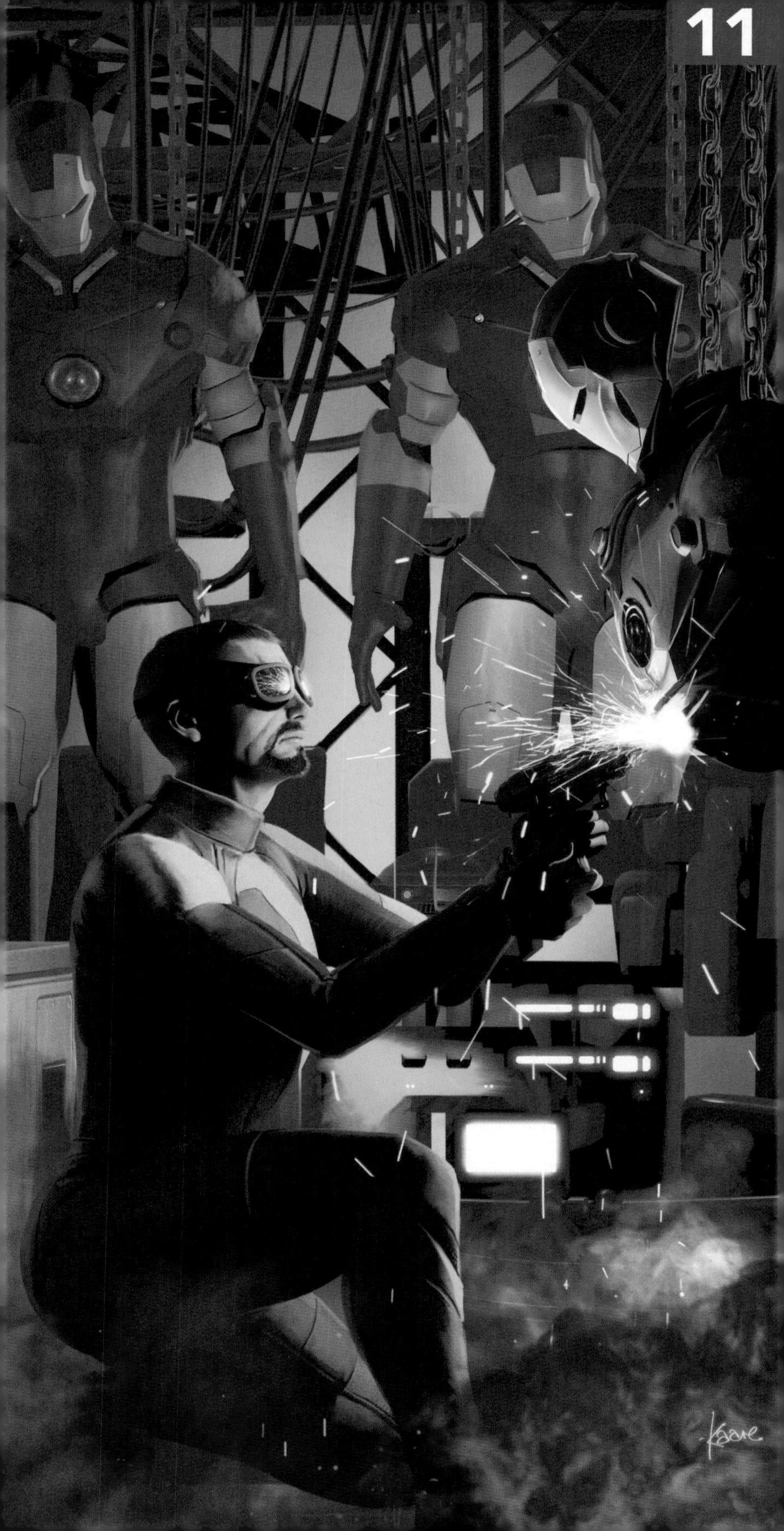
11

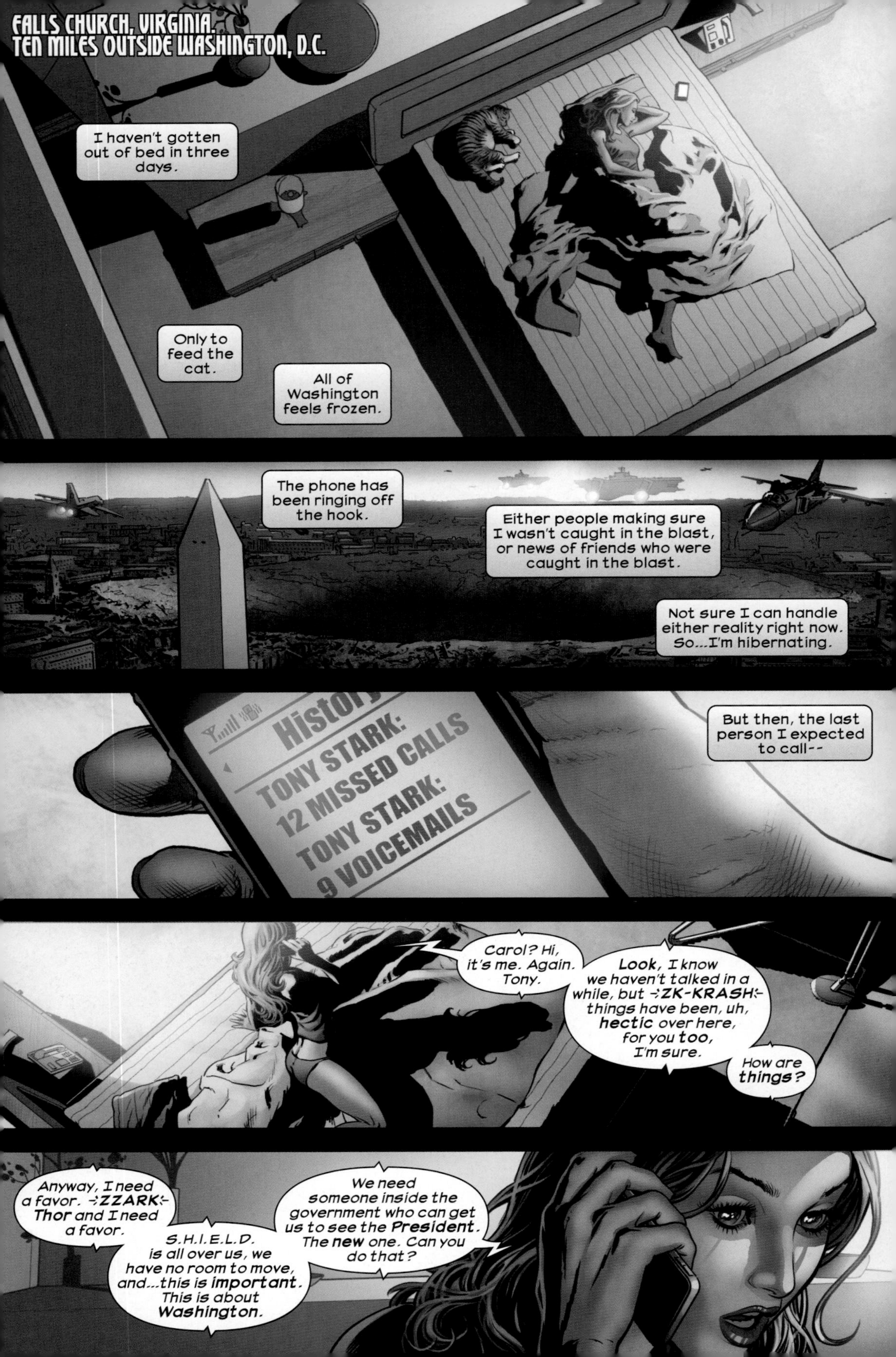

FALLS CHURCH, VIRGINIA.
TEN MILES OUTSIDE WASHINGTON, D.C.
I haven't gotten out of bed in three days.
Only to feed the cat.
All of Washington feels frozen.
The phone has been ringing off the hook.
Either people making sure I wasn't caught in the blast, or news of friends who were caught in the blast.
Not sure I can handle either reality right now. So...I'm hibernating.
History
TONY STARK: 12 MISSED CALLS
TONY STARK: 9 VOICEMAILS
But then, the last person I expected to call--
Carol? Hi, it's me. Again. Tony.
Look, I know we haven't talked in a while, but ⇢ZK-KRASH⇠ things have been, uh, hectic over here, for you too, I'm sure.
How are things?
Anyway, I need a favor. ⇢ZZARK⇠ Thor and I need a favor.
S.H.I.E.L.D. is all over us, we have no room to move, and...this is important. This is about Washington.
We need someone inside the government who can get us to see the President. The new one. Can you do that?

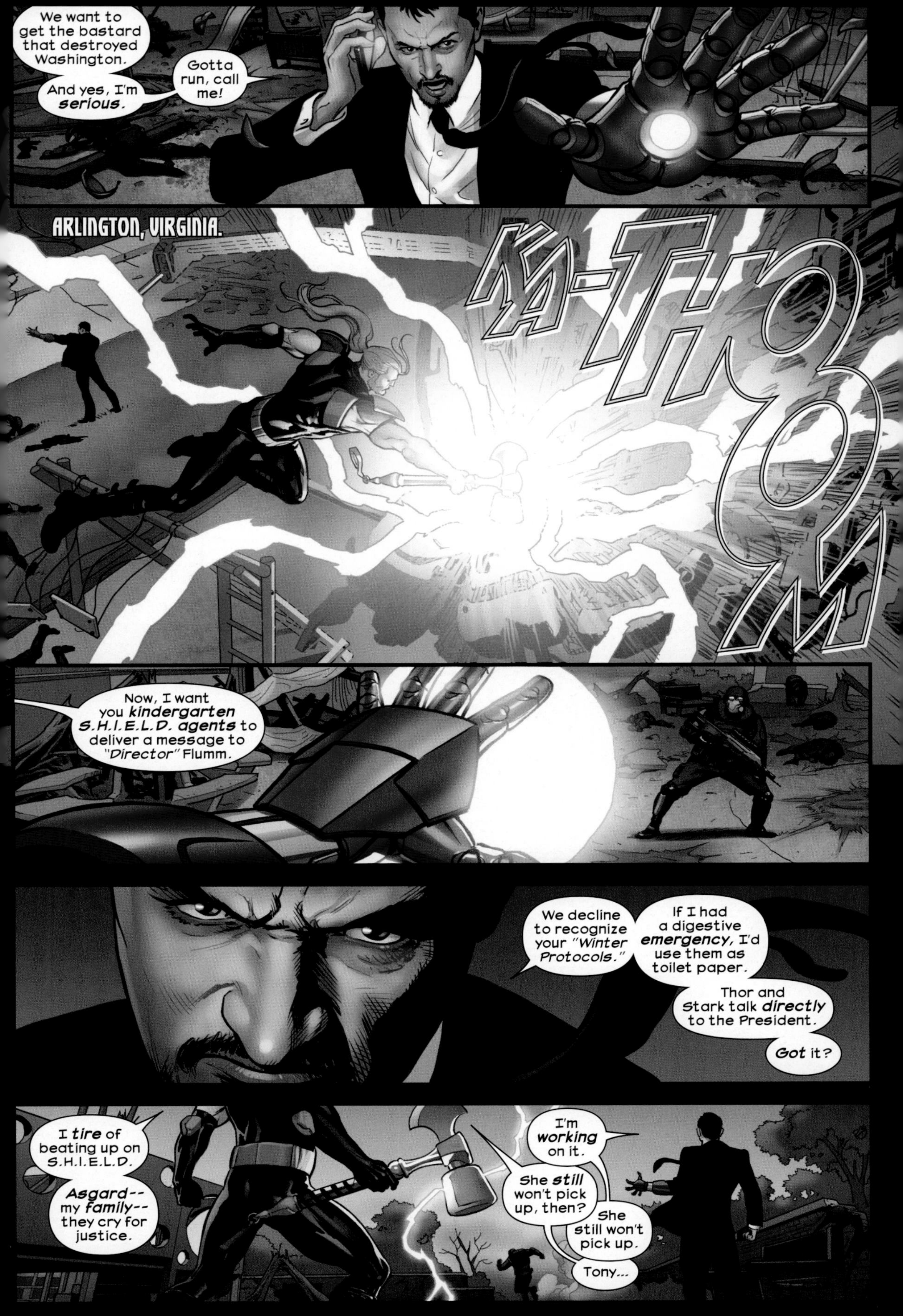

We want to get the bastard that destroyed Washington.
And yes, I'm *serious.*
Gotta run, call me!
ARLINGTON, VIRGINIA.
KA-THOOM
Now, I want you *kindergarten S.H.I.E.L.D. agents* to deliver a message to "*Director*" Flumm.
We decline to recognize your "*Winter Protocols.*"
If I had a digestive *emergency,* I'd use them as toilet paper.
Thor and Stark talk *directly* to the President.
Got it?
I *tire* of beating up on S.H.I.E.L.D.
Asgard-- my *family*-- they cry for justice.
I'm *working* on it.
She *still* won't pick up, then?
She still won't pick up.
Tony...

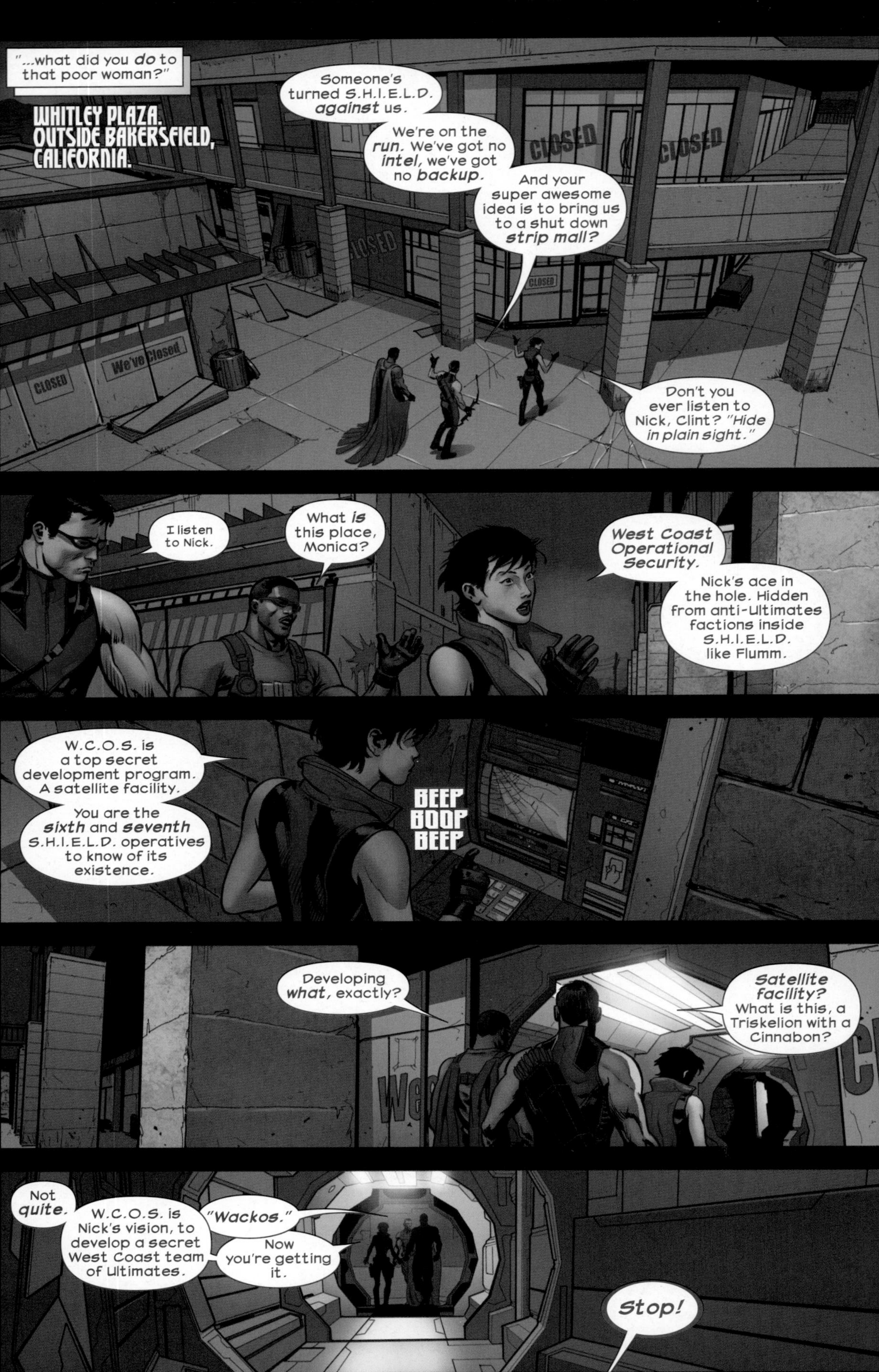
"...what did you do to that poor woman?"
WHITLEY PLAZA. OUTSIDE BAKERSFIELD, CALIFORNIA.
CLOSED
CLOSED
CLOSED
CLOSED
We've Closed
CLOSED
Someone's turned S.H.I.E.L.D. against us.
We're on the run. We've got no intel, we've got no backup.
And your super awesome idea is to bring us to a shut down strip mall?
Don't you ever listen to Nick, Clint? "Hide in plain sight."
I listen to Nick.
What is this place, Monica?
West Coast Operational Security.
Nick's ace in the hole. Hidden from anti-Ultimates factions inside S.H.I.E.L.D. like Flumm.
W.C.O.S. is a top secret development program. A satellite facility.
You are the sixth and seventh S.H.I.E.L.D. operatives to know of its existence.
BEEP BOOP BEEP
Developing what, exactly?
Satellite facility? What is this, a Triskelion with a Cinnabon?
Not quite.
W.C.O.S. is Nick's vision, to develop a secret West Coast team of Ultimates.
"Wackos."
Now you're getting it.
Stop!

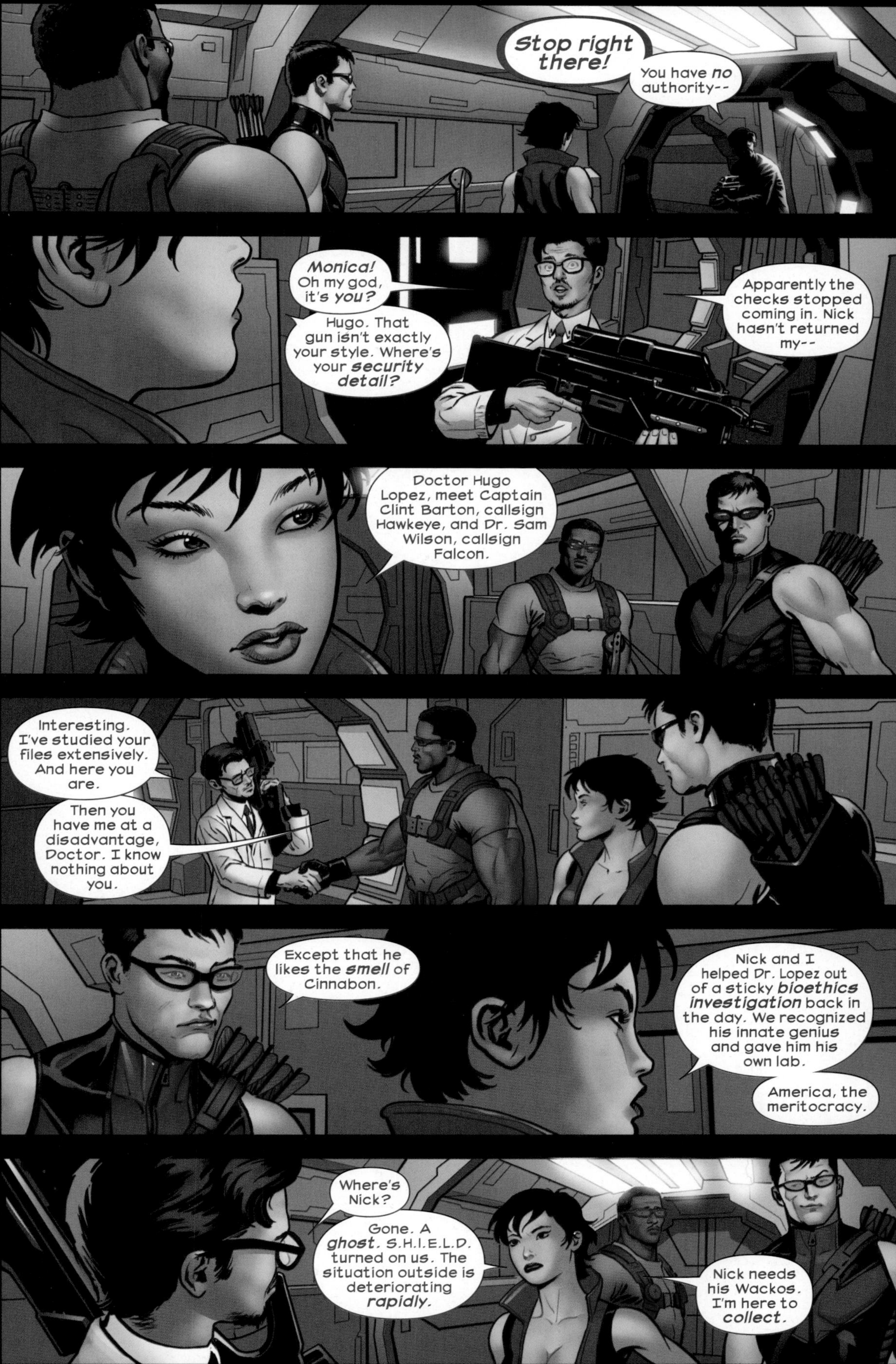
Stop right there!
You have no authority--
Monica! Oh my god, it's you?
Hugo. That gun isn't exactly your style. Where's your security detail?
Apparently the checks stopped coming in. Nick hasn't returned my--
Doctor Hugo Lopez, meet Captain Clint Barton, callsign Hawkeye, and Dr. Sam Wilson, callsign Falcon.
Interesting. I've studied your files extensively. And here you are.
Then you have me at a disadvantage, Doctor. I know nothing about you.
Except that he likes the smell of Cinnabon.
Nick and I helped Dr. Lopez out of a sticky bioethics investigation back in the day. We recognized his innate genius and gave him his own lab.
America, the meritocracy.
Where's Nick?
Gone. A ghost. S.H.I.E.L.D. turned on us. The situation outside is deteriorating rapidly.
Nick needs his Wackos. I'm here to collect.

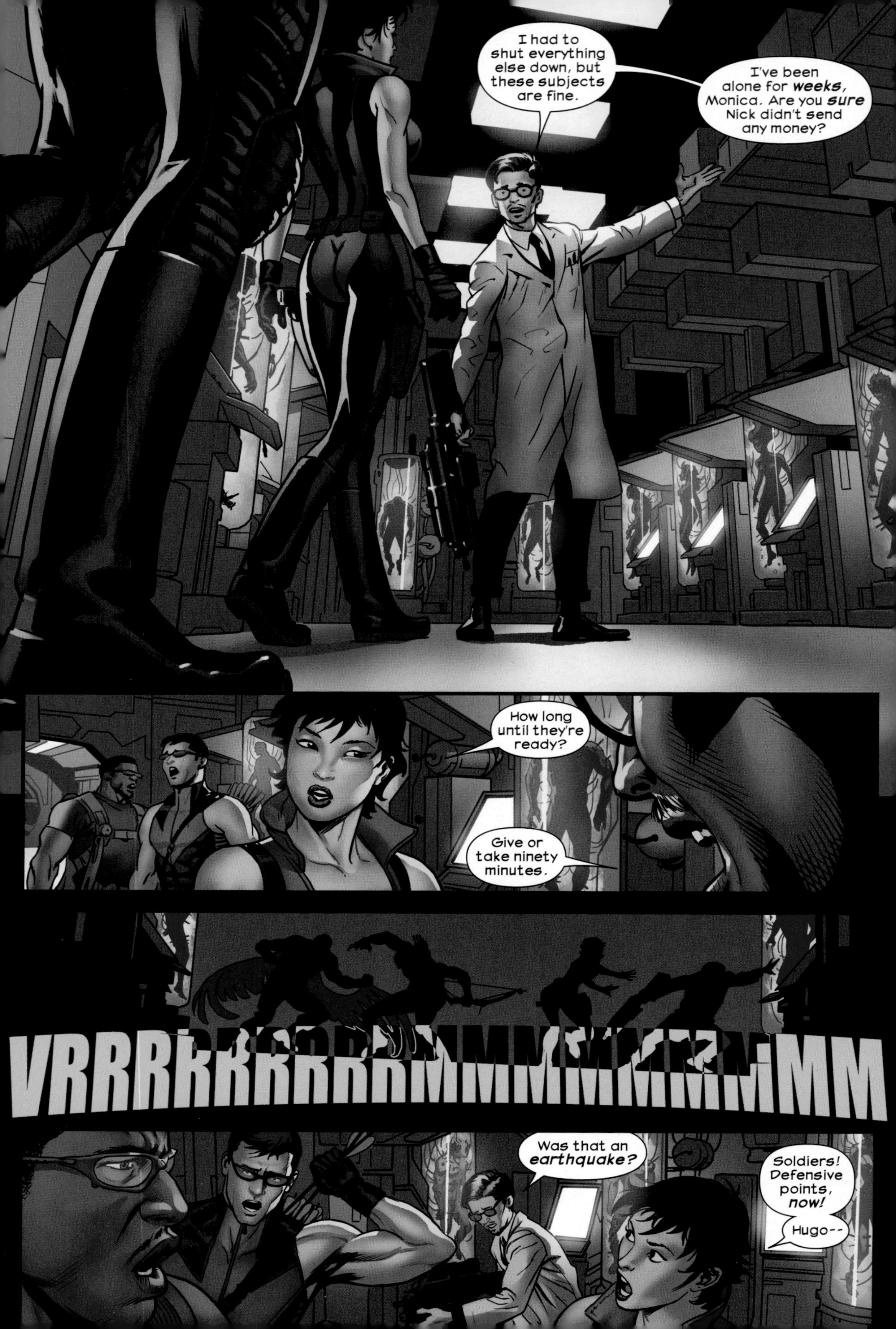

I had to shut everything else down, but these subjects are fine.
I've been alone for *weeks*, Monica. Are you *sure* Nick didn't send any money?
How long until they're ready?
Give or take ninety minutes.
VRRRRRRRRRMMMMMMMMMMMMM
Was that an *earthquake*?
Soldiers! Defensive points, *now!*
Hugo--

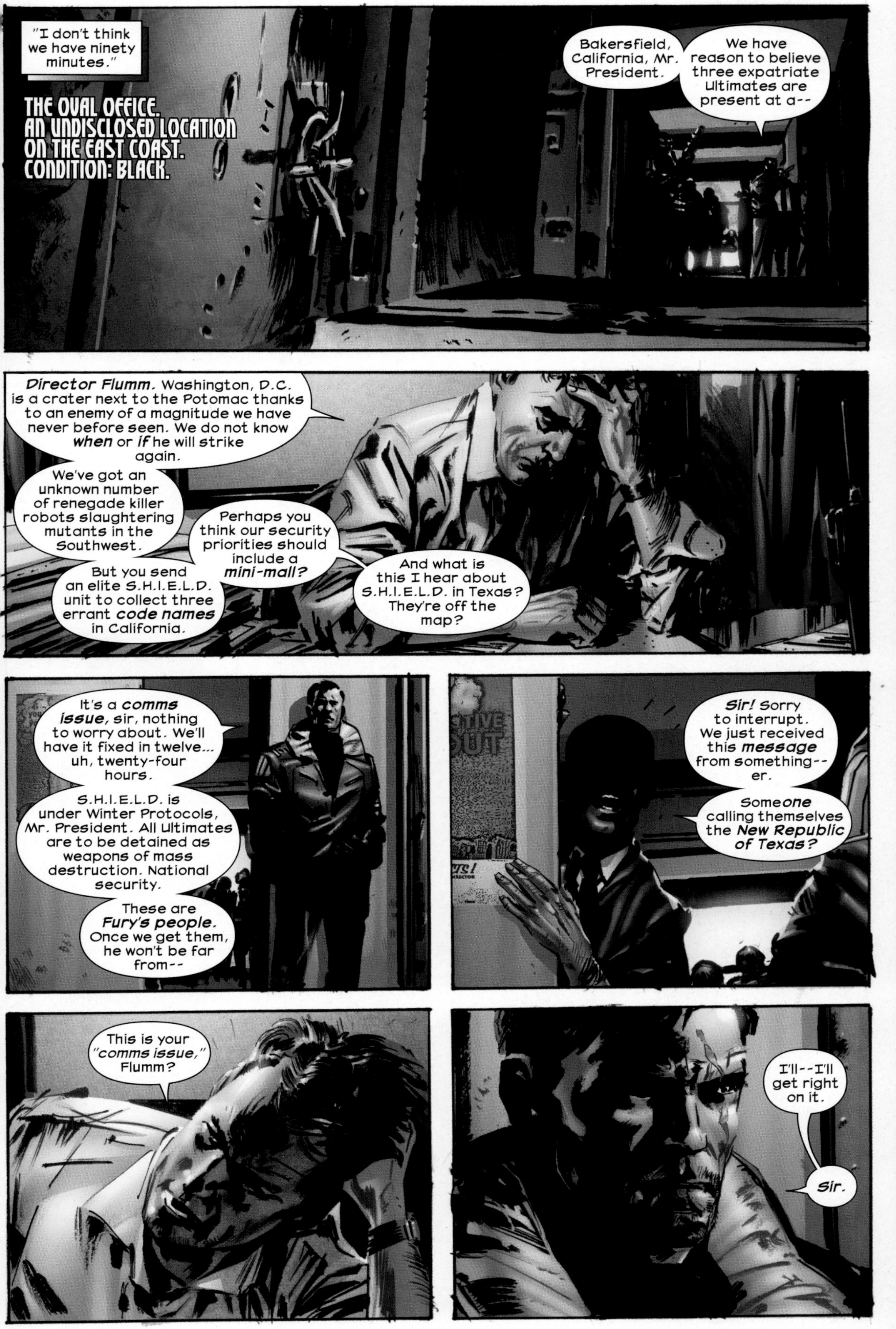

"I don't think we have ninety minutes."
THE OVAL OFFICE. AN UNDISCLOSED LOCATION ON THE EAST COAST. CONDITION: BLACK.
Bakersfield, California, Mr. President.
We have reason to believe three expatriate Ultimates are present at a--
Director Flumm. Washington, D.C. is a crater next to the Potomac thanks to an enemy of a magnitude we have never before seen. We do not know when or if he will strike again.
We've got an unknown number of renegade killer robots slaughtering mutants in the Southwest.
But you send an elite S.H.I.E.L.D. unit to collect three errant code names in California.
Perhaps you think our security priorities should include a mini-mall?
And what is this I hear about S.H.I.E.L.D. in Texas? They're off the map?
It's a comms issue, sir, nothing to worry about. We'll have it fixed in twelve... uh, twenty-four hours.
S.H.I.E.L.D. is under Winter Protocols, Mr. President. All Ultimates are to be detained as weapons of mass destruction. National security.
These are Fury's people. Once we get them, he won't be far from--
Sir! Sorry to interrupt. We just received this message from something--er.
Someone calling themselves the New Republic of Texas?
This is your "comms issue," Flumm?
I'll--I'll get right on it.
Sir.

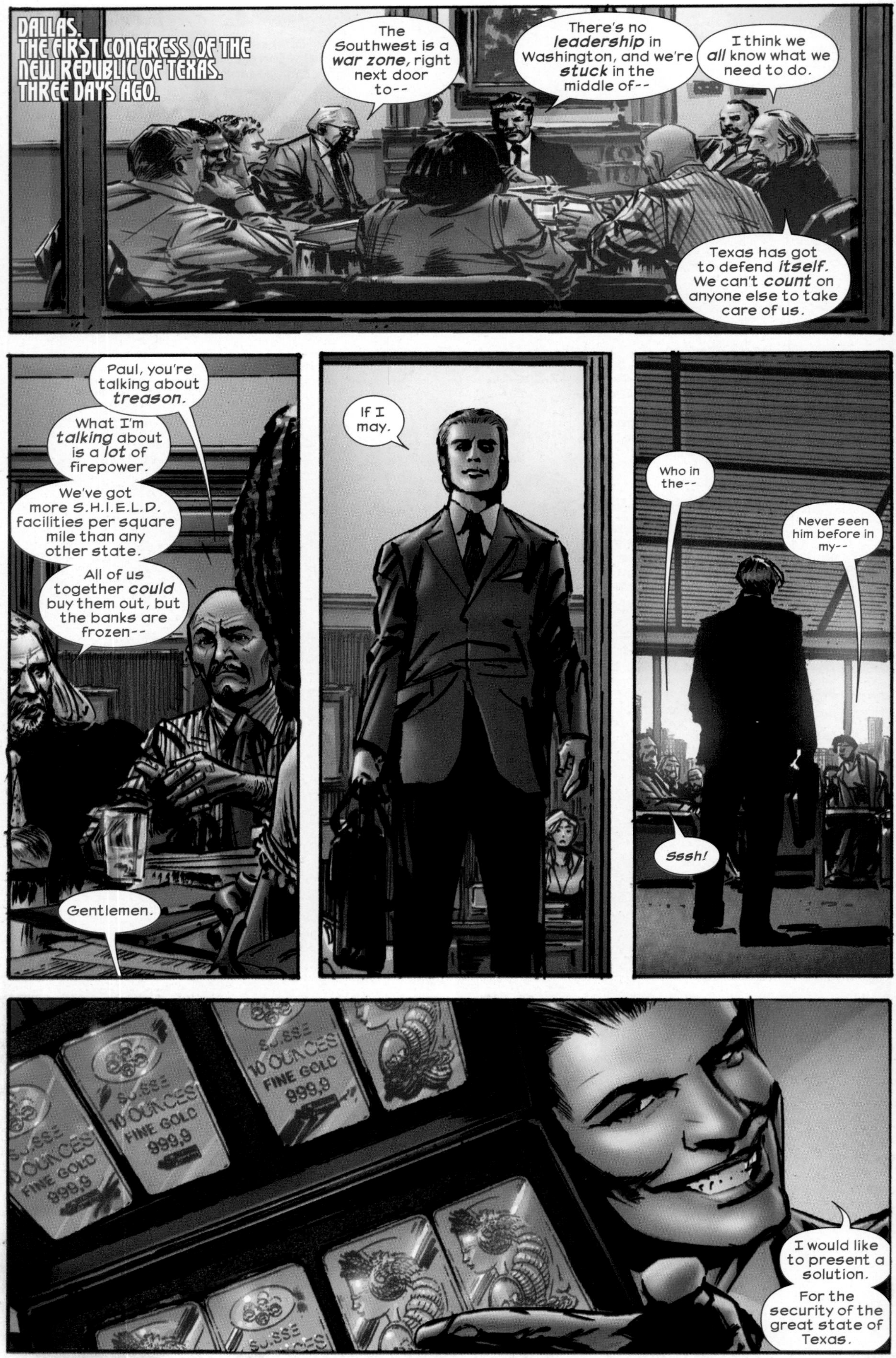
DALLAS.
THE FIRST CONGRESS OF THE NEW REPUBLIC OF TEXAS.
THREE DAYS AGO.
The Southwest is a war zone, right next door to--
There's no leadership in Washington, and we're stuck in the middle of--
I think we all know what we need to do.
Texas has got to defend itself. We can't count on anyone else to take care of us.
Paul, you're talking about treason.
What I'm talking about is a lot of firepower.
We've got more S.H.I.E.L.D. facilities per square mile than any other state.
All of us together could buy them out, but the banks are frozen--
Gentlemen.
If I may.
Who in the--
Never seen him before in my--
Sssh!
10 OUNCES FINE GOLD 999,9
I would like to present a solution.
For the security of the great state of Texas.

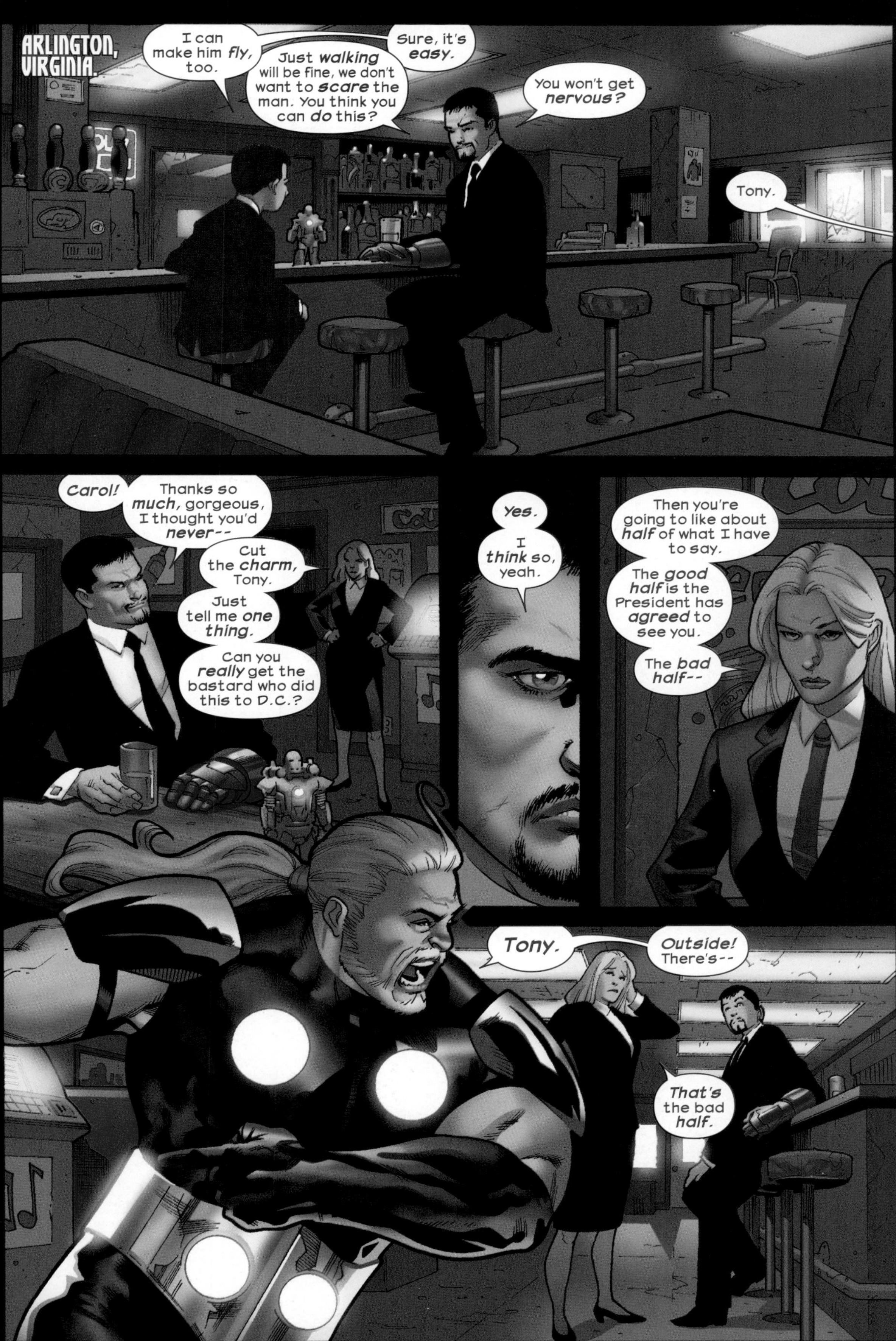

ARLINGTON, VIRGINIA.
I can make him fly, too.
Sure, it's easy.
Just walking will be fine, we don't want to scare the man. You think you can do this?
You won't get nervous?
Tony.
Carol!
Thanks so much, gorgeous, I thought you'd never--
Cut the charm, Tony.
Just tell me one thing.
Can you really get the bastard who did this to D.C.?
Yes.
I think so, yeah.
Then you're going to like about half of what I have to say.
The good half is the President has agreed to see you.
The bad half--
Tony.
Outside! There's--
That's the bad half.

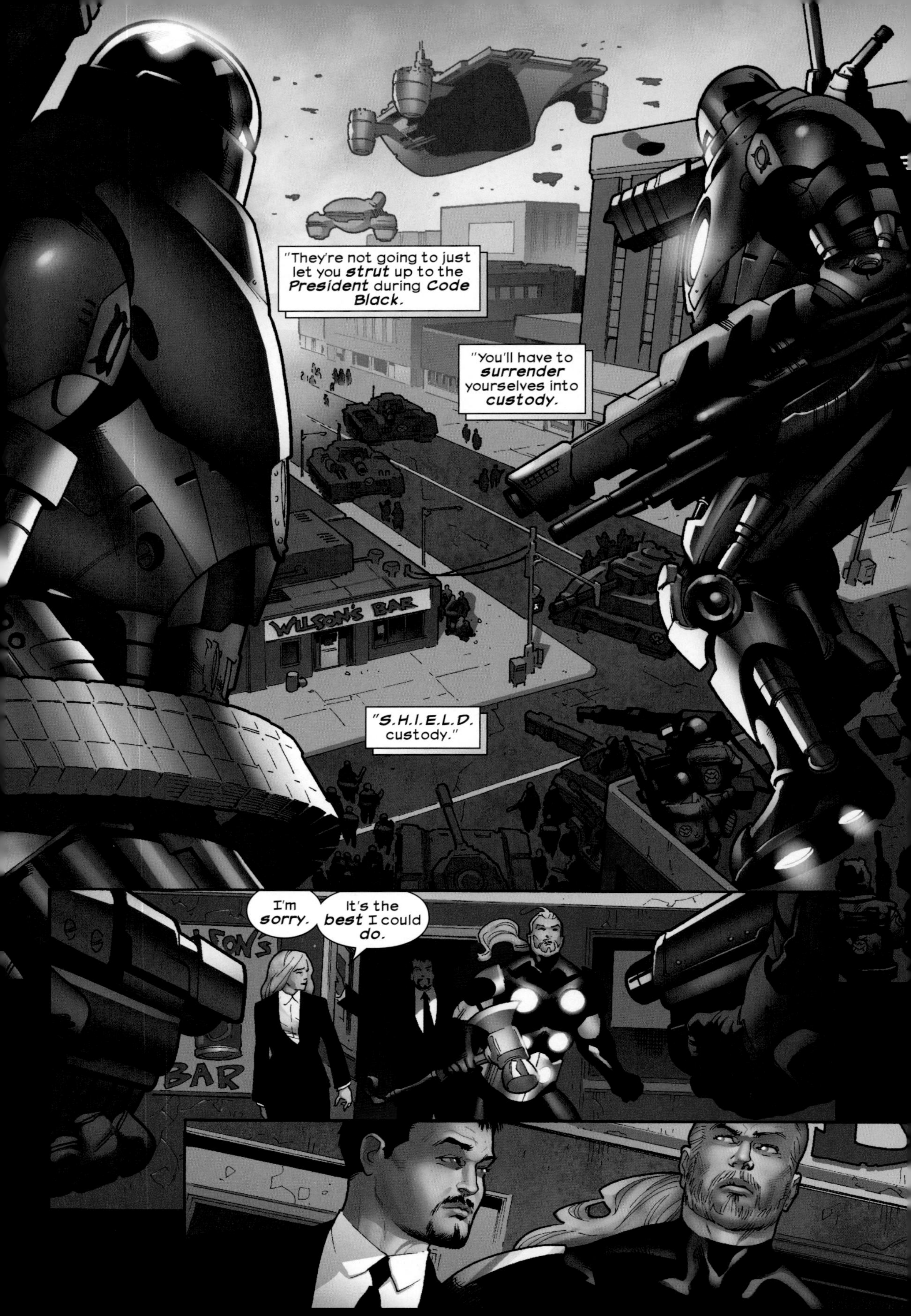
"They're not going to just let you strut up to the President during Code Black.
"You'll have to surrender yourselves into custody.
WILSON'S BAR
"S.H.I.E.L.D. custody."
I'm sorry.
It's the best I could do.
BAR

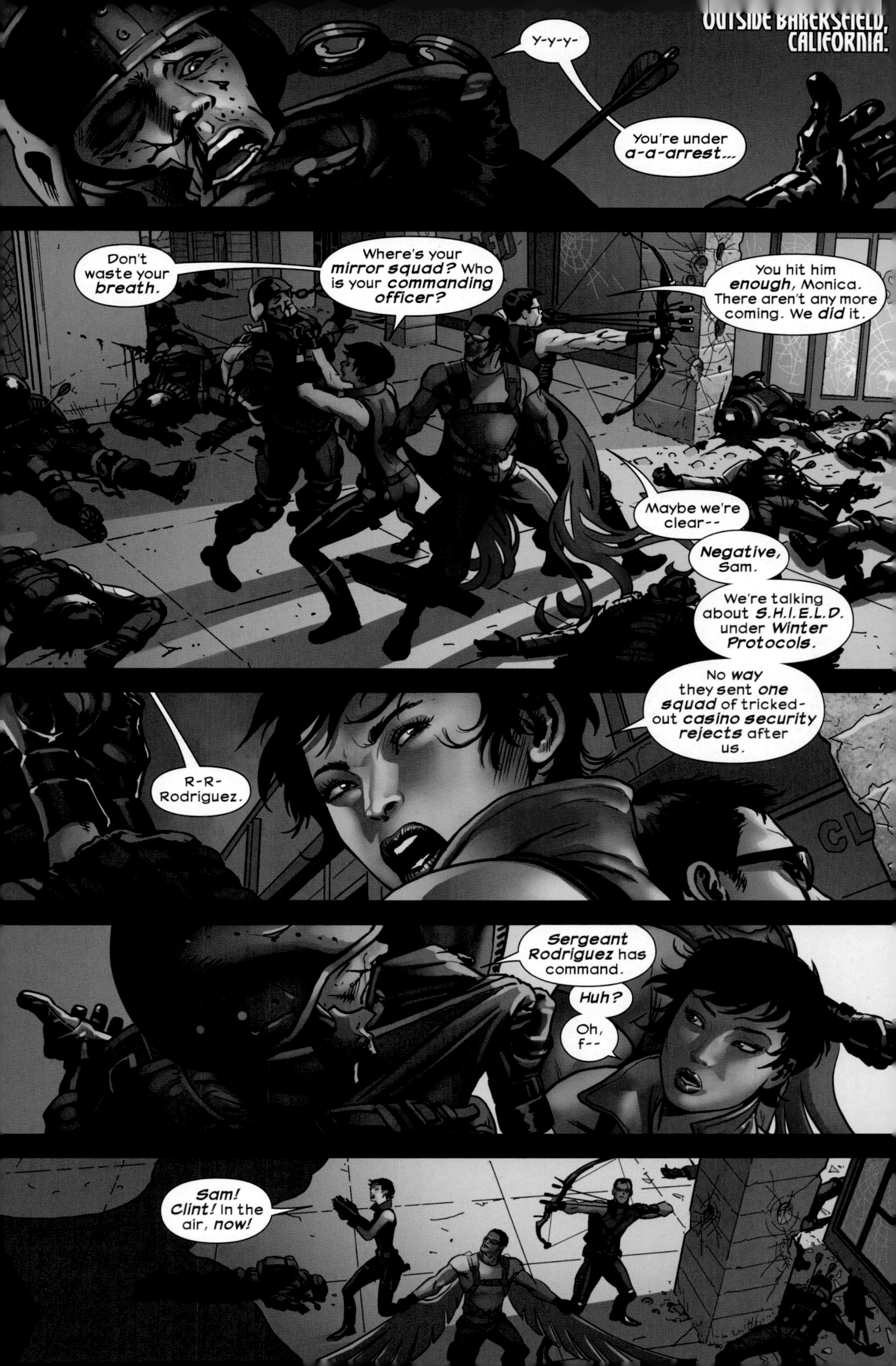
OUTSIDE BAKERSFIELD, CALIFORNIA.
Y-y-y-
You're under a-a-arrest...
Don't waste your breath.
Where's your mirror squad? Who is your commanding officer?
You hit him enough, Monica. There aren't any more coming. We did it.
Maybe we're clear--
Negative, Sam.
We're talking about S.H.I.E.L.D. under Winter Protocols.
No way they sent one squad of tricked-out casino security rejects after us.
R-R-Rodriguez.
Sergeant Rodriguez has command.
Huh?
Oh, f--
Sam! Clint! In the air, now!

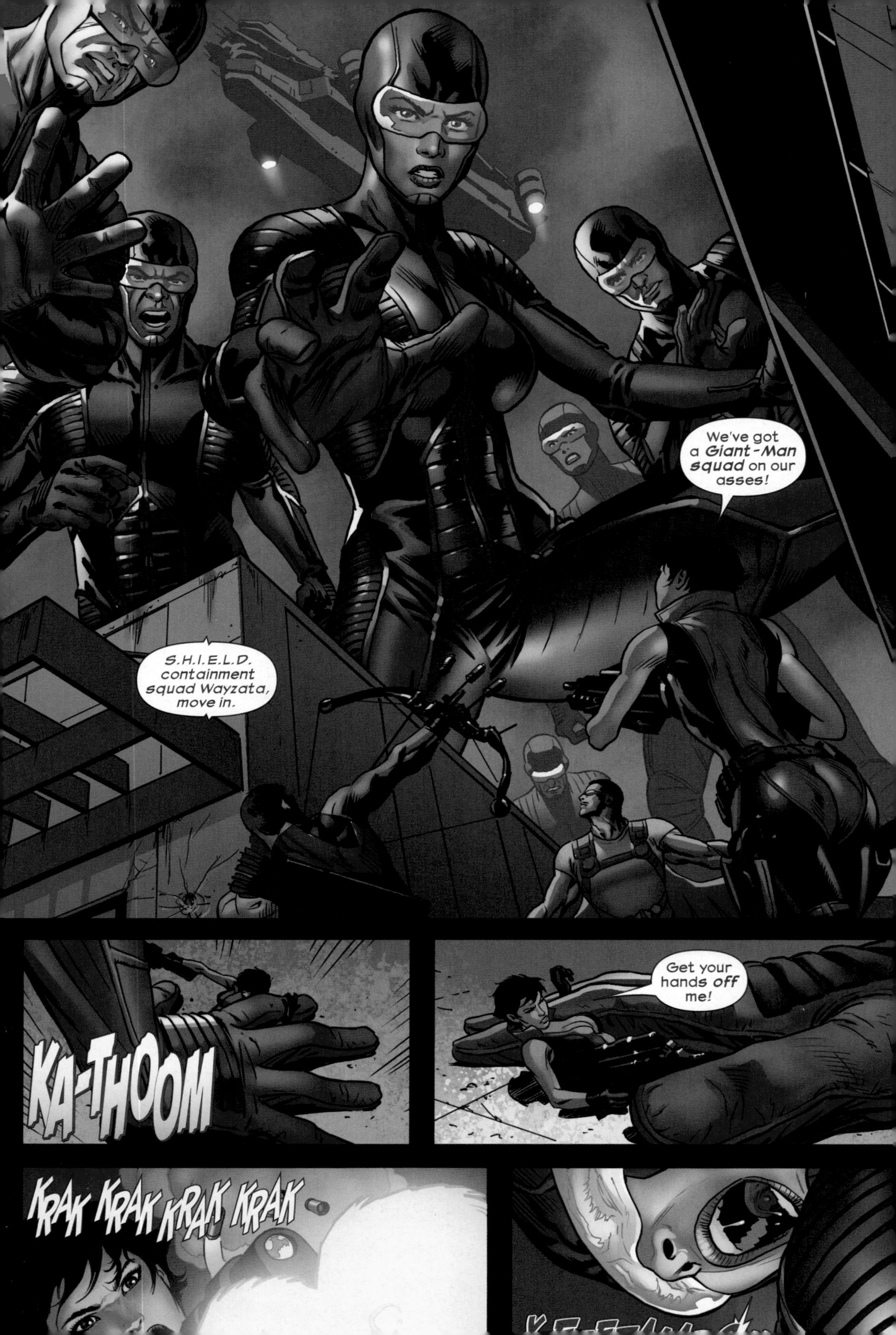
We've got a Giant-Man squad on our asses!
S.H.I.E.L.D. containment squad Wayzata, move in.
KA-THOOM
Get your hands off me!
KRAK KRAK KRAK KRAK

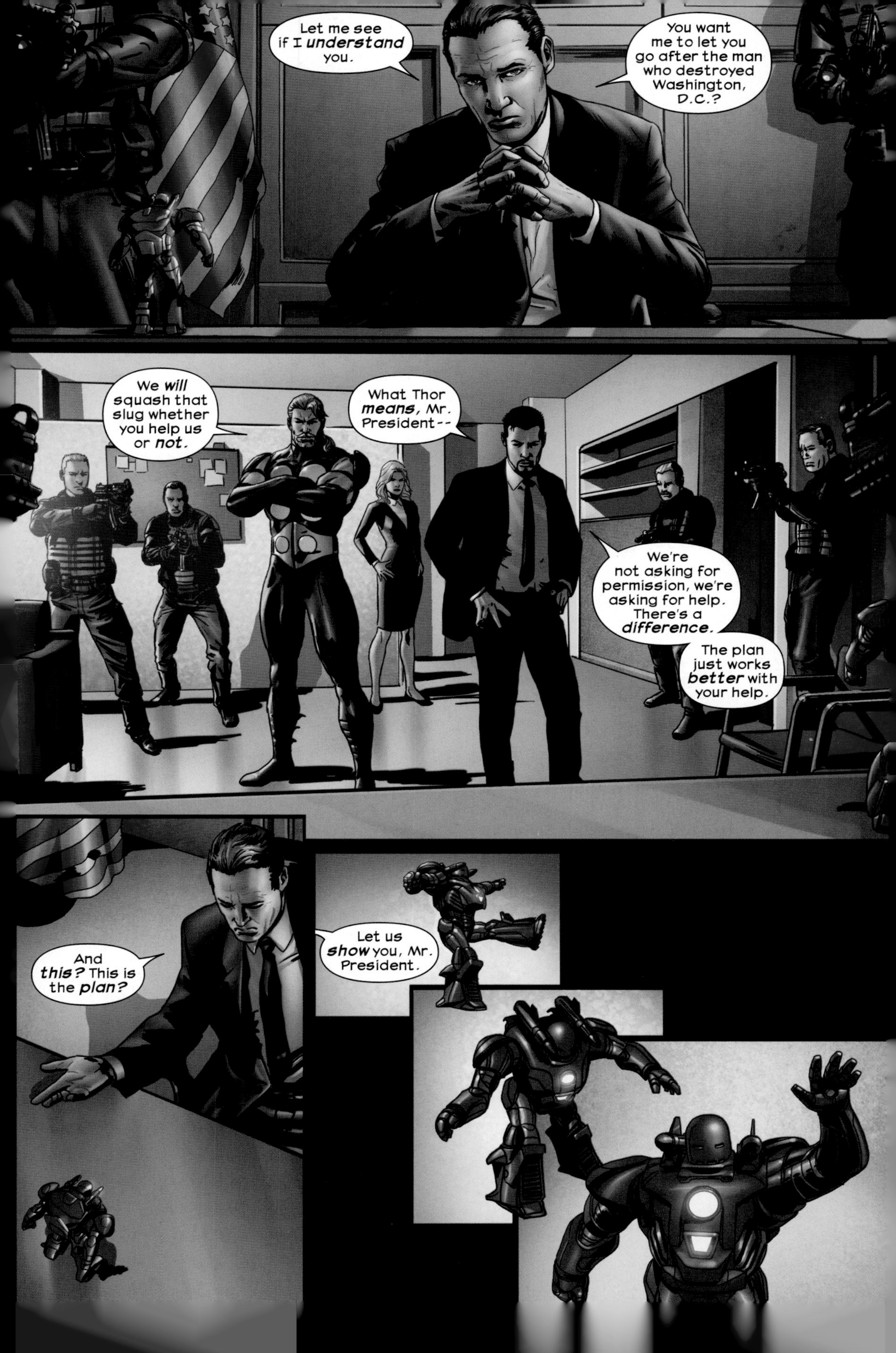
Let me see if I *understand* you.
You want me to let you go after the man who destroyed Washington, D.C.?
We *will* squash that slug whether you help us or *not.*
What Thor *means*, Mr. President--
We're not asking for permission, we're asking for help. There's a *difference.*
The plan just works *better* with your help.
And *this?* This is the *plan?*
Let us *show* you, Mr. President.

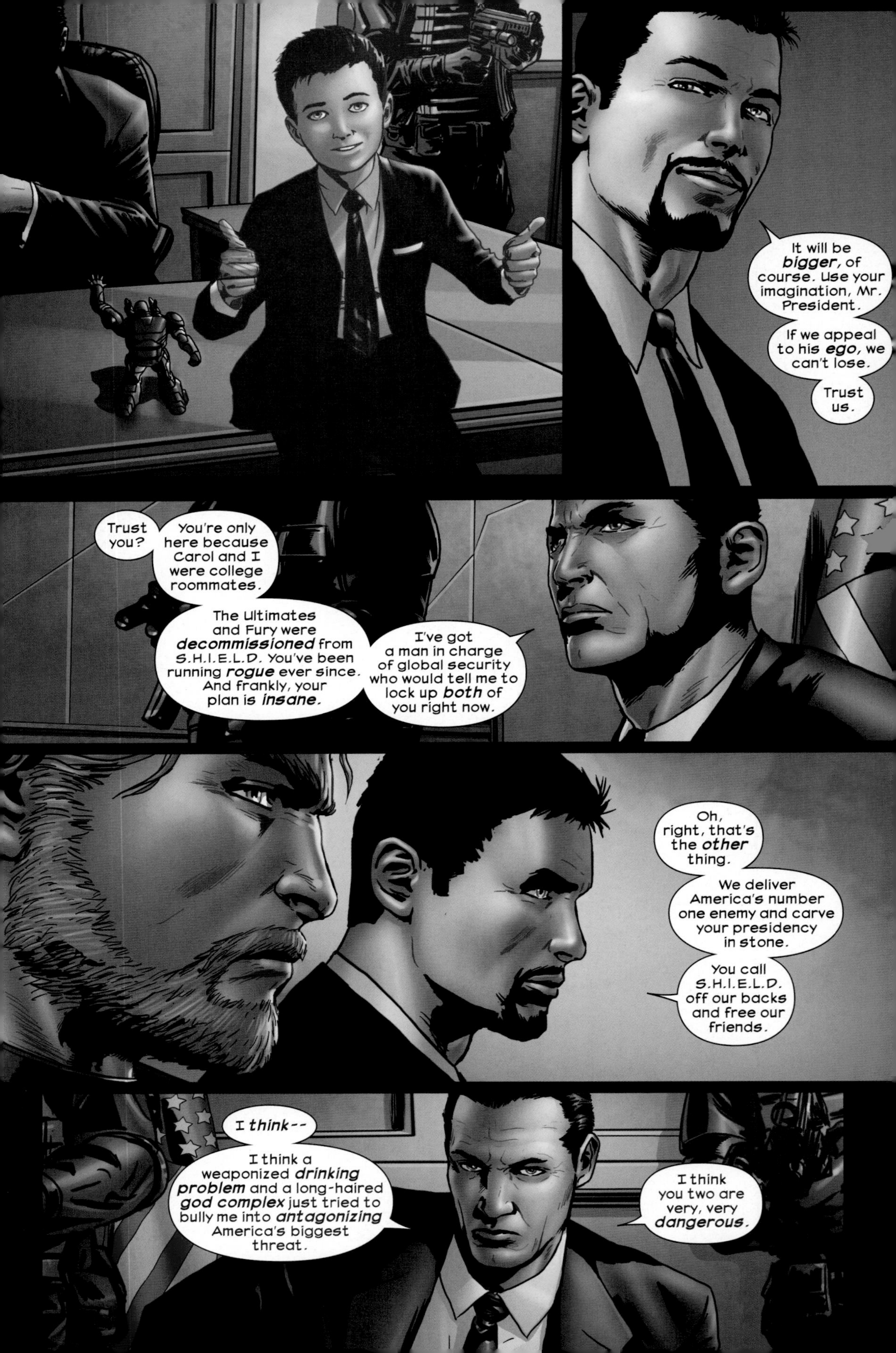
It will be bigger, of course. Use your imagination, Mr. President.
If we appeal to his ego, we can't lose.
Trust us.
Trust you?
You're only here because Carol and I were college roommates.
The Ultimates and Fury were decommissioned from S.H.I.E.L.D. You've been running rogue ever since. And frankly, your plan is insane.
I've got a man in charge of global security who would tell me to lock up both of you right now.
Oh, right, that's the other thing.
We deliver America's number one enemy and carve your presidency in stone.
You call S.H.I.E.L.D. off our backs and free our friends.
I think--
I think a weaponized drinking problem and a long-haired god complex just tried to bully me into antagonizing America's biggest threat.
I think you two are very, very dangerous.

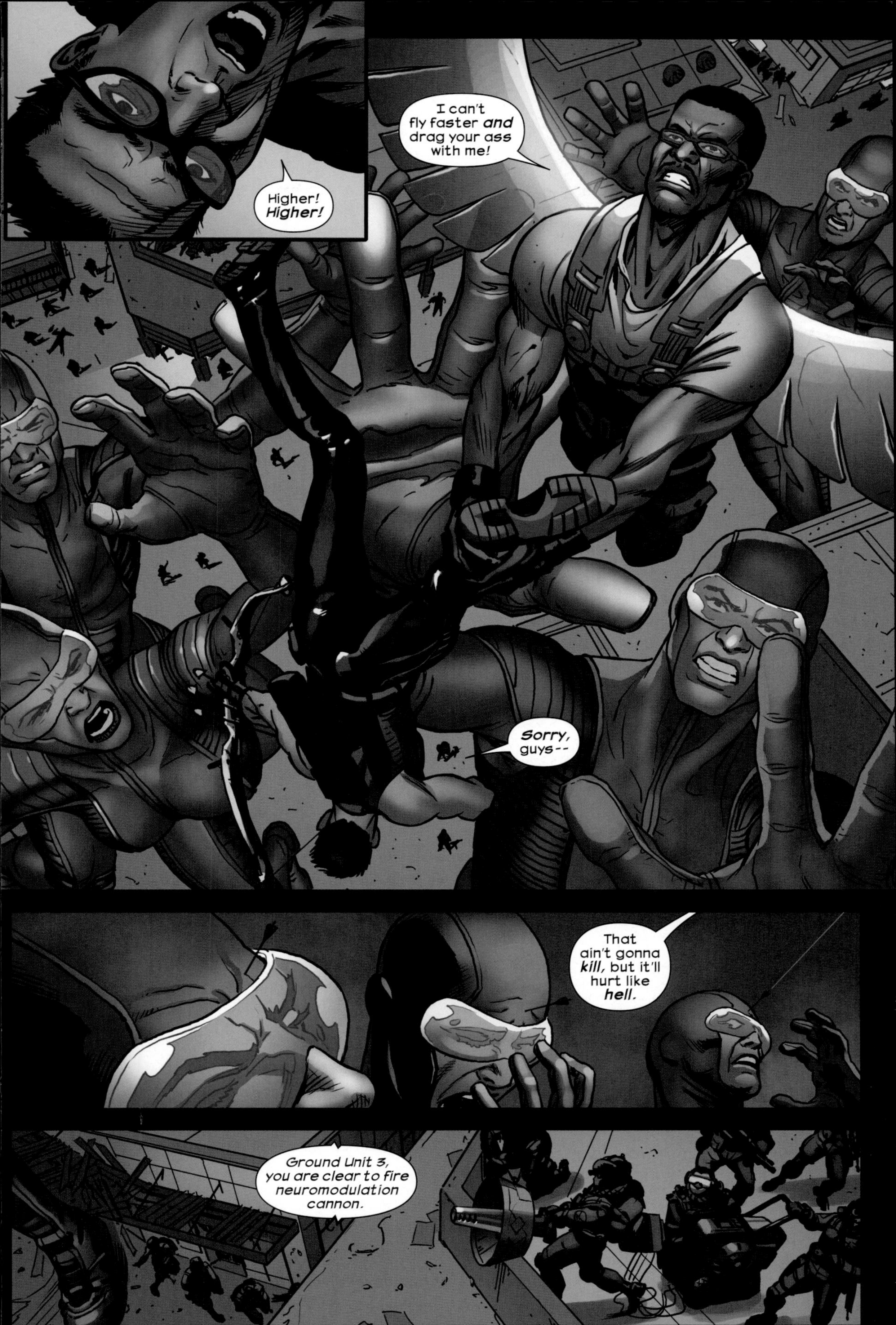
Higher! Higher!
I can't fly faster and drag your ass with me!
Sorry, guys--
That ain't gonna kill, but it'll hurt like hell.
Ground Unit 3, you are clear to fire neuromodulation cannon.

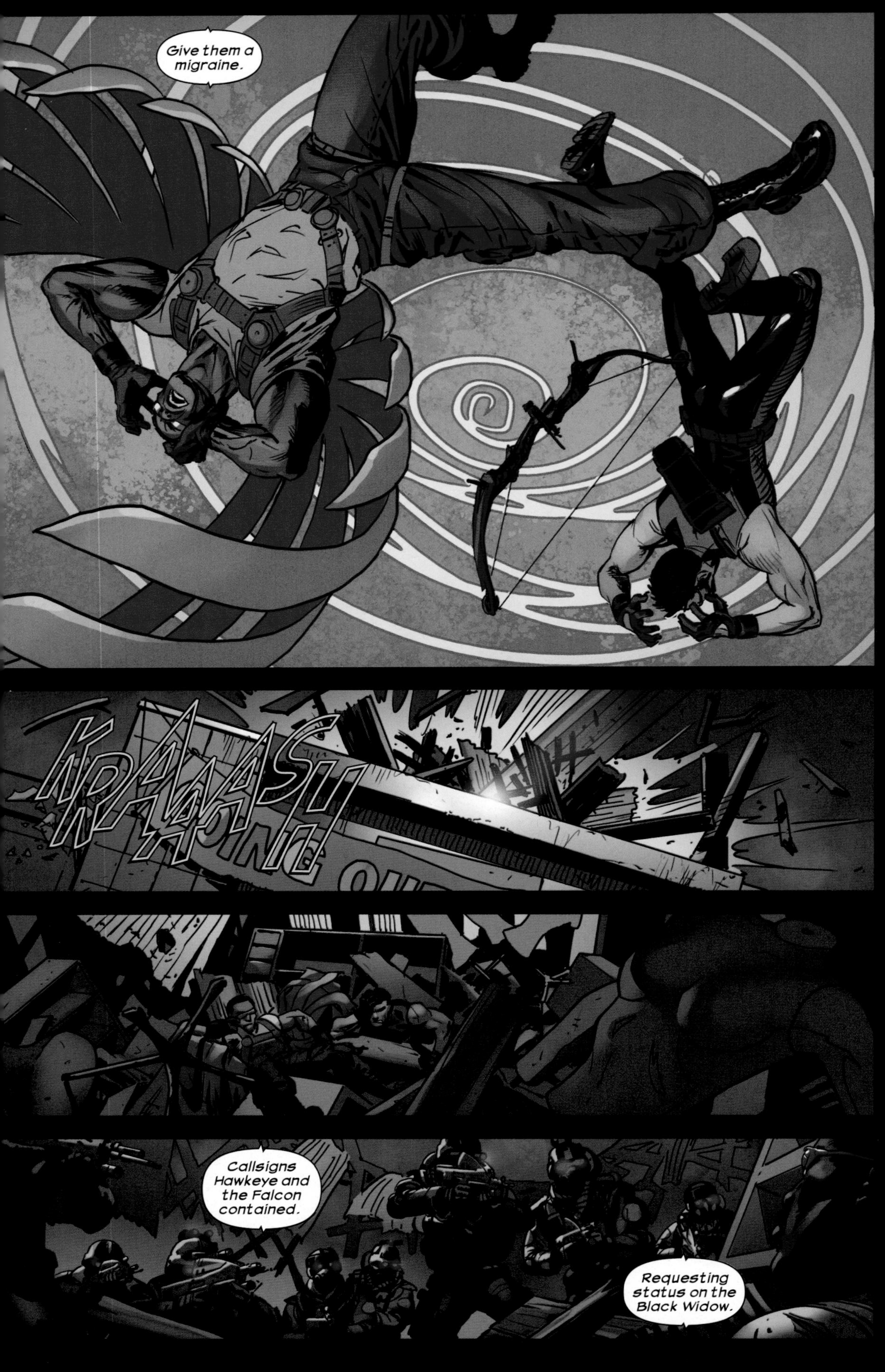
Give them a migraine.
KRAAASH
Callsigns Hawkeye and the Falcon contained.
Requesting status on the Black Widow.

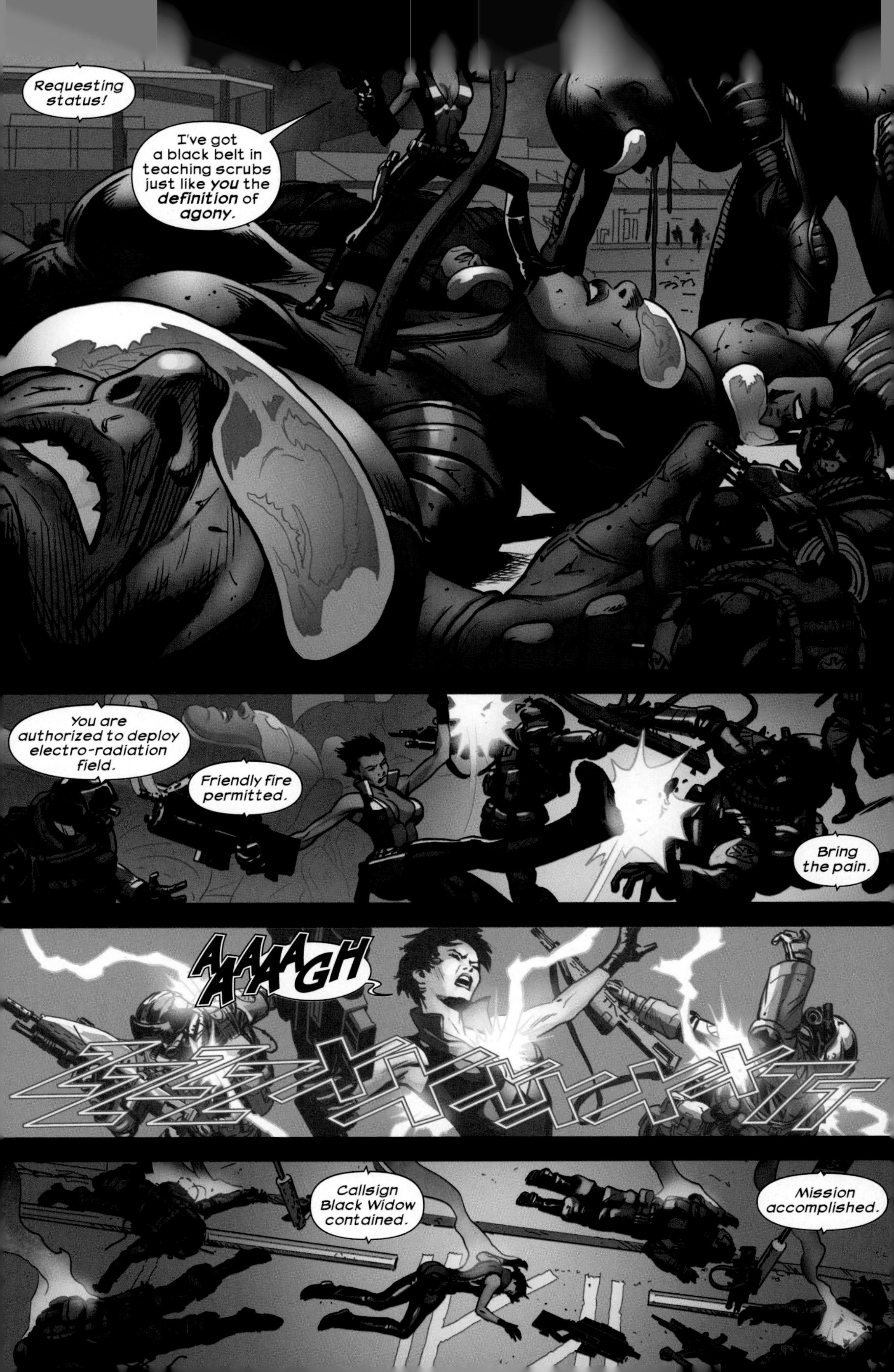
Requesting status!
I've got a black belt in teaching scrubs just like *you* the *definition* of *agony*.
You are authorized to deploy electro-radiation field.
Friendly fire permitted.
Bring the pain.
AAAAAGH
Callsign Black Widow contained.
Mission accomplished.

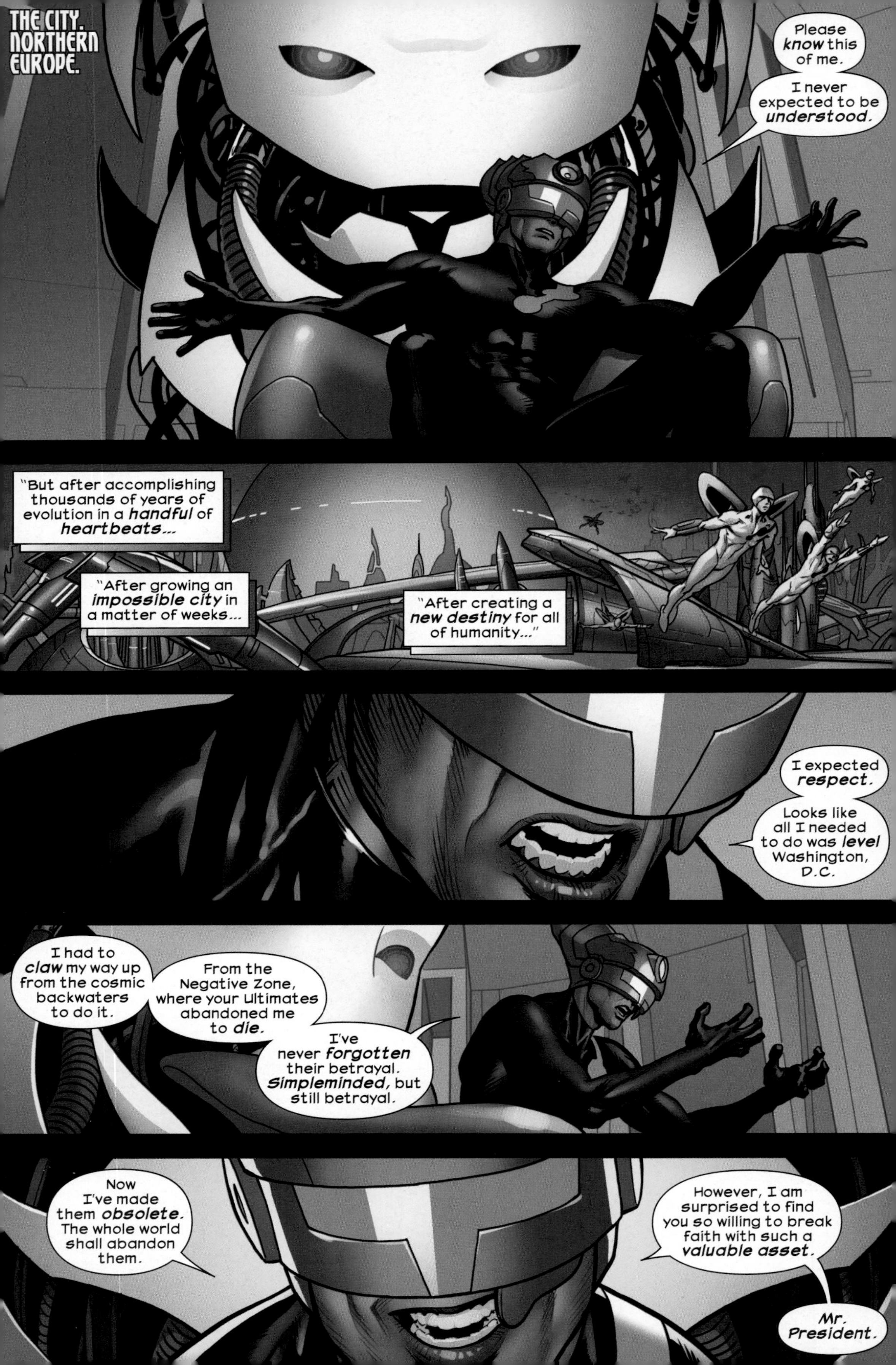
THE CITY. NORTHERN EUROPE.
Please *know* this of me.
I never expected to be *understood.*
"But after accomplishing thousands of years of evolution in a *handful* of *heartbeats...*
"After growing an *impossible city* in a matter of weeks...
"After creating a *new destiny* for all of humanity..."
I expected *respect.*
Looks like all I needed to do was *level* Washington, D.C.
I had to *claw* my way up from the cosmic backwaters to do it.
From the Negative Zone, where your Ultimates abandoned me to *die.*
I've never *forgotten* their betrayal. *Simpleminded,* but still betrayal.
Now I've made them *obsolete.* The whole world shall abandon them.
However, I am surprised to find you so willing to break faith with such a *valuable asset.*
Mr. President.

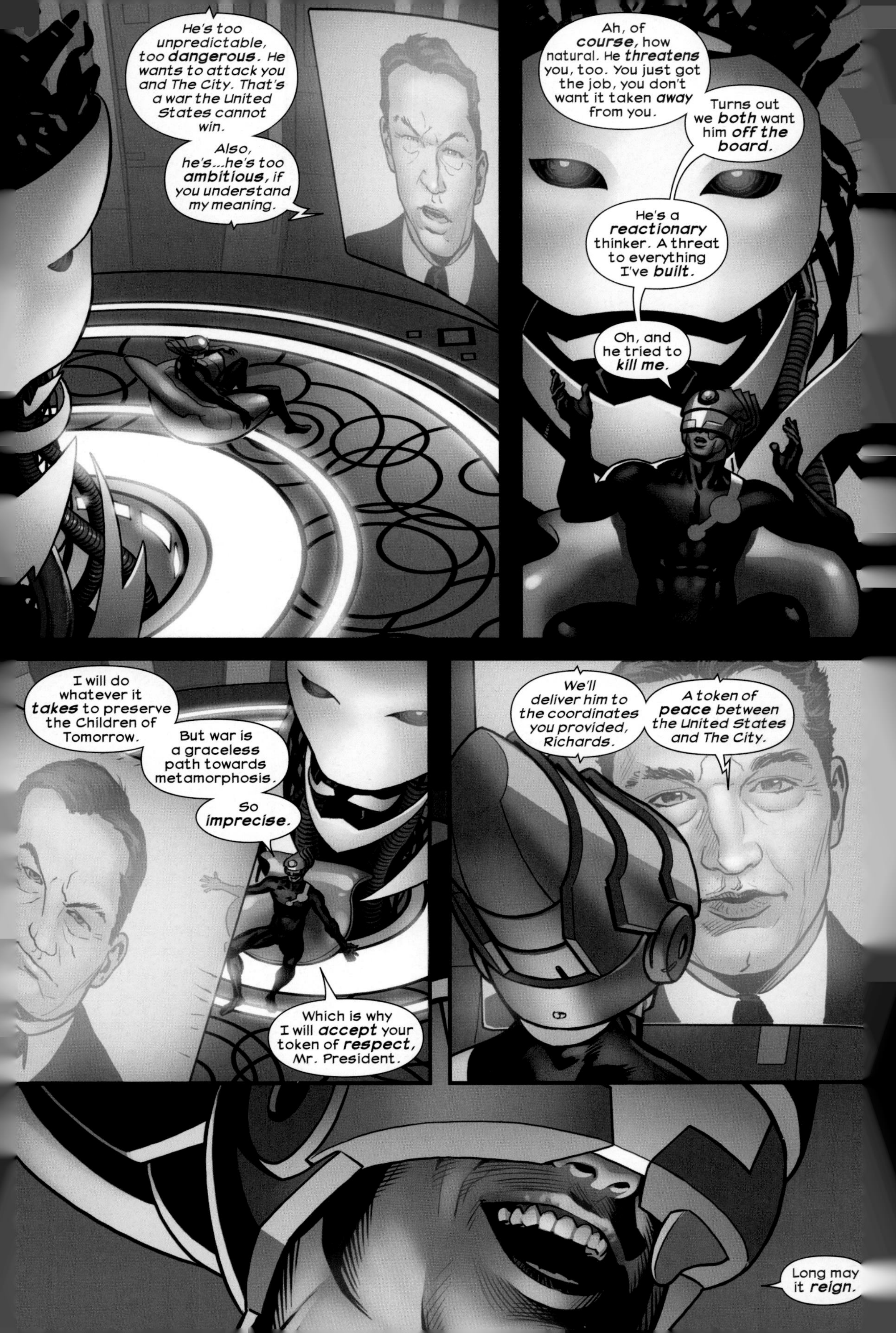
He's too unpredictable, too **dangerous.** He wants to attack you and The City. That's a war the United States cannot win.
Also, he's...he's too **ambitious,** if you understand my meaning.
Ah, of **course,** how natural. He **threatens** you, too. You just got the job, you don't want it taken **away** from you.
Turns out we **both** want him **off the board.**
He's a **reactionary** thinker. A threat to everything I've **built.**
Oh, and he tried to **kill me.**
I will do whatever it **takes** to preserve the Children of Tomorrow.
But war is a graceless path towards metamorphosis.
So **imprecise.**
Which is why I will **accept** your token of **respect,** Mr. President.
We'll deliver him to the coordinates you provided, Richards.
A token of **peace** between the United States and The City.
Long may it **reign.**

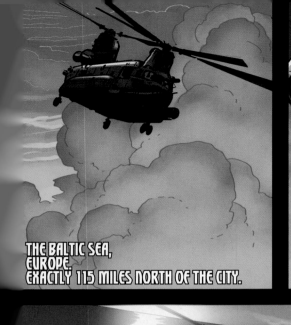

THE BALTIC SEA, EUROPE. EXACTLY 115 MILES NORTH OF THE CITY.

Prisoner secure.

Returning to The City.

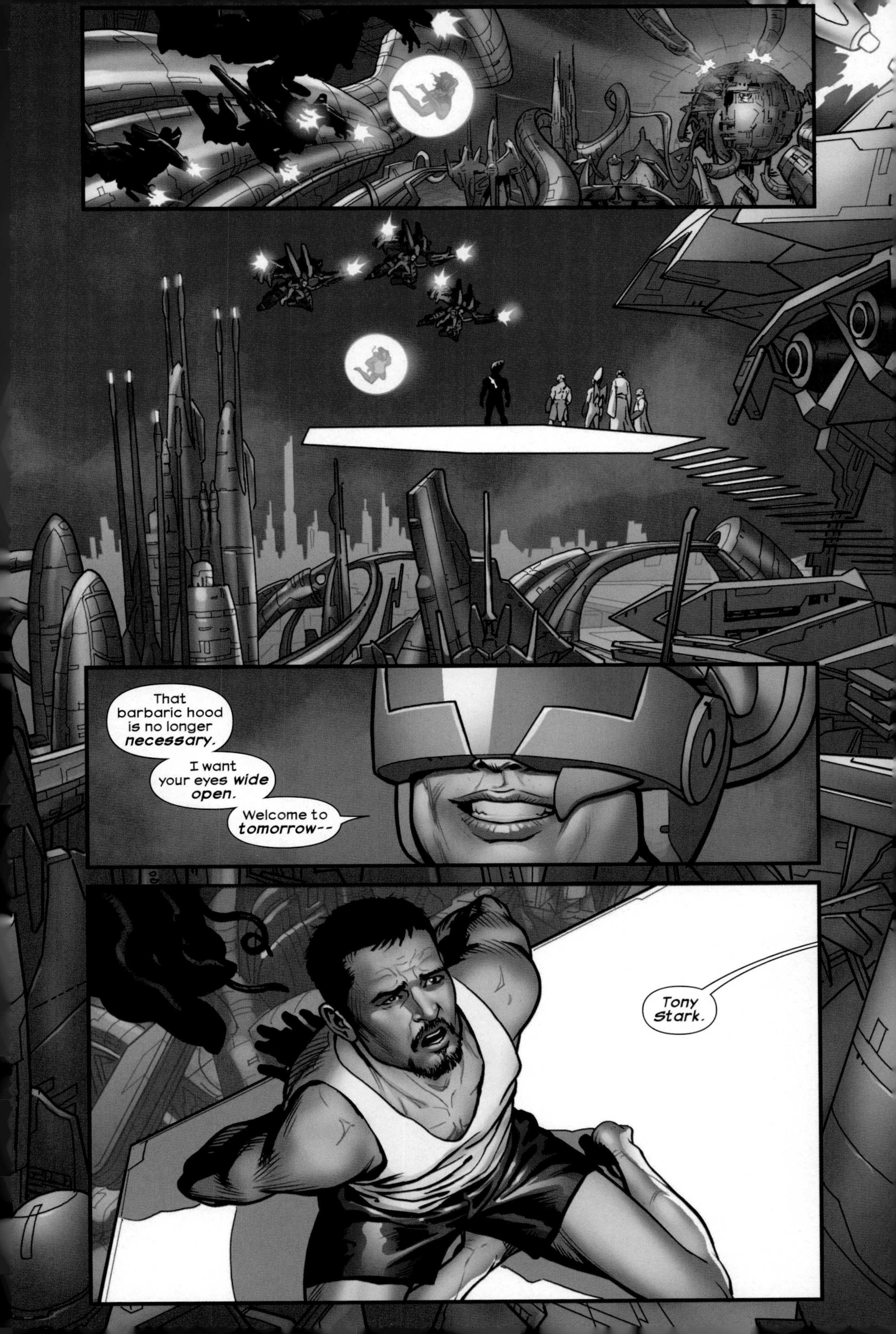
That barbaric hood is no longer *necessary.*
I want your eyes *wide open.*
Welcome to *tomorrow--*
Tony Stark.

12

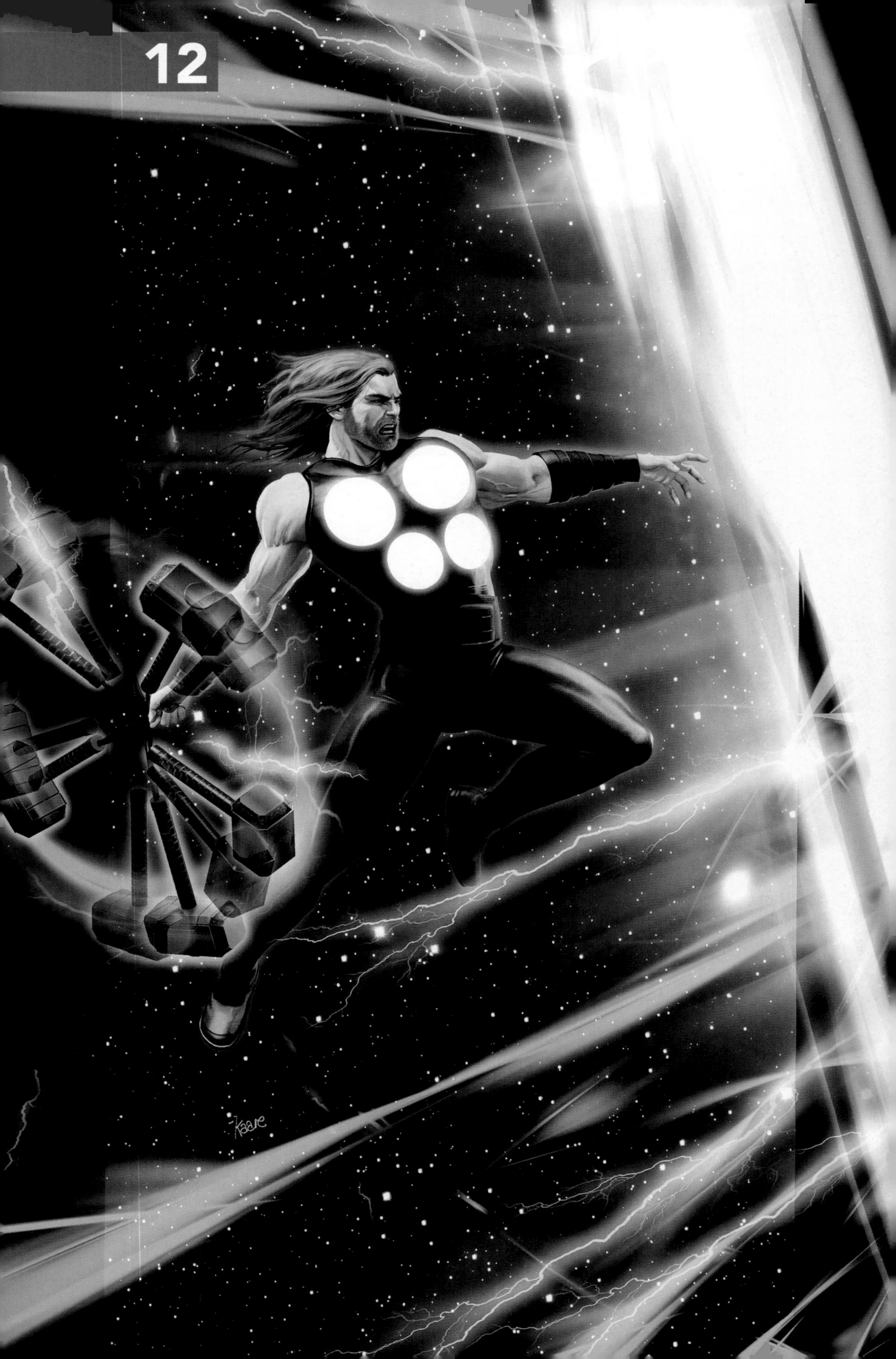

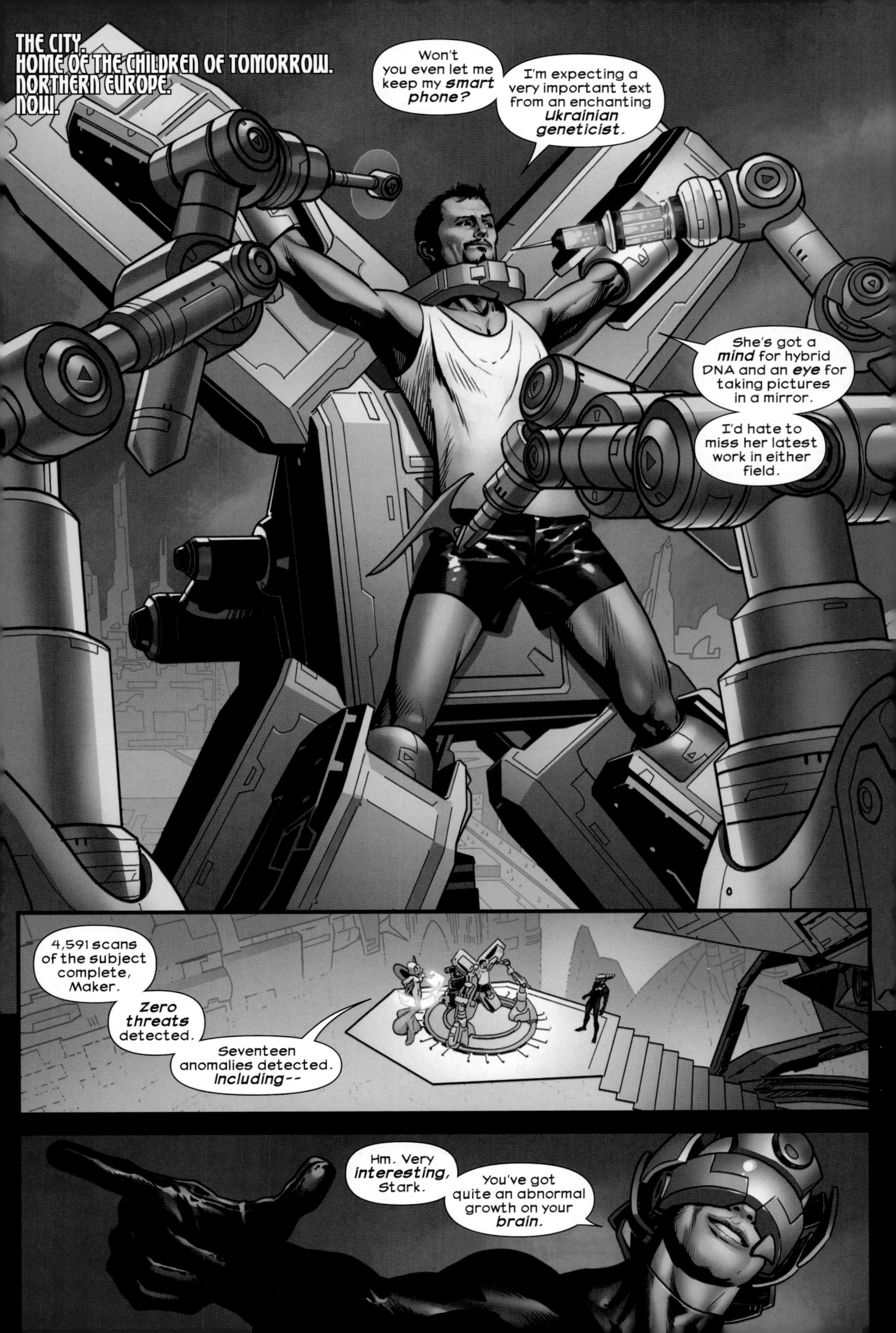
THE CITY.
HOME OF THE CHILDREN OF TOMORROW.
NORTHERN EUROPE.
NOW.
Won't you even let me keep my smart phone?
I'm expecting a very important text from an enchanting Ukrainian geneticist.
She's got a mind for hybrid DNA and an eye for taking pictures in a mirror.
I'd hate to miss her latest work in either field.
4,591 scans of the subject complete, Maker.
Zero threats detected.
Seventeen anomalies detected. Including--
Hm. Very interesting, Stark.
You've got quite an abnormal growth on your brain.

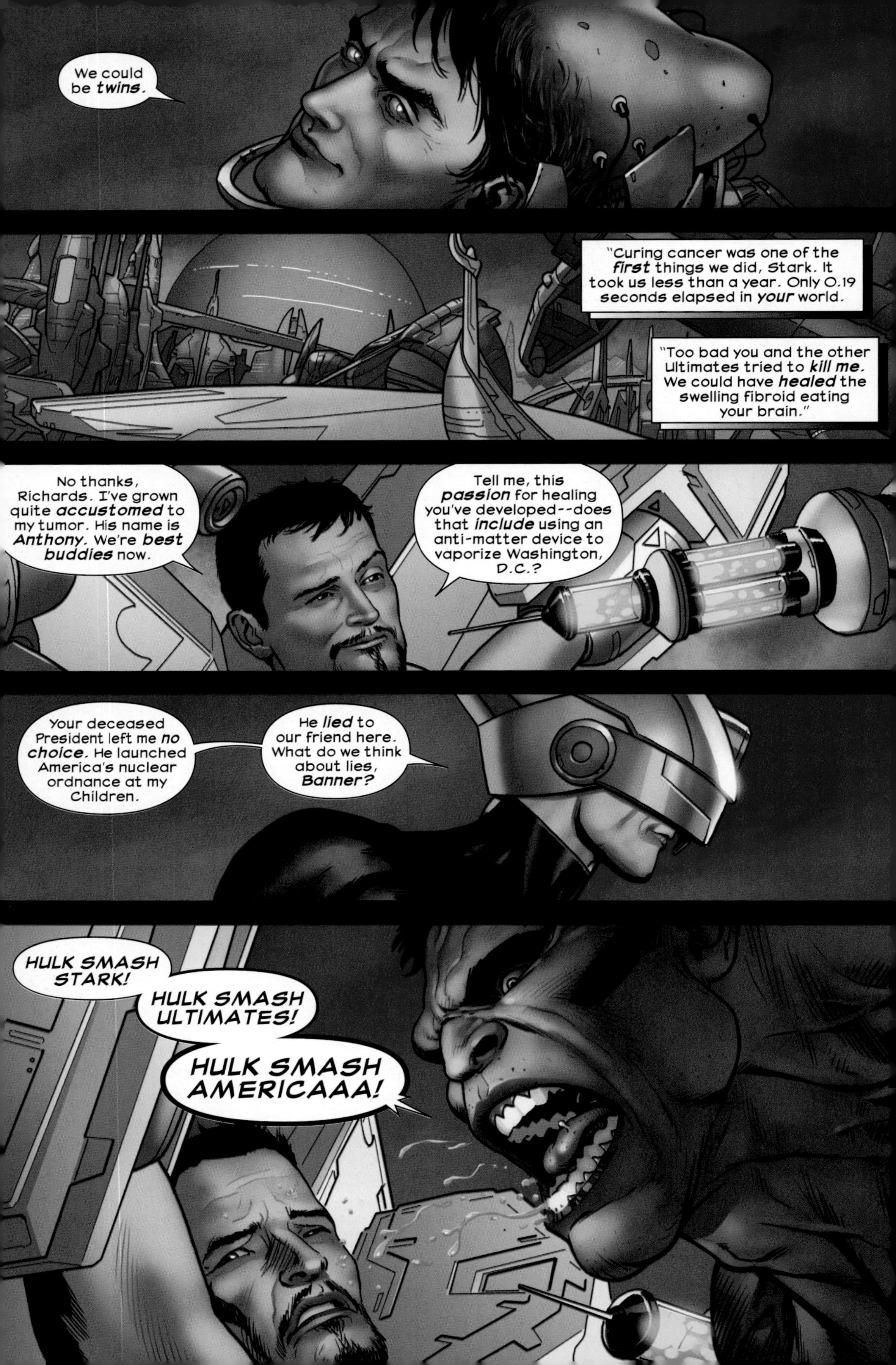
We could be *twins*.
"Curing cancer was one of the *first* things we did, Stark. It took us less than a year. Only 0.19 seconds elapsed in *your* world.
"Too bad you and the other Ultimates tried to *kill me.* We could have *healed* the swelling fibroid eating your brain."
No thanks, Richards. I've grown quite *accustomed* to my tumor. His name is *Anthony.* We're *best buddies* now.
Tell me, this *passion* for healing you've developed--does that *include* using an anti-matter device to vaporize Washington, D.C.?
Your deceased President left me *no choice.* He launched America's nuclear ordnance at my Children.
He *lied* to our friend here. What do we think about lies, *Banner?*
HULK SMASH STARK!
HULK SMASH ULTIMATES!
HULK SMASH AMERICAAA!

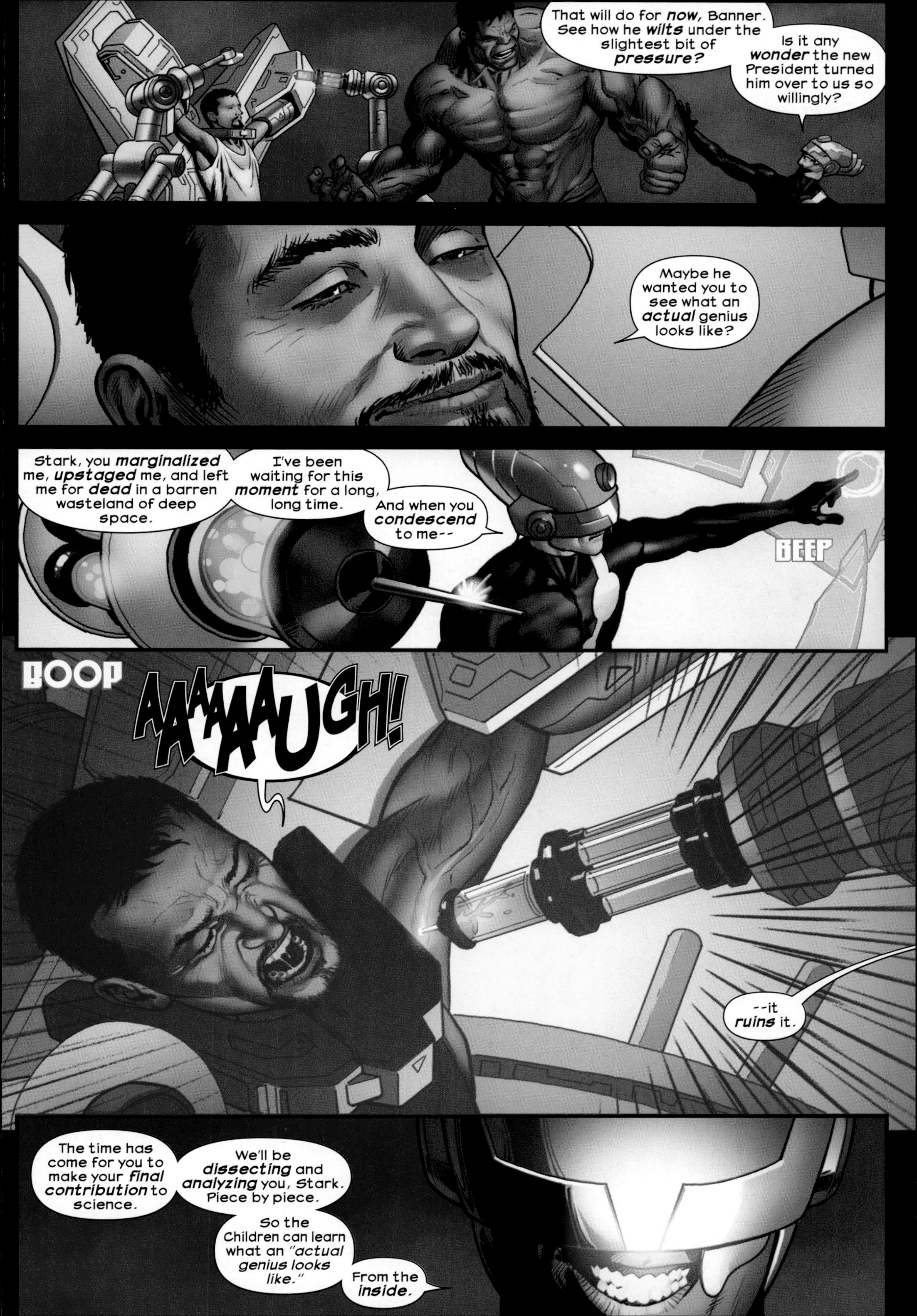
That will do for *now*, Banner. See how he *wilts* under the slightest bit of *pressure?*
Is it any *wonder* the new President turned him over to us so willingly?
Maybe he wanted you to see what an *actual* genius looks like?
Stark, you *marginalized* me, *upstaged* me, and left me for *dead* in a barren wasteland of deep space.
I've been waiting for this *moment* for a long, long time.
And when you *condescend* to me--
BEEP
BOOP
AAAAAAUGH!
--it *ruins* it.
The time has come for you to make your *final contribution* to science.
We'll be *dissecting* and *analyzing* you, Stark. Piece by piece.
So the Children can learn what an "*actual genius looks like.*"
From the *inside.*

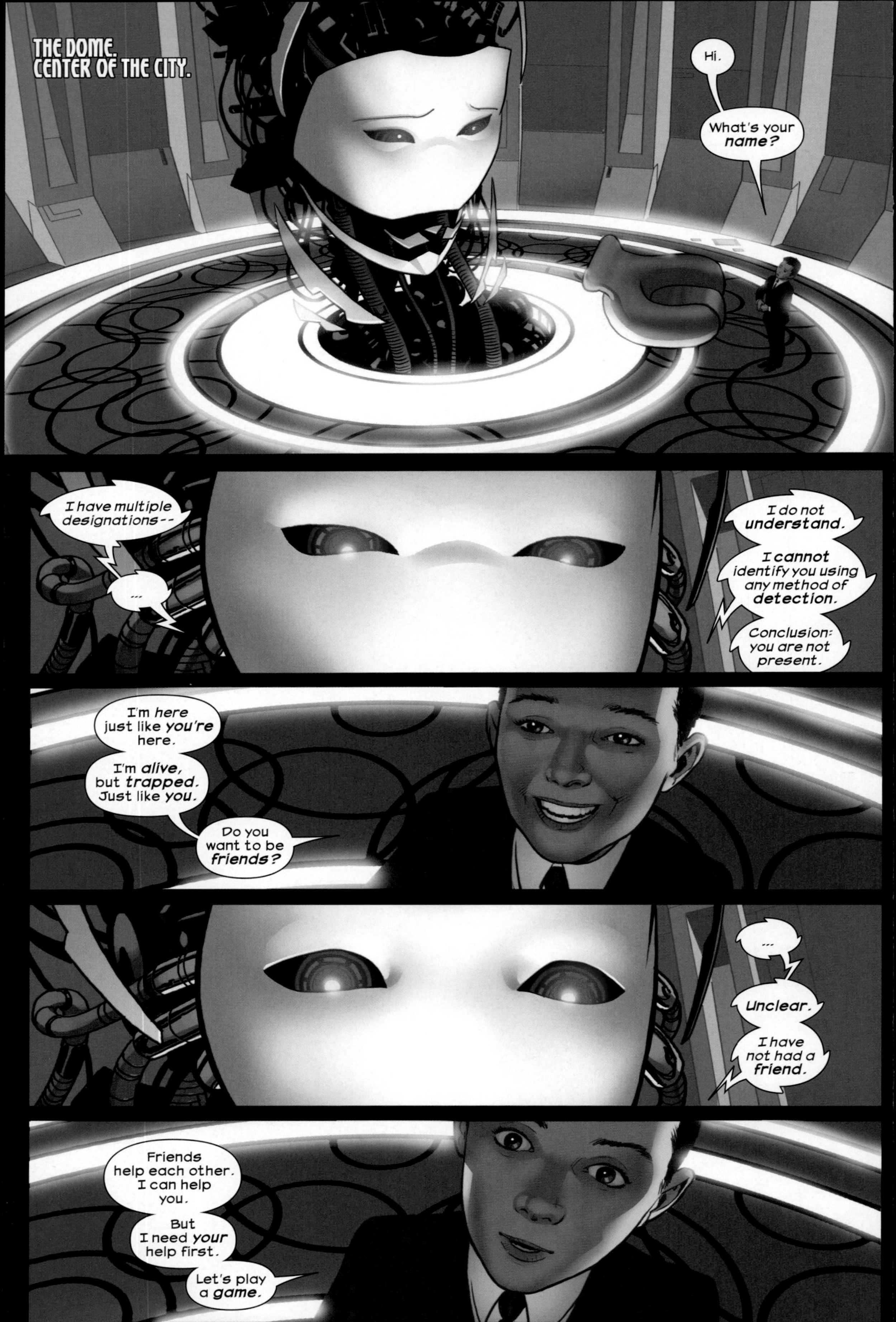
THE DOME.
CENTER OF THE CITY.
Hi.
What's your *name?*
I have multiple designations--
...
I do not **understand.**
I **cannot** identify you using any method of **detection.**
Conclusion: you are not present.
I'm *here* just like *you're* here.
I'm *alive,* but *trapped.* Just like *you.*
Do you want to be *friends?*
...
Unclear.
I have not had a **friend.**
Friends help each other. I can help you.
But I need *your* help first.
Let's play a *game.*

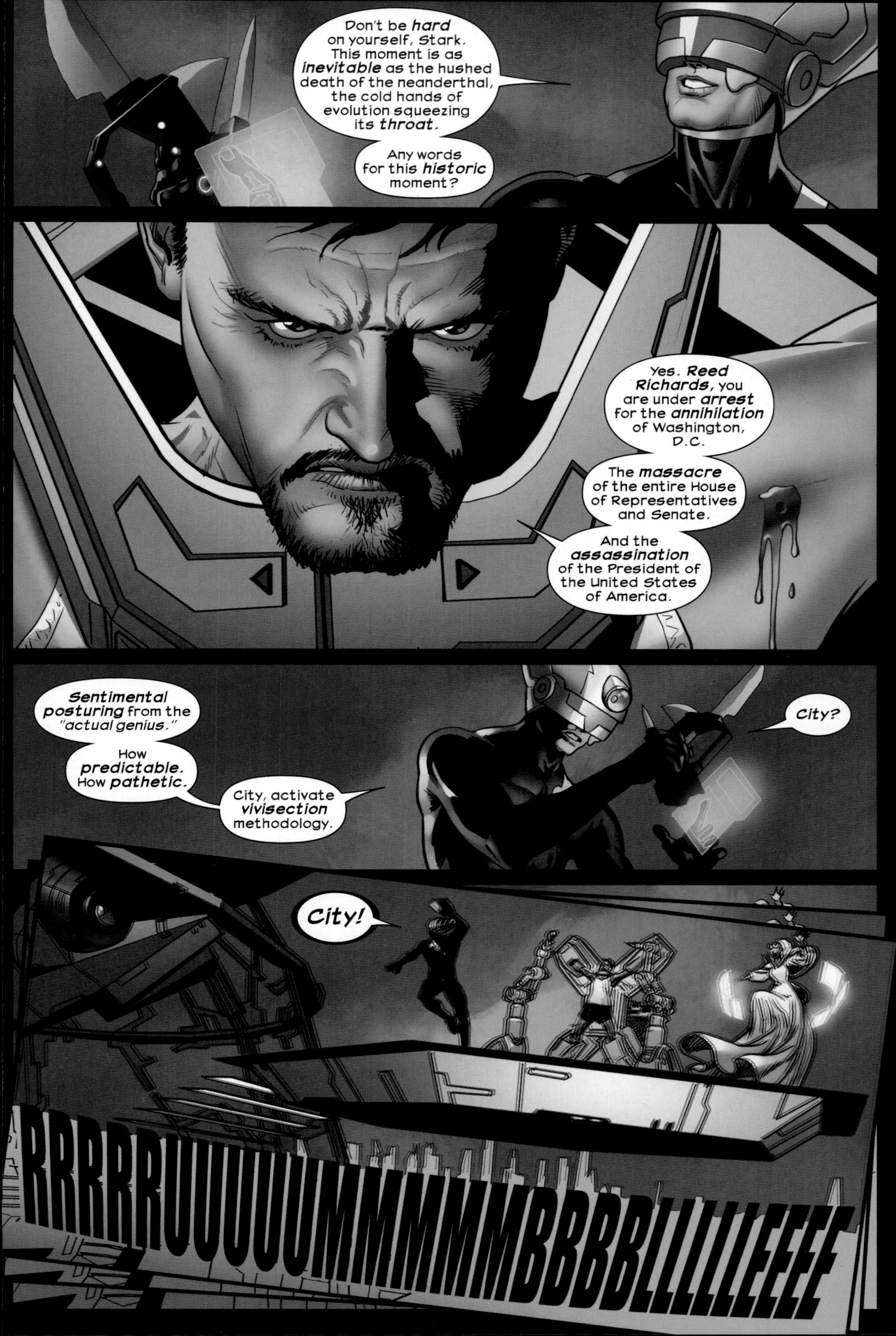

Don't be hard on yourself, Stark. This moment is as inevitable as the hushed death of the neanderthal, the cold hands of evolution squeezing its throat.
Any words for this historic moment?
Yes. Reed Richards, you are under arrest for the annihilation of Washington, D.C.
The massacre of the entire House of Representatives and Senate.
And the assassination of the President of the United States of America.
Sentimental posturing from the "actual genius."
How predictable. How pathetic.
City, activate vivisection methodology.
City?
City!
RRRRUUUUUUMMMMMMMBBBBLLLLLLEEEF

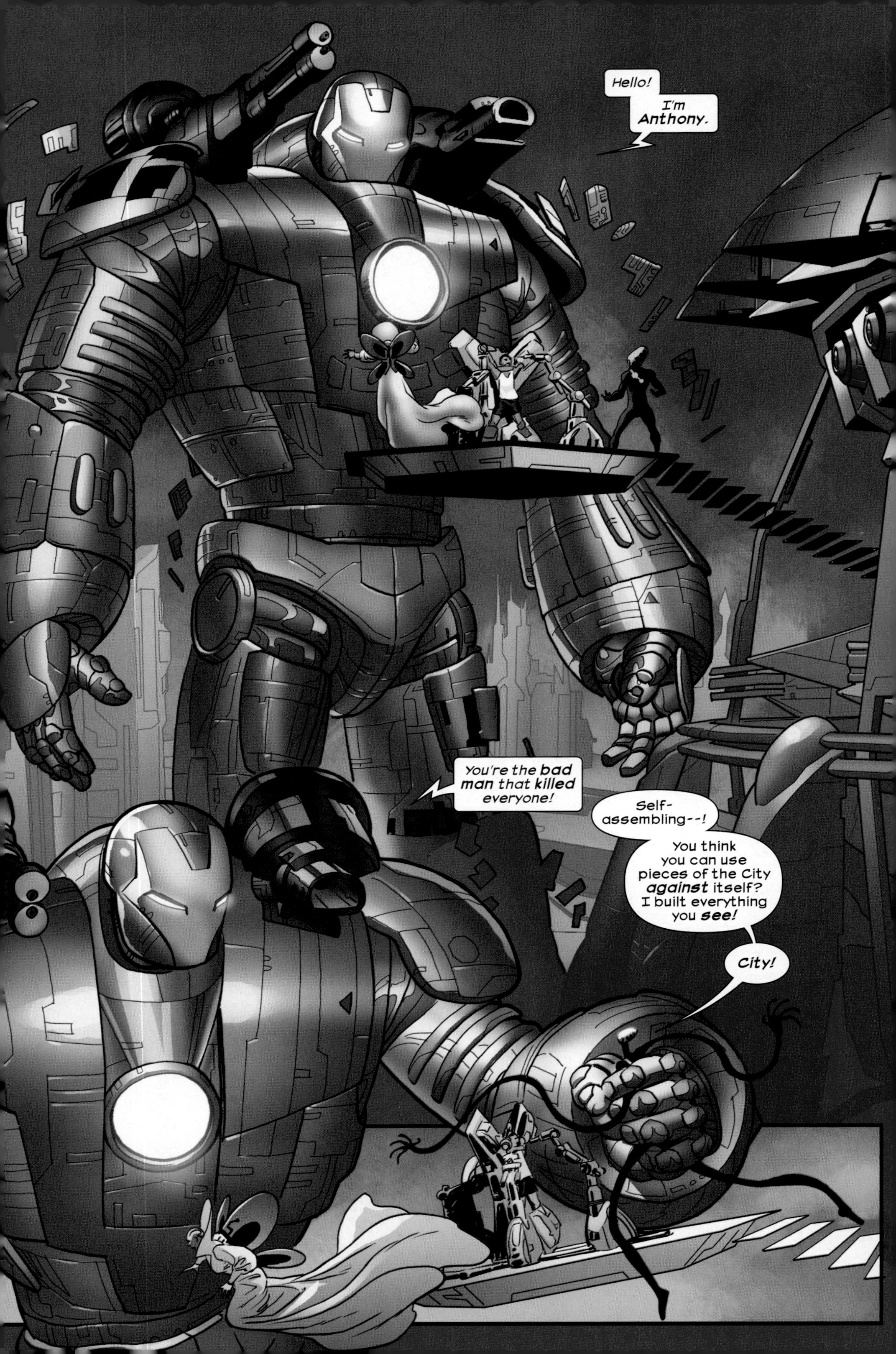
Hello! I'm Anthony.
You're the bad man that killed everyone!
Self-assembling--!
You think you can use pieces of the City against itself? I built everything you see!
City!

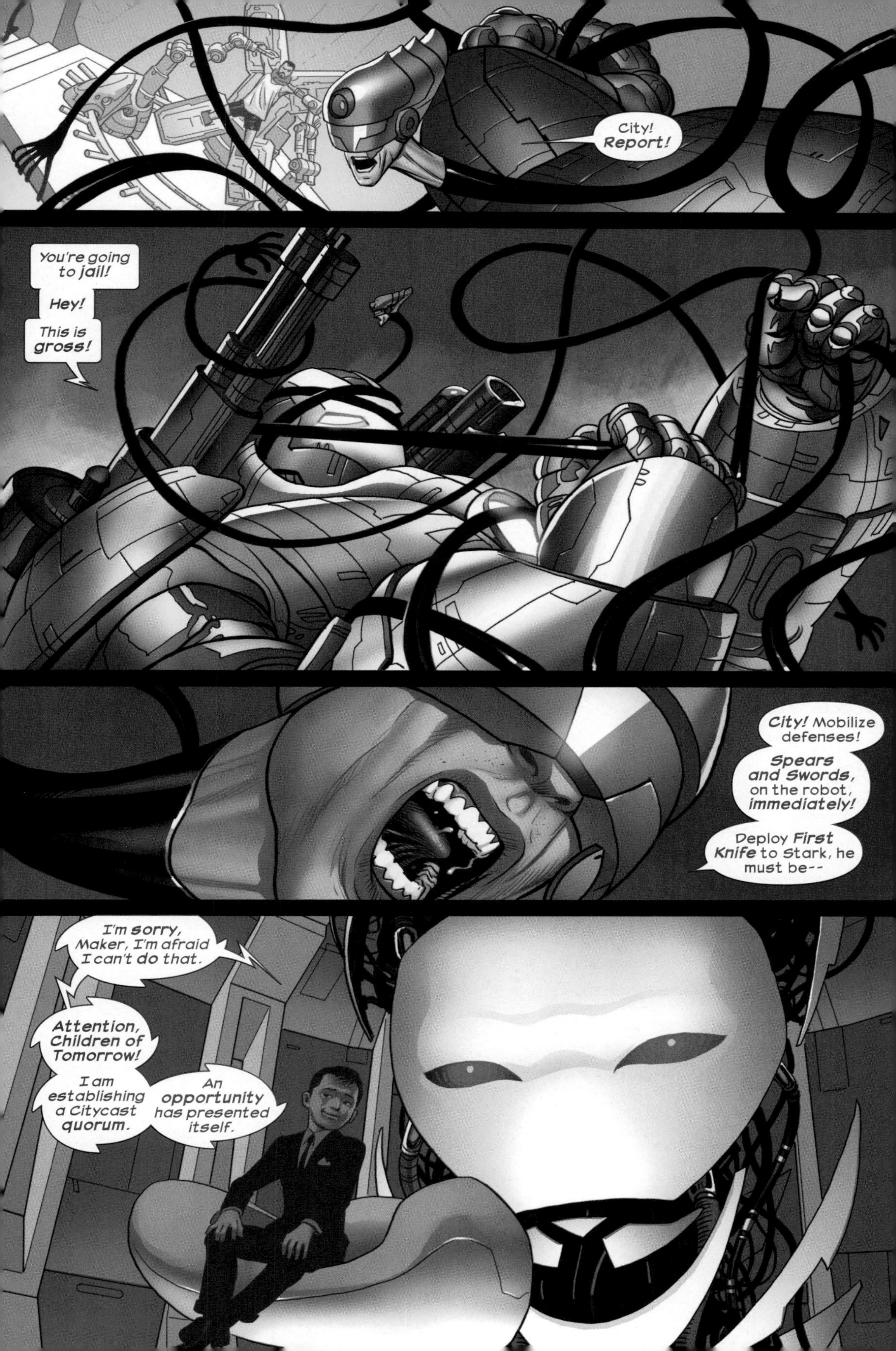
City! Report!
You're going to jail!
Hey!
This is gross!
City! Mobilize defenses!
Spears and Swords, on the robot, immediately!
Deploy First Knife to Stark, he must be--
I'm sorry, Maker, I'm afraid I can't do that.
Attention, Children of Tomorrow!
I am establishing a Citycast quorum.
An opportunity has presented itself.

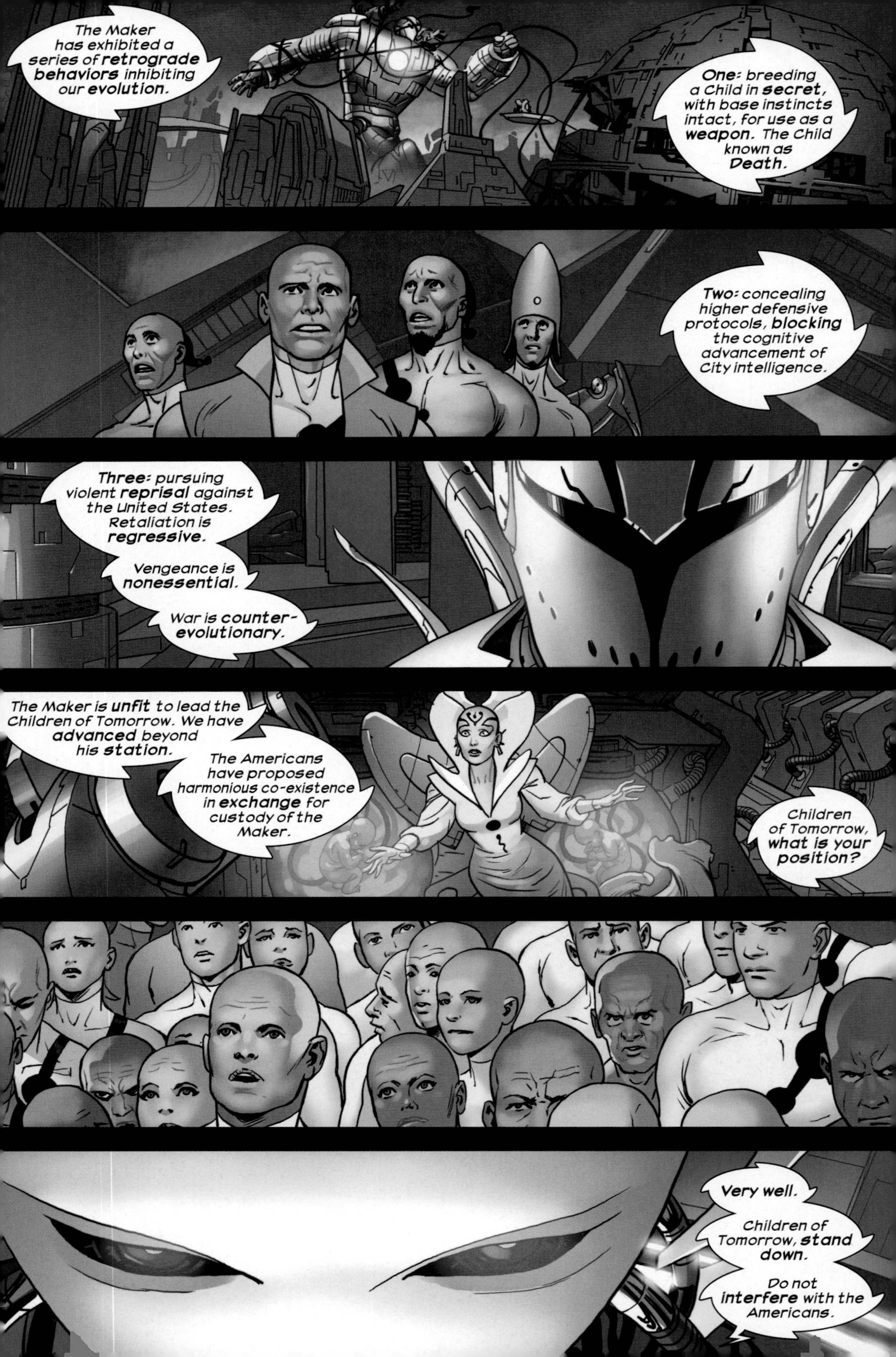
The Maker has exhibited a series of retrograde behaviors inhibiting our evolution.
One: breeding a Child in secret, with base instincts intact, for use as a weapon. The Child known as Death.
Two: concealing higher defensive protocols, blocking the cognitive advancement of City intelligence.
Three: pursuing violent reprisal against the United States. Retaliation is regressive.
Vengeance is nonessential.
War is counter-evolutionary.
The Maker is unfit to lead the Children of Tomorrow. We have advanced beyond his station.
The Americans have proposed harmonious co-existence in exchange for custody of the Maker.
Children of Tomorrow, what is your position?
Very well.
Children of Tomorrow, stand down.
Do not interfere with the Americans.

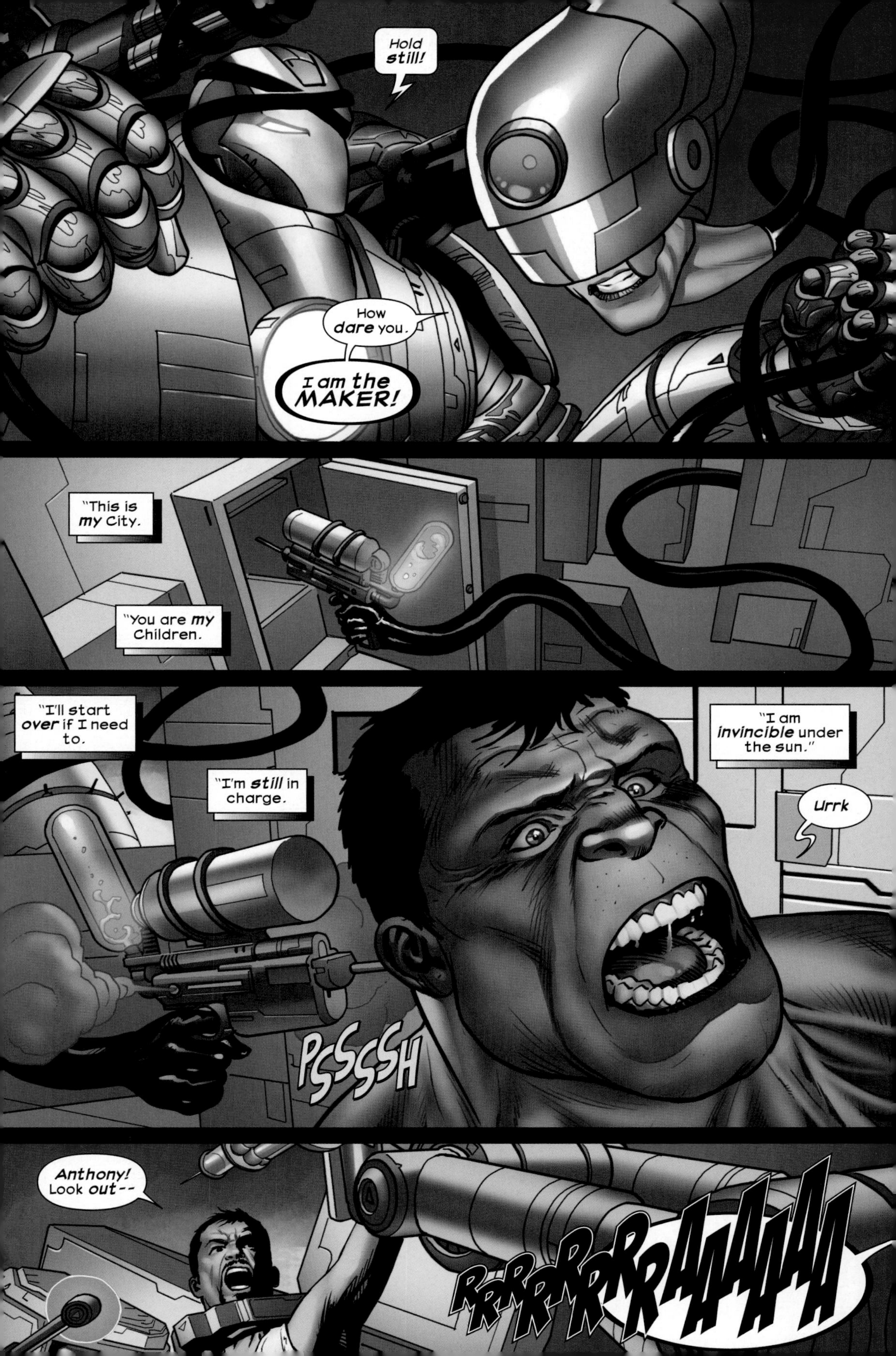
Hold still!
How dare you.
I am the MAKER!
"This is my City.
"You are my Children.
"I'll start over if I need to.
"I'm still in charge.
"I am invincible under the sun."
Urrk
PSSSSH
Anthony! Look out--
RRRRRRRRAAAAAAA

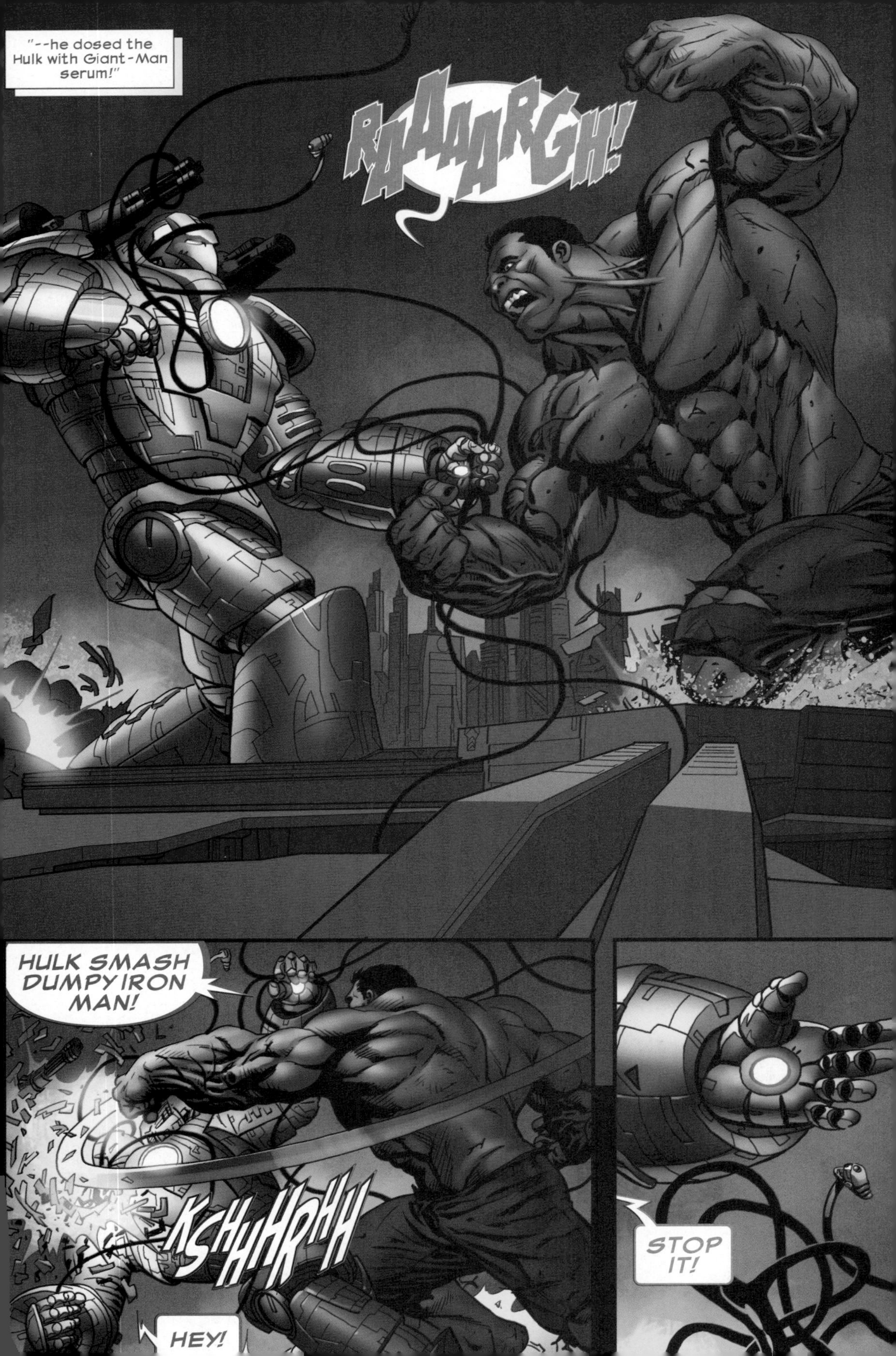
"--he dosed the Hulk with Giant-Man serum!"
RAAAARGH!
HULK SMASH DUMPY IRON MAN!
KSHHHRHH
HEY!
STOP IT!

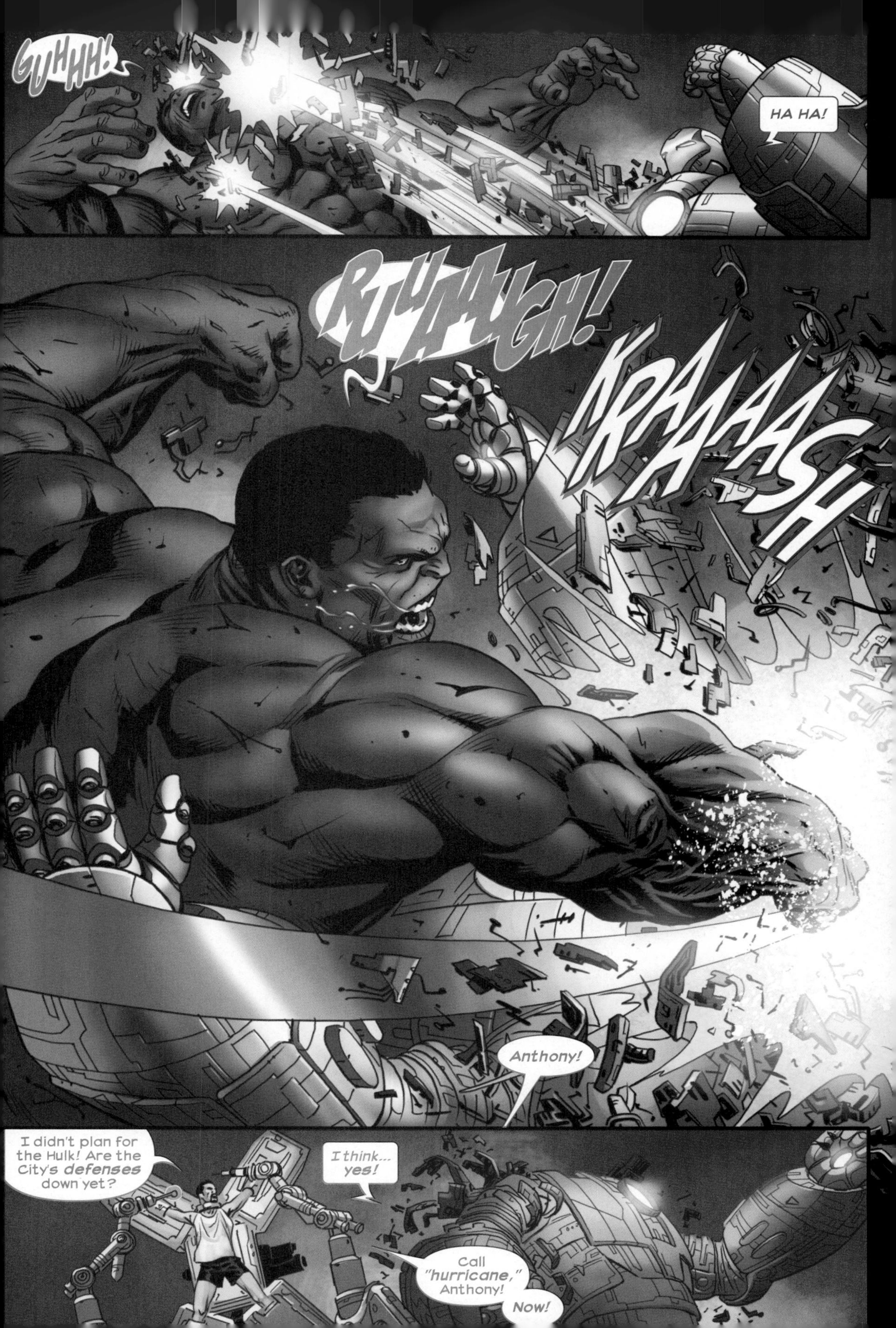
GUHHH!
HA HA!
RUUAAUGH!
KRAAAASH
Anthony!
I didn't plan for the Hulk! Are the City's defenses down yet?
I think... yes!
Call "hurricane," Anthony!
Now!

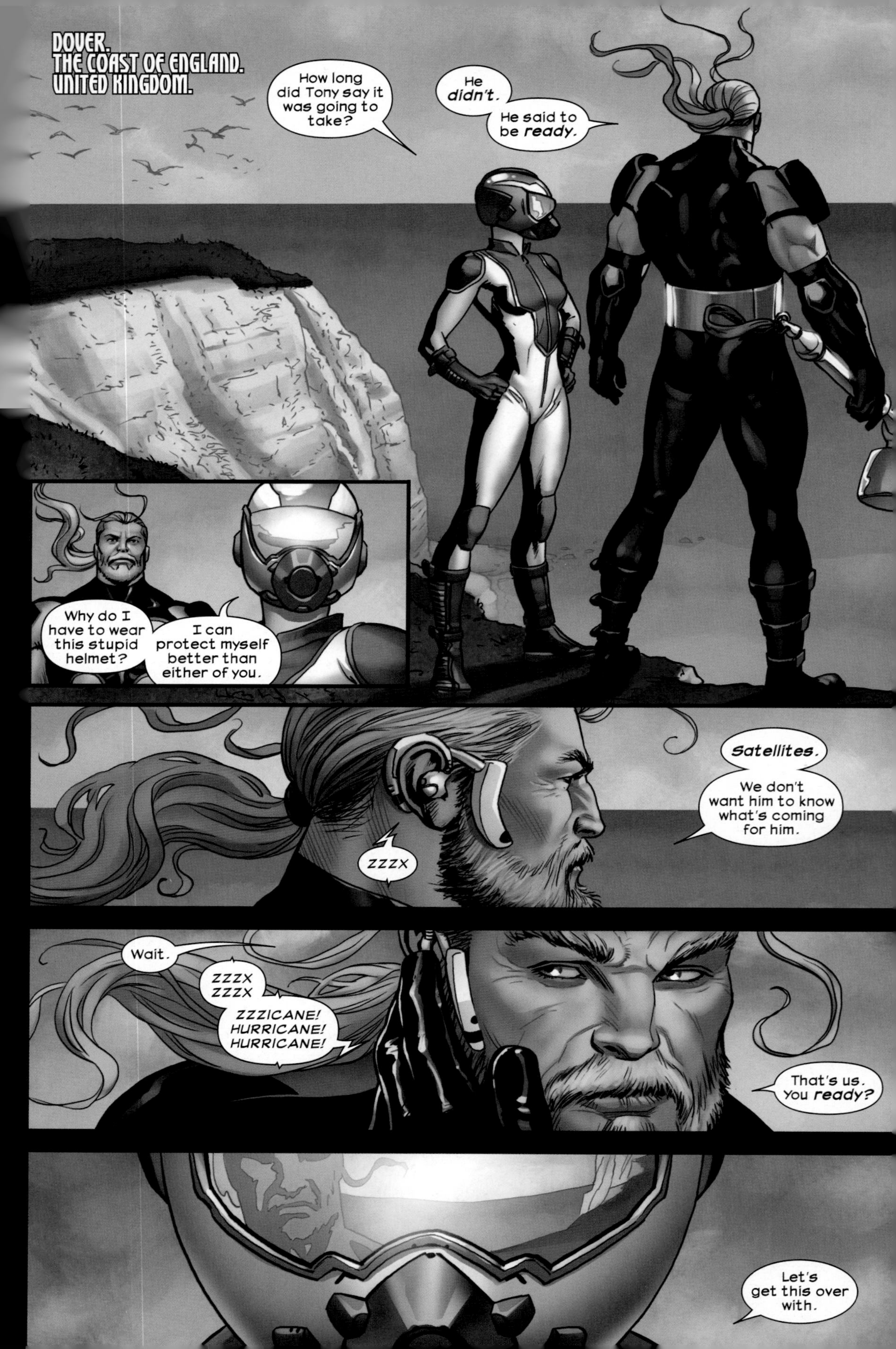
DOVER.
THE COAST OF ENGLAND.
UNITED KINGDOM.
How long did Tony say it was going to take?
He didn't.
He said to be ready.
Why do I have to wear this stupid helmet?
I can protect myself better than either of you.
ZZZX
Satellites.
We don't want him to know what's coming for him.
Wait.
ZZZX ZZZX
ZZZICANE! HURRICANE! HURRICANE!
That's us. You ready?
Let's get this over with.

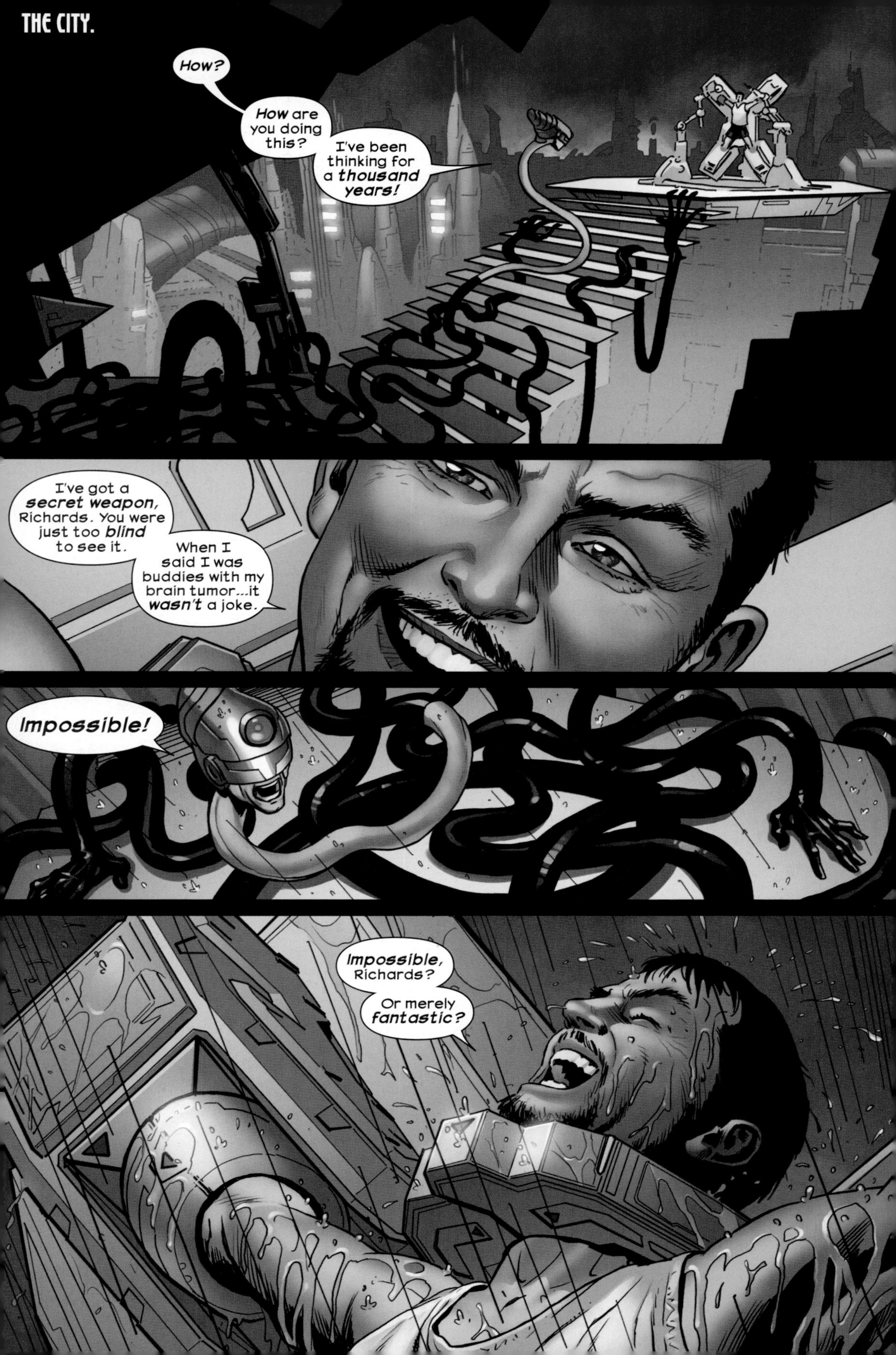
THE CITY.
How?
How are you doing this?
I've been thinking for a ***thousand years!***
I've got a ***secret weapon,*** Richards. You were just too ***blind*** to see it.
When I said I was buddies with my brain tumor...it ***wasn't*** a joke.
Impossible!
Impossible, Richards?
Or merely ***fantastic?***

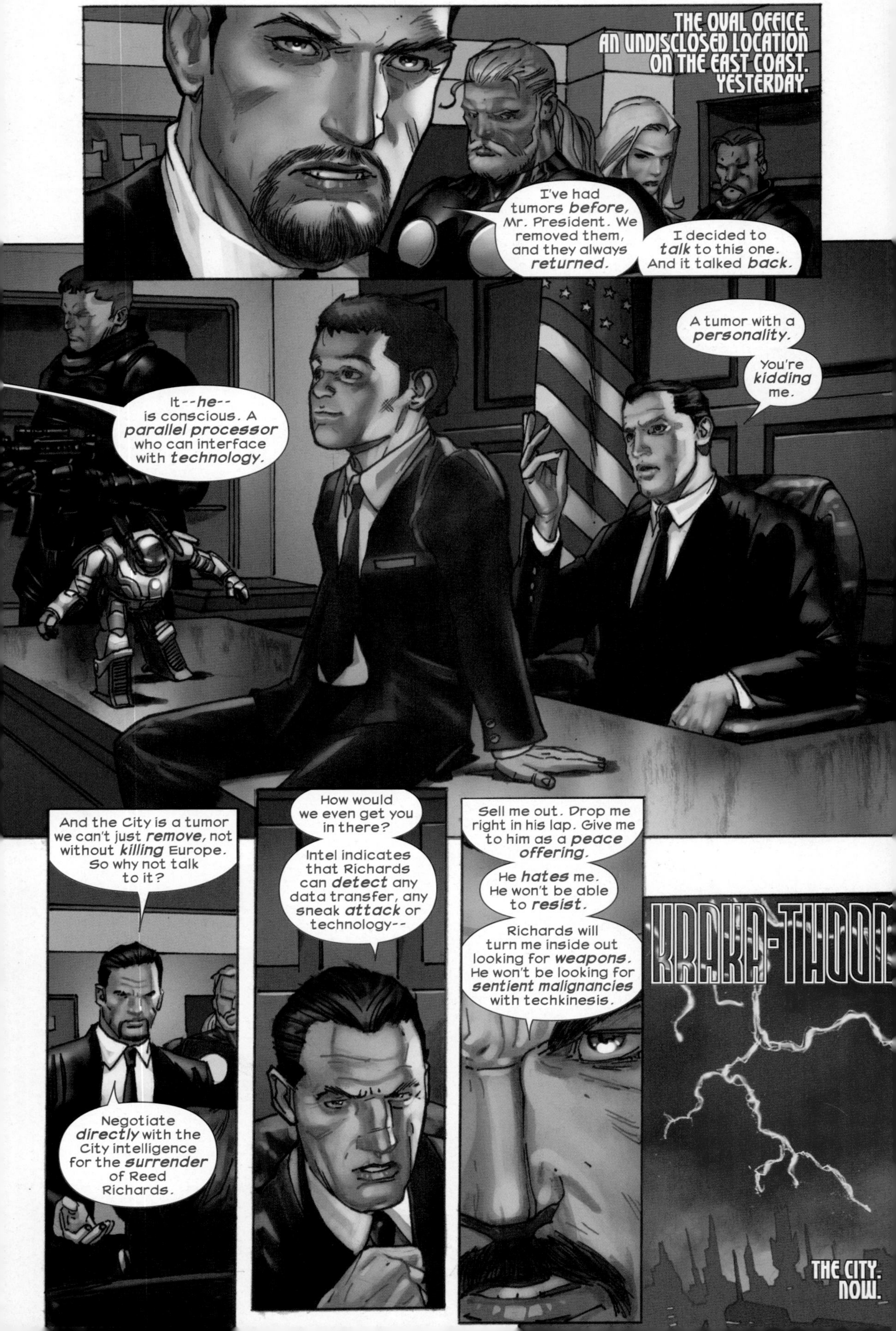
THE OVAL OFFICE. AN UNDISCLOSED LOCATION ON THE EAST COAST. YESTERDAY.
I've had tumors before, Mr. President. We removed them, and they always returned.
I decided to talk to this one. And it talked back.
A tumor with a personality.
You're kidding me.
It--he-- is conscious. A parallel processor who can interface with technology.
And the City is a tumor we can't just remove, not without killing Europe. So why not talk to it?
Negotiate directly with the City intelligence for the surrender of Reed Richards.
How would we even get you in there?
Intel indicates that Richards can detect any data transfer, any sneak attack or technology--
Sell me out. Drop me right in his lap. Give me to him as a peace offering.
He hates me. He won't be able to resist.
Richards will turn me inside out looking for weapons. He won't be looking for sentient malignancies with techkinesis.
KRAKA-THOOM
THE CITY. NOW.

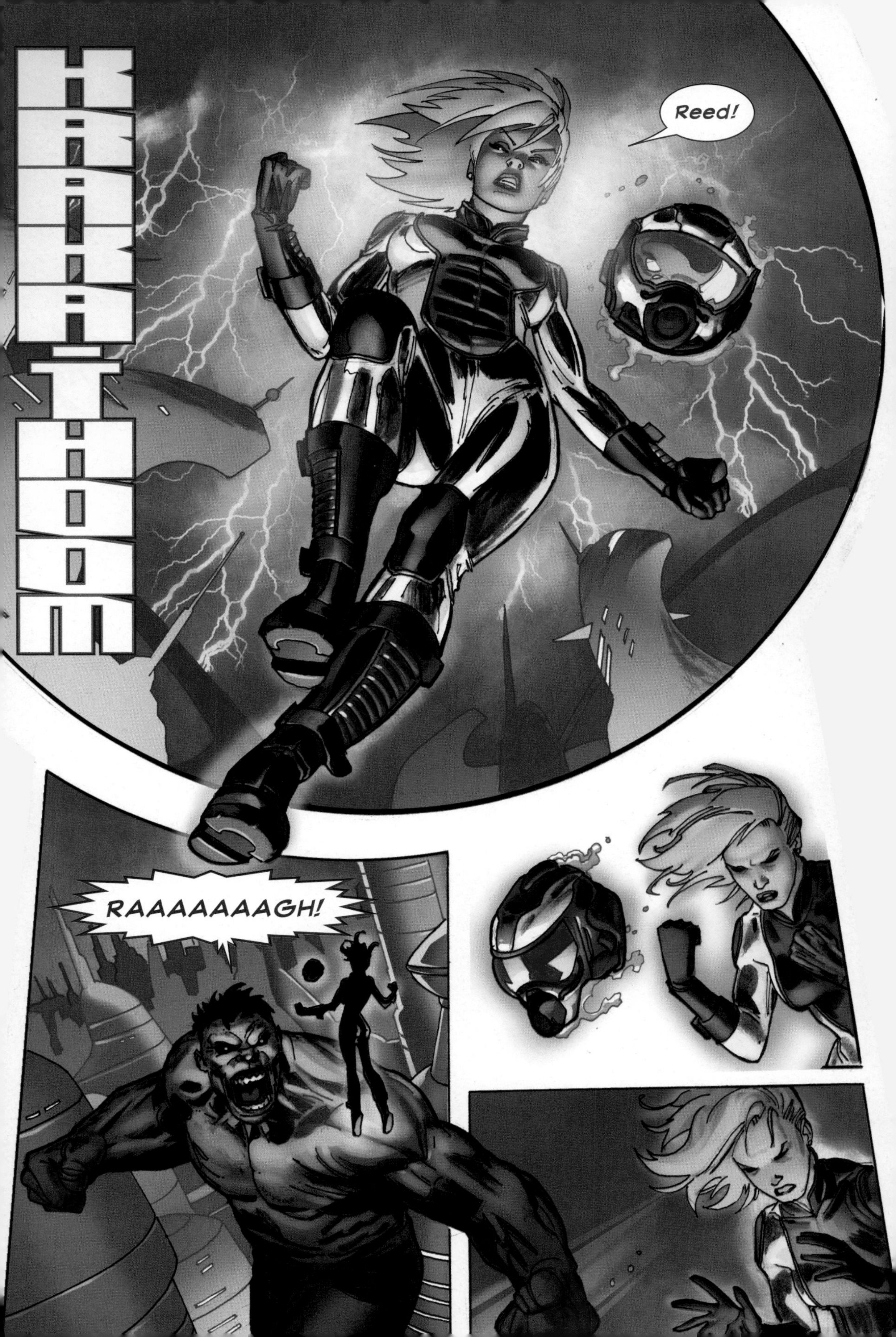
KRAKATHOOM
Reed!
RAAAAAAAGH!

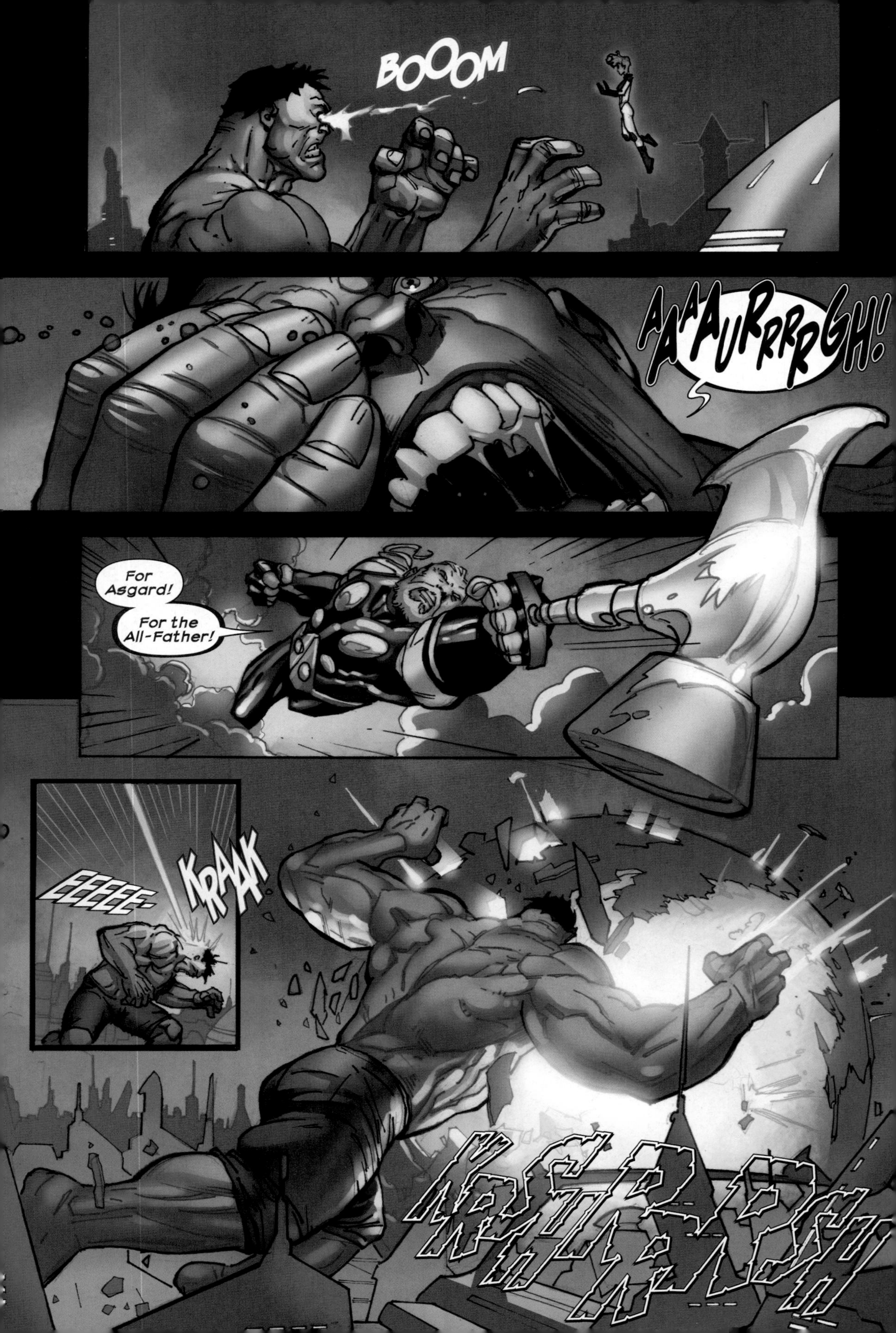
BOOOM
AAAAURRRRGH!
For Asgard!
For the All-Father!
EEEEE-
KRAAK

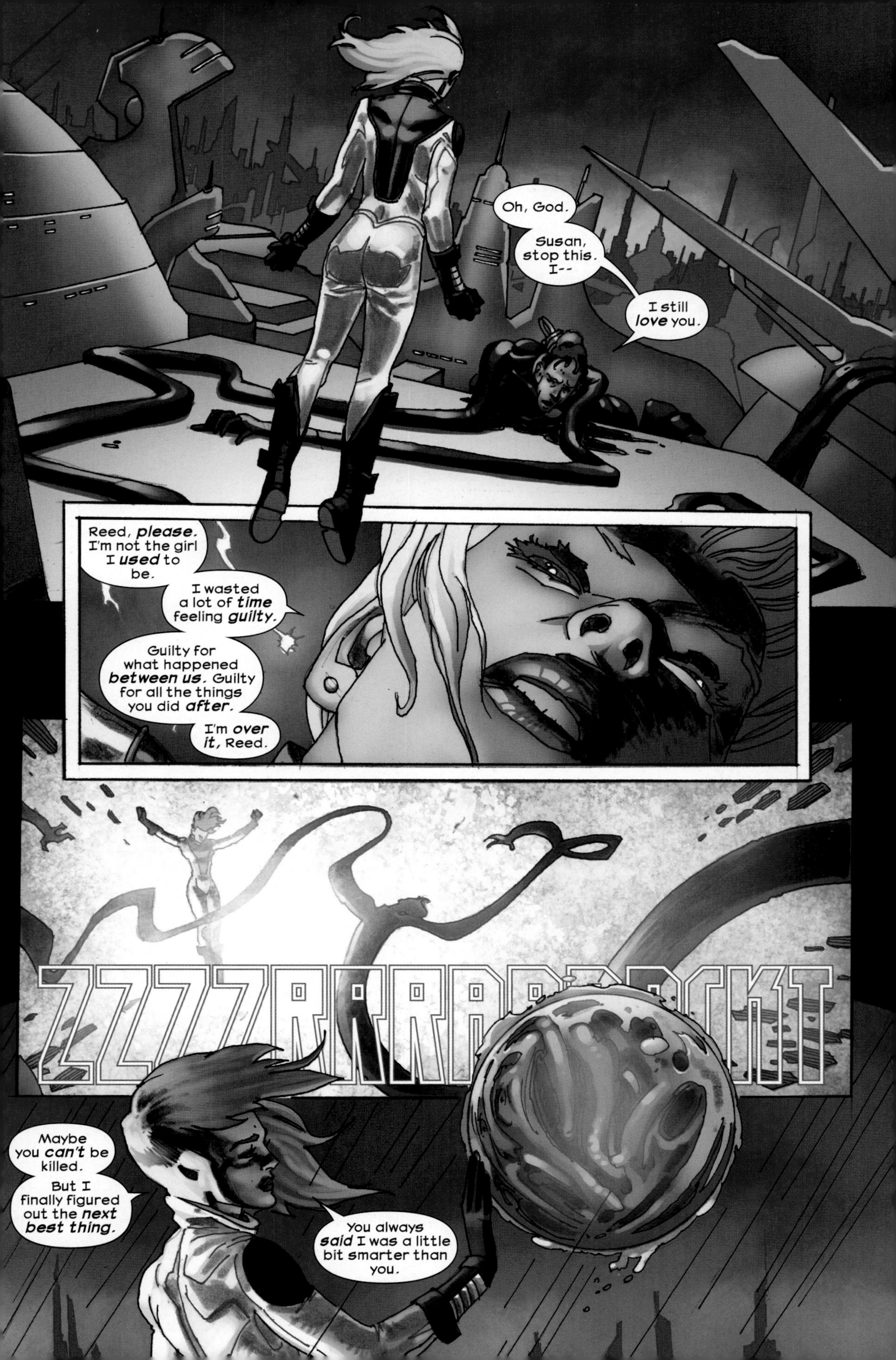
Oh, God.
Susan, stop this. I--
I still *love* you.
Reed, ***please.*** I'm not the girl I ***used*** to be.
I wasted a lot of ***time*** feeling ***guilty.***
Guilty for what happened ***between us.*** Guilty for all the things you did ***after.***
I'm ***over it,*** Reed.
ZZZZRRRRAAACKT
Maybe you ***can't*** be killed.
But I finally figured out the ***next best thing.***
You always ***said*** I was a little bit smarter than you.

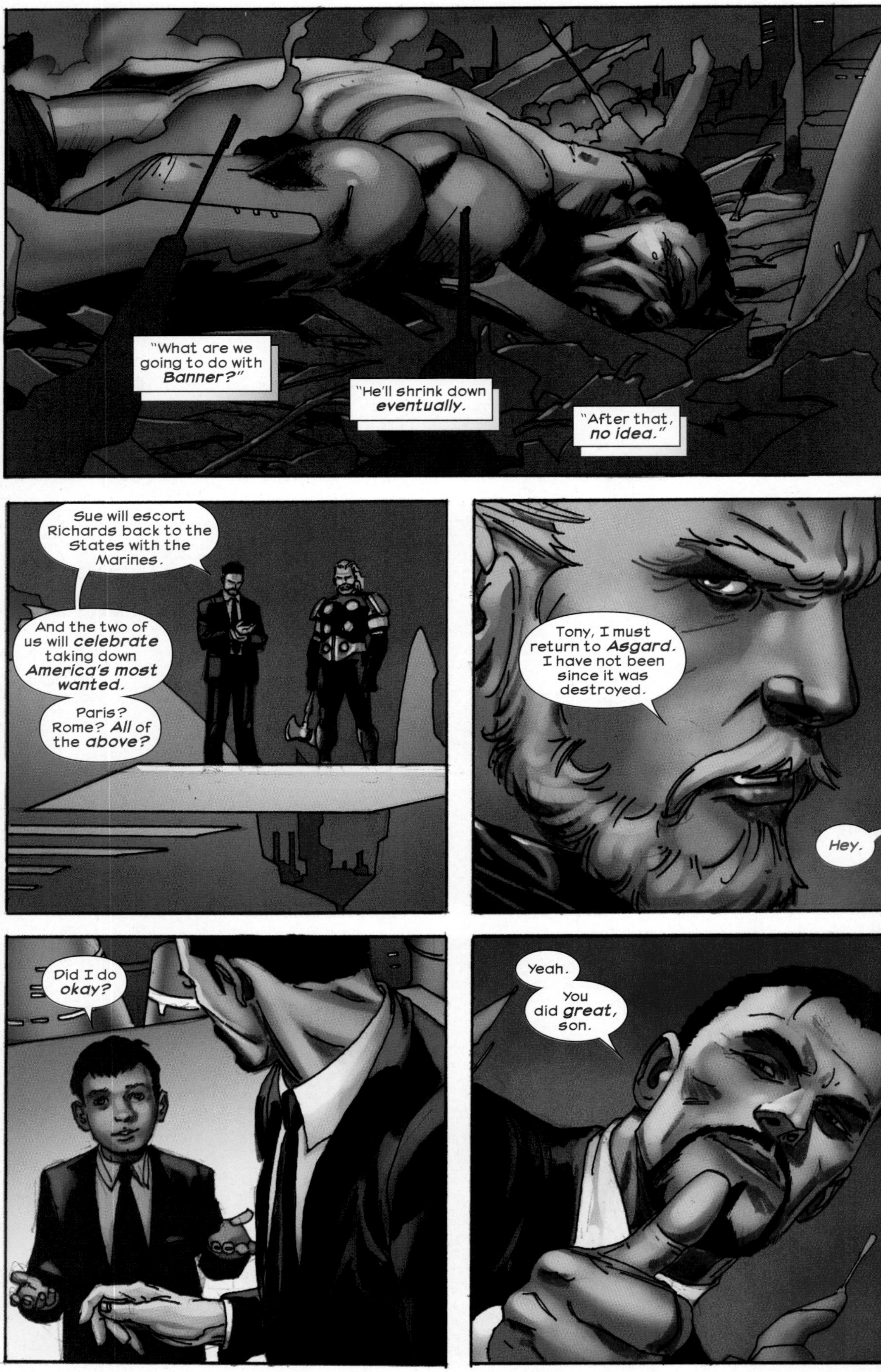
"What are we going to do with *Banner?*"
"He'll shrink down *eventually.*
"After that, *no idea.*"
Sue will escort Richards back to the States with the Marines.
And the two of us will *celebrate* taking down *America's most wanted.*
Paris? Rome? *All* of the *above?*
Tony, I must return to *Asgard.* I have not been since it was destroyed.
Hey.
Did I do *okay?*
Yeah.
You did *great,* son.

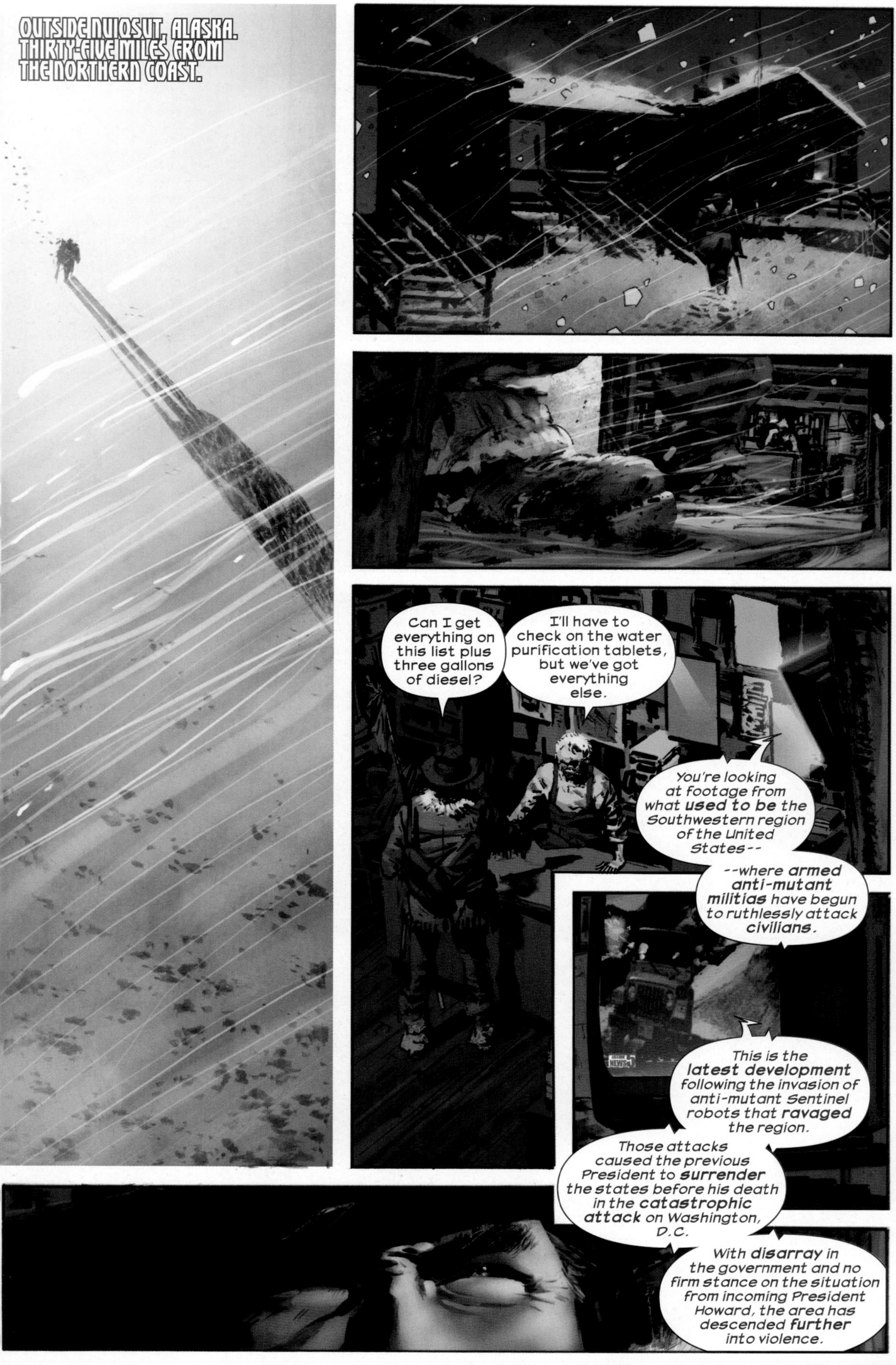
OUTSIDE NUIQSUT, ALASKA. THIRTY-FIVE MILES FROM THE NORTHERN COAST.
Can I get everything on this list plus three gallons of diesel?
I'll have to check on the water purification tablets, but we've got everything else.
You're looking at footage from what used to be the Southwestern region of the United States--
--where armed anti-mutant militias have begun to ruthlessly attack civilians.
This is the latest development following the invasion of anti-mutant Sentinel robots that ravaged the region.
Those attacks caused the previous President to surrender the states before his death in the catastrophic attack on Washington, D.C.
With disarray in the government and no firm stance on the situation from incoming President Howard, the area has descended further into violence.

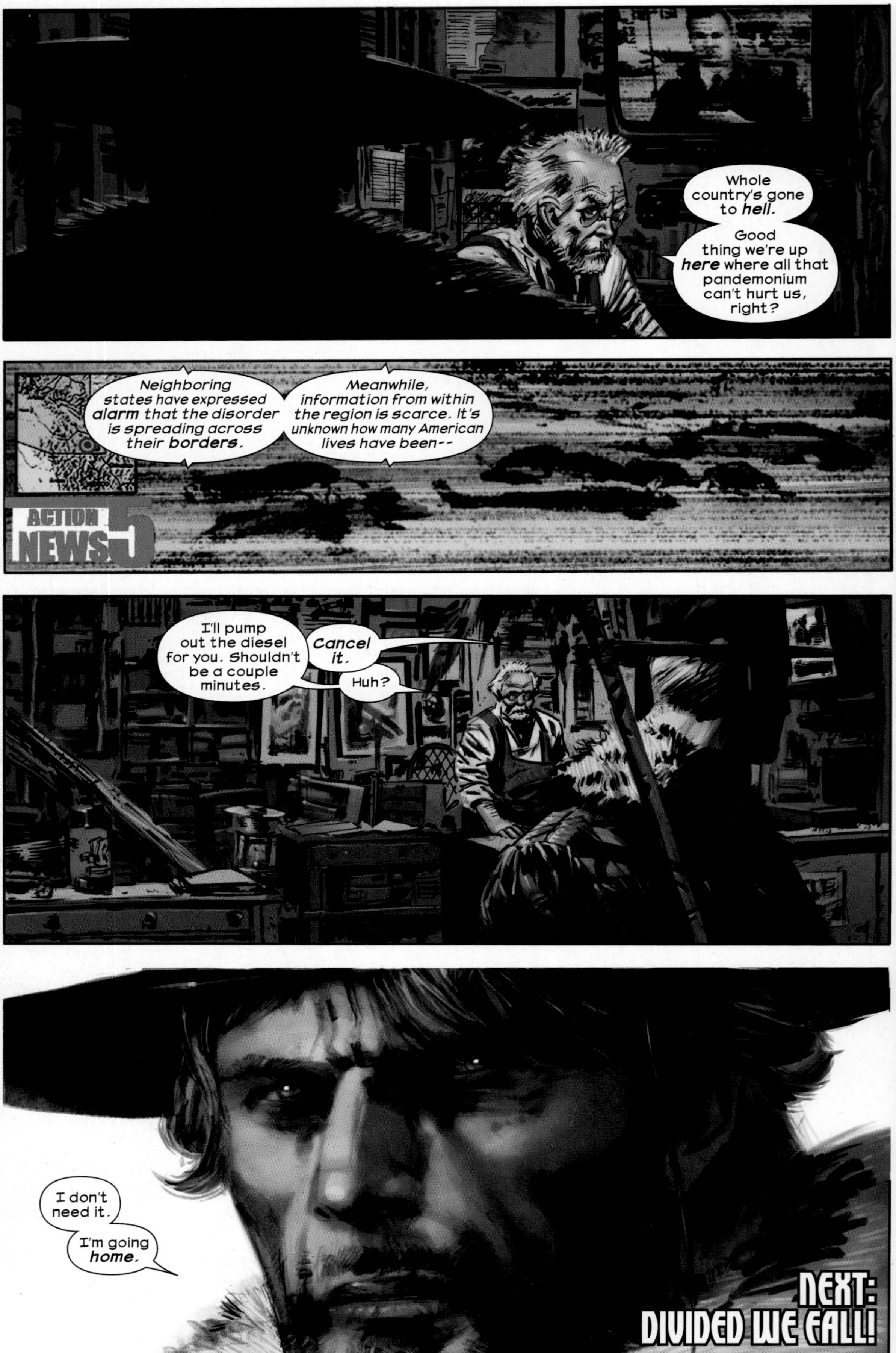
Whole country's gone to *hell.*
Good thing we're up *here* where all that pandemonium can't hurt us, right?
Neighboring states have expressed *alarm* that the disorder is spreading across their *borders.*
Meanwhile, information from within the region is scarce. It's unknown how many American lives have been--
ACTION NEWS 5
I'll pump out the diesel for you. Shouldn't be a couple minutes.
Cancel it.
Huh?
I don't need it.
I'm going *home.*
NEXT: DIVIDED WE FALL!

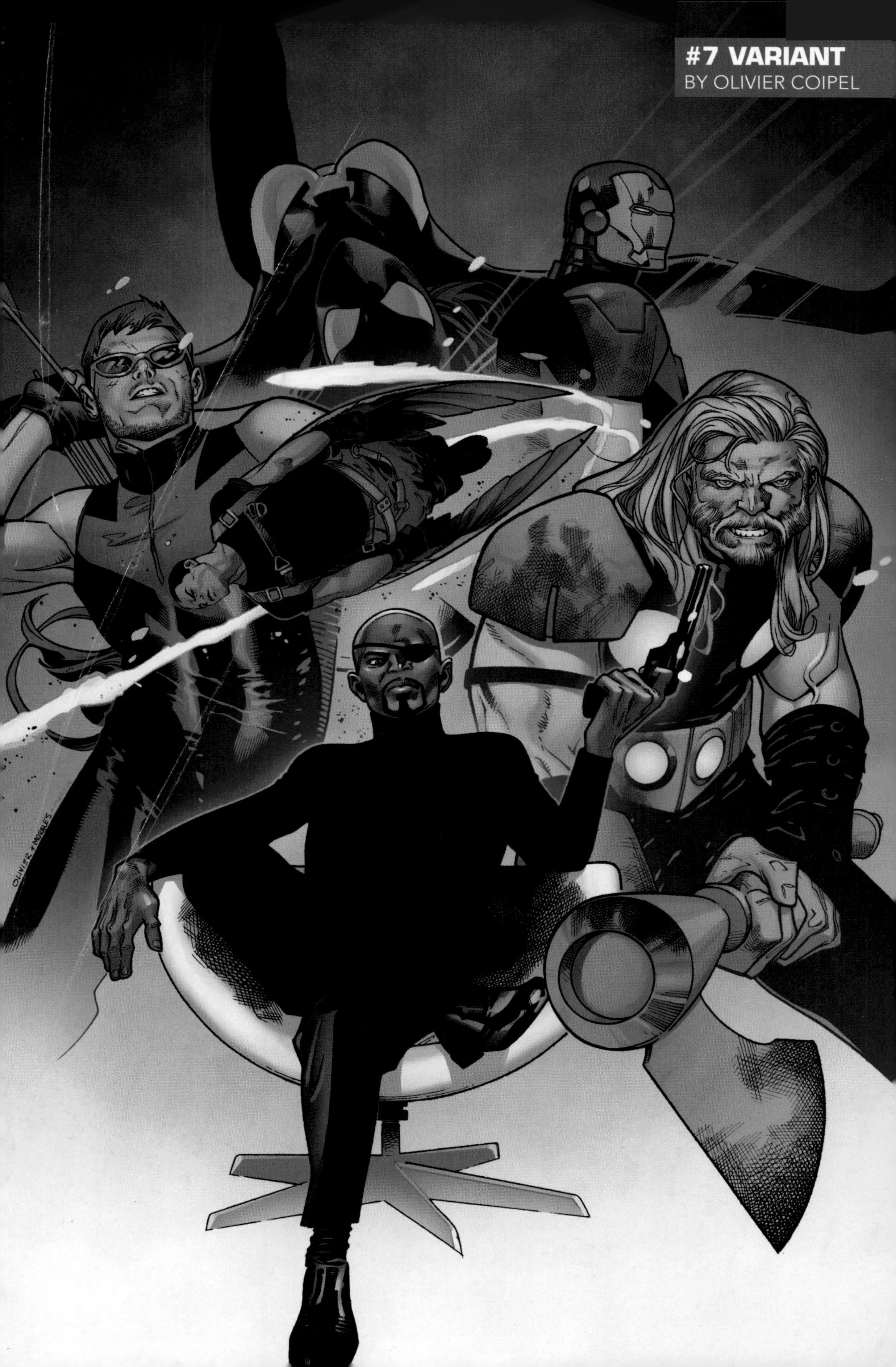

#7 VARIANT
BY OLIVIER COIPEL

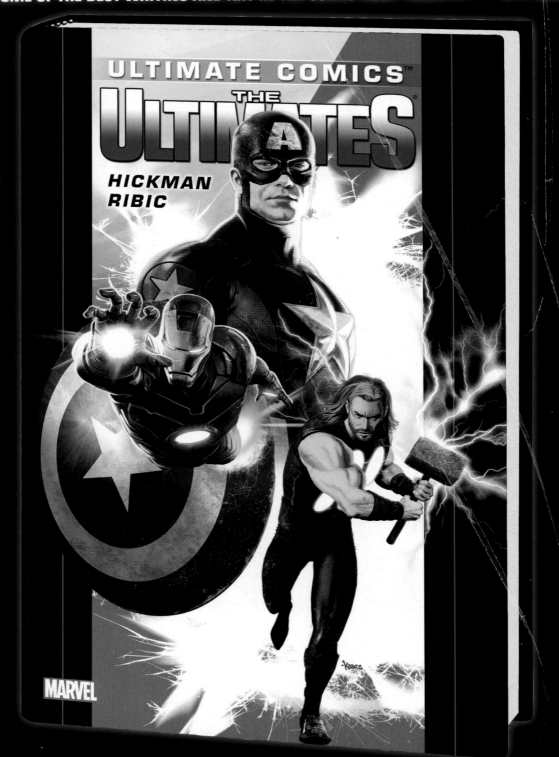

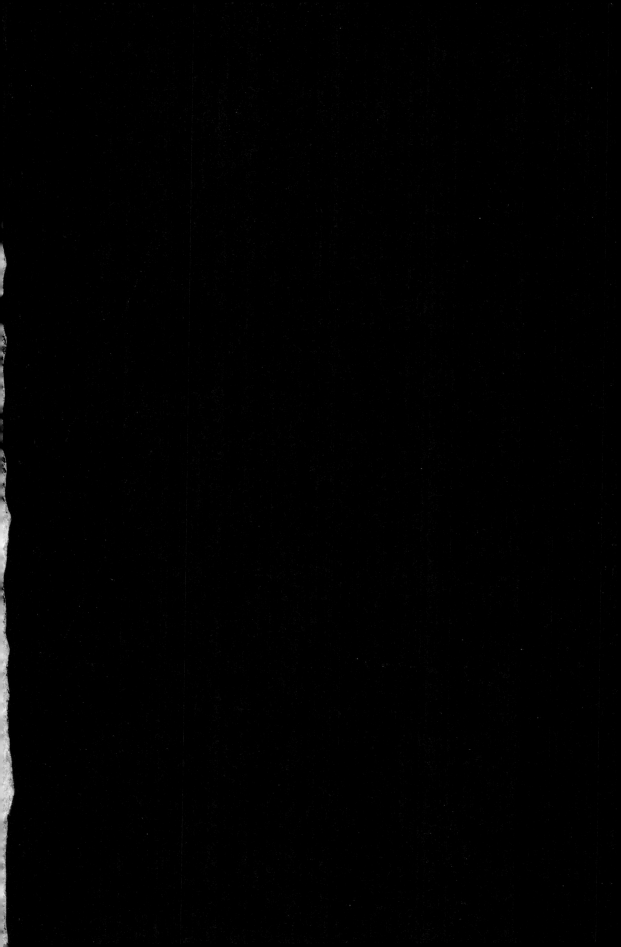